Hezekiah Butterworth

Zigzag Journeys on the Mediterranean

Hezekiah Butterworth

Zigzag Journeys on the Mediterranean

ISBN/EAN: 9783743316591

Manufactured in Europe, USA, Canada, Australia, Japa

Cover: Foto ©ninafisch / pixelio.de

Manufactured and distributed by brebook publishing software (www.brebook.com)

Hezekiah Butterworth

Zigzag Journeys on the Mediterranean

ON THE

MEDITERRANEAN.

BY

HEZEKIAH BUTTERWORTH.

FULLY ILLUSTRATED.

BOSTON:
ESTES AND LAURIAT,
PUBLISHERS.

PREFACE.

THE purpose of this book is to explain the Consular Service of the United States, and to relate those curious stories which are often told in the Consulates of the East and which resemble the "Thousand and One Nights," or the "Arabian Nights' Entertainments." The Consulates of the East sometimes become famous story-telling places in which caravan tales, sea tales, and travellers' tales are told in an original way; and it is with this peculiar lore that this, the fifteenth volume of the "Zigzag Series," seeks to interest the reader. Many of the tales of Consulates are geographically and historically instructive, and some of them have the peculiar flavor of old Oriental traditions. The pet animals and birds of Consulates are also interesting topics, and are introduced in these Consular museums.

The Zigzag books or annuals, like many magazines with a definite educational purpose, make use of interpolated stories to illustrate and to give interest to their pages. Most of these stories have been written by the author, but helps from other pens have sometimes been sought. In this book the author is indebted to George H. Coomes, of Warren, R. I., an old sailor, and a popular writer of sea stories, for helps which are credited in their places. He is also indebted to Messrs. Harper Brothers for permission to reproduce here some of his own stories, using the illustrations originally made for them. He has sought in this, as in former volumes, to make clear a useful subject by that sympathetic story-telling art, which, although a *mélange*, leaves the purpose at last clear in the mind. Few books have been written to make our diplomatic and consular service better known to the young people, and the author hopes that these Tales of the Consulates may serve this purpose of popular information.

The Oriental stories in this volume are selected and edited out of a careful study of books on Oriental folk-lore, it being the author's purpose to give to young people those which most interested him. The sources of these stories are fully credited, so that the lover of Oriental tales can follow the study, if he have access to the best libraries.

H. B.

28 WORCESTER STREET, BOSTON, MASS.

CONTENTS.

CHAPTER		PAGE
I.	A Zigzag Journey to Zag-a-Zig	13
II.	How Consuls are appointed. — Their Duties. — The Story-telling Garden. — The Capitol by Moonlight. — The Singing Mouse. — The Village Mystery	26
III.	A Plan for a Journey of Educational Travel	53
IV.	Caracas on the First Day of the Revolution, 1892. — Amusements at Sea	70
V.	Gibraltar	112
VI.	Algeria. — Tunis. — The Holiest Place in Africa	130
VII.	Marseilles	146
VIII.	Consular Pets and Parrots	156
IX.	Venice	165
X.	Stories and Studies while detained in Quarantine	191
XI.	The Mediterranean and its Legends	216
XII.	St. Sophia. — The Dervish's Fairy Tale	232
XIII.	Brindisi. — An odd Story-Teller	240
XIV.	Rienzi, the Last of the Roman Tribunes	258
XV.	Naples. — Roman Fairy Tales. — The Story of Sordello	277
XVI.	The White-Bordered Flag	308

ILLUSTRATIONS.

	PAGE		PAGE
The Mediterranean	*Frontispiece*	An Algerian Antelope-Hunter	135
Pitti Palace, Florence	15	An Algerian Beauty	141
On the Mediterranean	18	Tailpiece	145
"'Wait till the Sun goes into a Cloud,' said the Doctor"	41	Public Garden, Marseilles	147
		"The Old Red Settle by the Fire"	158
Faneuil Hall	44	"The Quaker smiled 'neath his Sunday Hat"	158
The Valley of Mexico	51		
Popocatepetl	55	"Silas the Bass-viol strung"	159
The God of Fire	57	"The Turnpike Coach"	160
The President's Palace	58	"Take that, and pay Ben's debts"	163
The Sacrificial Stone	59	"The old Man powdered his Wig"	164
Top of Sacrificial Stone	61	The Great Bridge of Rialto	166
Sculpture on the Side of the Sacrificial Stone	62	Pigeons of St. Mark's	167
		Venetian Glass	168
The Cathedral	63	Foot of Flagstaff in front of St. Mark's, Venice	169
The Tomb of Juarez	66		
Main Plaza, Monterey, Bishop's Palace	67	Masquerading in Venice	173
Statue of Chitaahuac	69	Ca D'Oro, Venice	175
The Plaza and La Mitra, Monterey	70	Library of St. Mark's, Venice	179
Statue of Columbus, Mexico	75	A Venetian Garden	183
Bolivar	80	Sciollo and Colleoni, Venice	187
La Guayra	81	A Vision of Egypt	193
Statue of Bolivar, Caracas	83	A Camping-Place in Sight of Biskra	197
A youthful Beggar of Caracas	84	A Daughter of Egypt	201
Ancient House in Caracas	85	Florence	217
Grand Opera House, Caracas	87	The Duomo, Florence	221
A Donkey Car, Caracas	88	Loggia di Lanzi, Florence	225
Old Mission near Caracas	107	Fountain of Neptune, Florence	229
The Rock of Gibraltar	113	Turkish Woman	233
The Grinding over young	117	Interior of a Mosque	235
The City of Morocco	123	Moslem at Prayer	241
Nemours	127	Appian Way	244
Travelling in Algeria	131	Tomb of Cecilia Mattella, Appian Way	249

LIST OF ILLUSTRATIONS.

	PAGE		PAGE
The Baptistery, Duomo, and Campanile of Giotto, Florence	253	Monument of Vico, Naples	284
The Campagna	258	Morning in Venice	293
The Aventine	261	The Tower of St. Mark's	301
St. Paul Basilica	265	Capri	309
Square of the Capitol, Rome	269	National Villa, Naples	311
House of Cola di Rienzi	274	Roman Gate, Genoa	318
Old Entrance to National Villa, Naples	278	Pilo Gate, Genoa	319
Naples and Mount Vesuvius	279	South Bastion, Genoa	319
The Aquarium, Naples	282	Tailpiece	320

ZIGZAG JOURNEYS

ON THE

MEDITERRANEAN.

CHAPTER I.

A ZIGZAG JOURNEY TO ZAG-A-ZIG.

"THE days of the caliphs and the palaces of the caliphates are gone. The United States and the English consular offices of the ports of the Mediterranean are the interesting story-telling places of to-day. How I have enjoyed the hours spent in the consular offices of the Southern ports of Europe! It was once my good fortune to visit all the American and English consulates on the coasts of the Mediterranean and of the Red Sea to the ports of Mecca. In other words, I made a journey under Government instructions from Washington to Zag-a-zig, as a town near Suez was called; a Zigzag journey of the Mediterranean from Cadiz to Zag-a-zig. The evenings in half of the consulates I visited were spent in story-telling, and I collected at the time a library of English, French, and Oriental story-books."

The speaker was Captain John Van der Palm, a veteran in the consular service of the United States. The place was the picnic-grounds of the old Van Ness mansion near the White House in Washington.

John Van der Palm was a middle-aged man, a widower, with an only son, named Percy. This boy had accompanied his father in several journeys to consular ports, in the interest of the State Department. Mr. Van der Palm had once served as a consul in several ports, but in late years had been employed as a general agent of the State Department in the consular service.

Percy Van der Palm was a story-loving boy. He early developed a lively appreciation of sea tales, wonder tales, and Oriental imagination. It was his delight to accompany his father to the social rooms of the State Department, and meet there old foreign ministers, consuls, and commercial agents, and to listen to their narratives, which often had all the interest and force of the best story-telling.

The Van der Palms were friends of the occupants of the old Van Ness mansion, who used often to invite their friends to the famous garden of the house to spend the spring and summer evenings. These friends were usually consuls or commercial agents. So stories of all lands came to be told here, in this unconventional way, greatly to the delight of Percy. He himself began to wish to travel, and he formed a plan to study to make himself an acceptable candidate as a consular clerk.

"Well, Percy," said his father one day, "what profession will you choose for life? Your education should now be turned into some preparation for a single thing. Life is too short for many things. The age demands superior fitness for one thing to open the door to one's success. Your story-telling days are now over. The time for fables has passed."

"No, father; my story-telling days have only begun. Let me study languages, commercial book-keeping, and commercial law. I intend to apply to the President for a place as consular clerk."

"And what would you do then?"

"After such a clerkship?"

"Yes, you would not wish to be a consular clerk for life?"

PITTI PALACE, FLORENCE.

"I would seek to become a secretary of legation, a diplomatic agent, a naval *attaché*, or a consul, such as you have been. Let me qualify myself for some place in the service of the Department of State. I would like a government position in that department above all things. Such people are in touch with all the world. They study everything. The world is their country, and their countrymen are all mankind. Their minds have no latitude or longitude; they take the world as a whole. Their very forms of conversation make other men seem small. Other men *suppose*; they *know*."

"Well, my son, I am glad that you take such a philosophical view of the State service. I am pleased with your decision. But I once heard of a man who had a son who wished to see the world, and—"

"Well, father?"

"He went to his father and said, 'Father, I want to travel and see the world.'"

"And what did his father say?"

"He said, 'My son, I am very willing that you should travel and see the world, but I would be sorry to have the world see *you*.'"

"Oh, father, you do not mean that!"

"I should be unwilling that you should seek employment in the office of the State Department without a long and a thorough preparation. Our diplomatic service in the past has often not been a credit to our country. Politicians have been given places that should have been filled only by trained men. Your education must begin now. It must be first in languages, then in mathematics, then in law, and in general knowledge always."

"Where shall I begin in languages?"

"Your education in languages must begin in the countries where those languages are spoken. I shall send you to the city of Mexico to study Spanish, and then, perhaps, to my friends in Caracas. I shall then send you for a year to the ports of the Mediterranean, to study French, Italian, and the eastern tongues, and to learn commercial usages. I have friends in nearly all those ports. I may be able to go with you myself; we may be able to make together a sort of a Zigzag journey from Washington to Port Said, or Zag-a-Zig. Should you go to Caracas to study, you would indeed make such a journey around the world as well as across the Mediterranean. The famous railway up the Andes from La Guayra to Caracas is called the Zig Zag. I will think over your plan. Your education must consist largely in educational travel; this is the highest education, and will become a

ON THE MEDITERRANEAN.

part of intellectual training of the future. Let us go down to the Garden. I have been promised a story to-night by one who knows the history of the Van Ness house."

"The ghost story?"

"Yes."

The two passed down the avenue and turned into the monument grounds. It was near sunset, and the western trees seemed glimmering with golden fruitage. Light airs rippled the leaves. The day had been hot, but was cooling.

The Garden?

All Washington knows of that strangely beautiful place. How shall I describe it? I cannot better do so than in the story of the place as it existed in former years, which an old visitor that night related to the Van der Palms as they sat under the trees in the mellow air: —

THE MYSTERY OF THE MYSTERY.[1]

AN OLD WASHINGTON GHOST STORY.

ONE keen December day, a few years after the war, I arrived in Washington to spend a few weeks with a friend who was making his home at this old Van Ness mansion, near the White House, and adjoining the grounds where the Washington Monument now stands. The mansion is almost a ruin now, and its beautiful grounds are broken and faded, but it was in its glory then, with its quaint porticos, its halls and gardens and beautiful trees.

In the same yard with the fine house, which had been associated with the best social life of many administrations, stood the so-called Marcia Burns's cottage, in which Sir Thomas Moore was entertained in Jefferson's days, on the occasion of his unhappy visit to Washington. In this cottage lived Davie Burns, the stubborn Scotchman, whom General Washington compelled to sell his plantation for the site of the city.

"Your position," said Davie Burns to Washington, "makes you feel that all is grist that comes into your hopper. Who would you have been, I should like to know, if you had n't 'a' married the Widow Custis?"

I had loved the songs of Tom Moore in my boyhood. My mother used to sing them. The "Last Rose of Summer," the "Vale of Avoca," "The Harp that once through Tara's Halls," came ringing back in memory; and after an hour with my friend in the Van Ness hall, I went out into the yard and sat down on one of the benches, and looked at the little gray cottage where the famous author of "Lallah Rookh" and the "Loves of the Angels" had been entertained when the city was new.

An old negress came sauntering by. With my Northern freedom I said to her, —

"Auntie, this all seems to me a place of mysteries."

"A place of mysteries, dat is wot it is, Massa Nof, — dat am wot it is. Dat am de suller [cellar] whar dey was goin' to prison Linkem [Lincoln] in de las' days ob de war. Wot you think of dat, Massa Nof? De 'spirators did n't intend on killin' him at first; dey had planned to 'duct him, an' jus' hide him

---

[1] Originally published by the author in the "Household." Used by permission.

in dat dar suller. An' den a *still* boat was to come ober de ribber, like de white hosses, wid *still* oars, movin' up an' down so *still*, an' dey were to steal him away, an' hold him for a ransom. Dat story sort o' haunts dat suller yet. It nebber happened, but de ghost of it all am dar jus' de same.

"Dar be some ghosts dat nebber happened, Massa Nof. De white hosses ain't de only ghosts that come round here o' nights. Marcia Burns, she come on summer nights, when de roses all hang in de dews in de thin light ob de moon, an' de mockin' bird am singin' his las' song.

"De white hosses, dey come on Christmas nights, — six white hosses on seven Christmas nights, Massa Nof, widout any heads on dem an' dar necks all smokin'. It may be you'll stay ober Christmas time, Massa Nof, an' see 'em wid your own eyes."

Of what was this old negress talking? Her eyes dilated as she spoke of the six white hosses, and she raised her arm and looked like a seeress.

"What are the six white horses?" I asked. "I never heard of them before."

"You did n't! Now dat am strange! I must call you Massa Up-Nof. Eberybody knows about 'em here. Dey am ghosts, — jus' ghosts. Dey are de ghosts ob de six white hosses dat all dropped right down dead wid broken hearts on de night dat Marcia Burns, as dey call Mrs. Van Ness, gabe up her soul to de angels. Dat am wot dey am."

My friend came out of the house. The old negress heard the door close, and gave her head a toss, and with an air of mystery moved away.

"It is rather cool for you to be sitting here," my friend said. "You need your overcoat. We have kindled the fires."

"Dwight," said I, "what is it the old negress has been telling me about six white horses? — one of the oddest things I ever heard."

"Oh, nonsense, Herbert. An old Christmas tale; the negroes believe it yet. I am going to the station; will be back soon. You had better go in. There's a chill in the air."

He passed out of the gate.

I did not go in. The ancient place seemed to throw over me a spell. I had heard that the early Presidents used to be entertained here; that Marcia Burns Van Ness was a kind of Washington saint; that she founded the orphan asylum, and that the government stopped on the day that she was buried.

"The government stopped," I said to myself, absently, "but did the six white horses really fall down dead?"

"Dat dey did."

The words seemed to come out of the air. I looked up, and the old negress again stood before me. She was on her way to some place outside the gate.

"An' Massa Up-Nof, jus' you let me tell you somethin': De white hosses am a mystery, but dar am a *mystery ob de mystery*. I'll tell you some day, I will."

She passed out of the gate. The sun was setting; the last breeze seemed to die, and I sat in the silence trying to picture to myself the past of this most wonderful place.

Dwight refused to talk to me about the six white horses. I went to Fortress Monroe to spend a week or two, and while there I wrote to a lady in Georgetown, who well knew the history of the Van Ness place, and asked her about the legend of the six white horses. The return letter intensely interested me. It was as follows: —

GEORGETOWN, December 20.

DEAR HERBERT, — Scrapbooks, old notes, a few letters from friends living near Seventeenth Street in Washington, bring to me about the same data you seem to possess.

The "headless horses" number "*six*," because General Van Ness drove to his *best* coach six, when guests were many and distinguished. He died at the age of seventy-six. He married the beautiful Marcia Burns when he was thirty; he was then a New York member of Congress. During all those years he gave annually a large, gay, fashionable entertainment to all of Congress, during the holidays. They were *the* Christmas events of society.

On the anniversary of that event, the six headless horses are said to appear "to this day"! They are seen at twelve o'clock at night, any or all nights during Christmas week. (You know, in the South, the Christmas revelry lasts all the week.) An old lady of eighty tells me, "The horses *do* gallop round and round the mansion in Mansion Square, and sometimes stop right in front of the old pillars of the porch and rock to and fro and moan and sigh. They are white as snow, with smoke and mist and white flame, like burning brandy, going upward from their shoulders."

They stop in their midnight gallops and listen at the door for the old voices of George Washington, Hamilton, Clay, Jefferson, the Taylors, and hundreds of distinguished men of that time. They come *over* the river, as most of the men are buried there. The unseen spirits of the great dead hover about the grounds, and make the aspen trees shiver, the willows moan, as the horses dash past.

Old Mr. Van Ness comes with his own horses, and it is his spirit appearing in them.

Tom Moore spent one week there, and comes generally at Christmas time, his voice repeating verses composed for the beautiful Marcia Van Ness, and as repeated at one entertainment *to her*, is still heard as the clock strikes *twelve*.

One old man says, "Dey los' dere heads [the horses] when ole massa was put in de big, gran' mos-lem!" (The mausoleum now stands in Oak Hill Cemetery. We see it often.) "An' dey lay in de dus'; an' when dey was seen nex' day, smoke was dere heads, like onto de day ob jedgment."

Another theory says: "The six beautiful, fiery horses *died* of grief, and were buried on the place. A rise in the Potomac River washed them far away. The next Christmas they returned "like death on the pale horse," in bodily form, with cloudy heads, and the general's eyes flashing through the smoke and flames. Sometimes the very faces of the guests appeared plainly."

Montgomery Blair used to say that the six headless horses *did* appear to the servants annually, and that his own slaves had repeated to him their stories "until he himself believed them."

The lonely Taylor family of "The Octagon House," whose collection of curios are now in the Corcoran building, told funny stories of the "ghosts," credited up to the eighties:

"Six headless horses gallop round the old house and grounds annually; always white and large, and with heads of *fire*. The servants run, and more courageous, intelligent persons spend the night trying to hold the horses. They fly past them, and *dissolve* before their eyes! A noise of rushing wind and voices in the distance, a splash in the water, and all is still."

One note of 1885 says: "The headless horses are, of course, a myth, but few of the neighbors care to pass a night in the place, near Christmas time. We have hidden behind the brick wall, but found it a ghostly spot."[1]

The story had grown with the letter, and my imagination grew. The incidents of the smoking necks of the horses, of Tom Moore's songs at Christmas at the midnight hour, of the terrified servants, and the dissolving spectres, all fixed themselves on my mind, and haunted my sleeping and waking dreams. On the 24th of December I returned to Washington, to pass the holidays with my friends at the old Van Ness house.

As I passed the gate into the great garden, I met the old negress again.

"De land! am you come back? Don' you be frightened now; you listen right now to wot you' Auntie Wisdom 's gwine to say. Dar am a mystery ob de mystery. I 'se found it out, I dun has.

> "Dem beliebs dat dar are witches.
> Dar de witches are;
> Dos dat tink dar ain't no witches,
> Dar ain't no witches dar.

Now. Massa Up-Nof, don' you be 'fraid. I 'll tell you somethin' befo' you go. Dar 's got to be a *mental* mind to see dem tings; de 'maginations

---

[1] These are extracts from a real letter, for nearly every incident of this strange story is true. I have used only a slight framework of fiction, and that framework does not include any essential historical event.

got to hab eyes; you 'member now wot yo' Auntie Wisdom says, an' don' you get scared at anyting dey tells you. Dar 'll be libely times about midnight. Glad to see ye. But I mus' hurry on; wot Massa Blair, he say, if he heard me talkin' dis way wid a gent'man from up Nof! No account nigger like me. But I 'se yer true frien', I 'se am! I likes peoples wot live up Nof!"

It was a beautiful night. The Capitol seemed to stand in the air like a mountain of marble, and when the moon rose and illumined the grand porticos of the nation's halls, the air, as it were, became enchanted, as if it held a celestial palace of light. The Capitol by moonlight is one of the most beautiful scenes on earth. It rivals the visions of the Taj, and impresses the imagination as the very genius of American destiny.

There was a gay party in the old house on that Christmas eve. Amid the social entertainments I once or twice heard an allusion to the "six white horses," as though the legend were merely a joke. The guests departed by eleven o'clock, and a half hour later I found myself in the guest-chamber, looking out of the window on Marcia Burns's cottage, the evergreens, and the Potomac. The house became still, but sounds of merriment from time to time broke on the air from the negro quarters. I wondered where Auntie Wisdom might be, and, but for the impropriety, I would have been glad to talk with her as the critical hour of twelve drew nigh.

Tom Moore probably wrote the once famous song, "The Lake of the Dismal Swamp" here, on returning from Norfolk, or here formed it in his mind. As I sat by the window, gazing across the Potomac, under the high moon, I could almost hear my old mother singing that song again: —

> "They made her a grave too cold and damp
>   For a heart so warm and true;
> And she's gone to the Lake of the Dismal Swamp,
> Where all night long by her fire-fly lamp,
>   She paddles her white canoe.
>
>   . . . . .
>
> "Away to the Dismal Swamp he speeds,
>   And his path is rugged and sore;
> Through tangled juniper, beds of reeds,
> Through many a fen where the serpent feeds,
>   And man never trod before.
>
> "And near him the she-wolf stirs the brake,
>   And the copper snake breathes in his ear,
> Till he starting cries —"

A shriek rent the air at this point of my mental recitation. It came from the negro quarters. The yard was soon filled with colored servants, and among them was Aunt Chloe, the woman of wisdom.

"Comin', comin', comin' on de wings ob de wind!" the old negress began to exclaim in a wild, high, gypsyish tone, bowing backwards and forwards and waving her hands in a circle. The negroes around her seemed beside themselves with terror.

What was coming?

I looked out on the Potomac over the motionless trees. On the margin of the river was rising a thin white mist, which formed itself into fantastic shapes as it rolled along and broke over the marshes in the viewless currents of the air. One of these mist forms began to condense, and drift toward the gardens of the house.

"Comin', comin', on de winds! The Revelations am comin', an' wot's gwine to sabe us now?"

I opened the window. The clocks were striking twelve in the church towers.

"The Powers above, sabe us!" shrieked Aunt Chloe. "Fall upon yo' knees. The dead are upon ye all. You that has bref, rend de skies!"

"Jerusalem and Jericho!" cried a negro who was called Deacon Ned. He seemed to think that in the union of these two words was prophylactic virtue, and repeated them over and over again. Then a cry went up, which might have reached the skies, had the celestial scenery been as near as it appeared on that still December morning. Deacon Ned followed the piercing cry with the startling declaration: —

"De yarth am comin' up an' de hebens am comin' down!"

With this thrilling announcement in my ears, I left my room, and went down into the hall, and out into the air. A Christmas carol from the chimes of some unknown tower was floating through the sky like an angel's song.

Aunt Chloe, the woman of occult wisdom, rose up when she saw me.

"Oh, Massa Up-Nof, dey is comin'! Wot you say now?"

"Where?"

"*Dere*—don' ye see 'em? Clar as de mornin'! Hain't ye got de clar vision?"

She pointed wildly to one of the forms of the night mist, and stood with one arm raised and white-orbed eyes.

"Don' ye see dat white hoss dar, widout any head, an' smokin'? An' don' ye see dem five white hosses dat am bein' *created* behind him?"

Then she pointed again toward the marshes, and I saw them.

There, as plainly as I ever saw anything, was a white horse without a head, his neck smoking. Behind him were five other white horses rising from the marshes.

"You see, now?"

"Yes."

"You hab de clar vision? Wot did I tell ye!"

"I see."

"You can't discern dese tings widout de seein' eye. Wot did I tell ye!"

The forms rolled over the marshes, and through the outward shrubbery of the gardens, and disappeared, dissolving as they approached the higher part of the city. The negroes stood like statues.

"It has passed by," said Deacon Ned. "Bress de Laud!"

"Aunt Chloe," said I, "you said there was a mystery of the mystery. What is it? I must know."

She heaved a deep sigh, but as of relief, and then said, slowly, "Massa Up-Nof, nobody sees 'em as hosses until dey are told dat dey *be* horses. Den dey hab de seein' eye. Do ye see?"

"I see." I did, indeed.

"Dey was hosses, warn't dey now, Massa Up-Nof?"

"Yes, Aunt Chloe, I saw them as plainly as I saw the President's horses on Inauguration Day."

The negroes disappeared in the shadows.

I slept serenely, and when I awoke, all the Christmas bells were ringing. There was a mystery of the mystery, and that key will unlock many doors.

But I shall never forget the impressions made upon my mind that night at the old Van Ness house; and wherever Christmas may find me, that haunting memory will always return again. No American Christmas story ever made such a vivid impression upon me, or left in my mind so many suggestive lessons. And the story is substantially true.

CHAPTER II.

HOW CONSULS ARE APPOINTED.—THEIR DUTIES.—THE STORY-TELLING GARDEN.—THE CAPITOL BY MOONLIGHT.—THE SINGING MOUSE.—THE VILLAGE MYSTERY.

A YOUNG mind with an inborn purpose is haunted by ideals. Dreams of life which shall be realities float before it. Percy Van der Palm loved to loiter about the old Washington garden, and read books that related to the duties and opportunities of the foreign offices of the Department of State. The "Register" of the State Department is a very simple document, but he was often found reading it, and making the catalogue a wonder-book by associating with some name in it a mental picture. For example, one would usually find pages like that on our next page of little interest. Some (like that on page 28) relate to the consulates of Spain and Italy, to which Percy's dreams somehow seemed to be tending after what his father had said.

But however dry such pages of official history may seem to our readers, they were leaves of story books to Percy, as we have said; they were titles of fictions which were founded, like old novels, on facts, which his interpretative fancy filled.

There was another book issued by the Department of State which his imagination used in a like way. It was entitled "United States Consular Regulations." It was a large book for a record, handsomely bound.

Many afternoons found him in the old haunted Garden, studying in this book facts that he hoped might have a bearing on his future.

REGISTER OF EXISTING OFFICERS, EMPLOYÉS, ETC.

OFFICERS AND CLERKS OF THE DEPARTMENT OF STATE.

Offices, salaries, and names.	Where born.	Whence appointed.	Service in the Department.
Secretary of State ($8,000). JOHN W. FOSTER	Ind.	Ind.	Commissioned June 29, 1892.
Assistant Secretary of State ($4,500). William F. Wharton	Mass.	Mass.	Commissioned April 2, 1889.
Second Assistant Secretary of State ($3,500). Alvey A. Adee	N. Y.	D. C.	Appointed Secretary of Legation at Madrid September 9, 1870; *Chargé d'Affaires* at different times; transferred from Madrid and appointed clerk class four July 9, 1877; appointed Chief of Diplomatic Bureau June 11, 1878; commissioned Third Assistant Secretary July 18, 1882; commissioned Second Assistant Secretary August 3, 1886.
Third Assistant Secretary of State ($3,500). William M. Grinnell	N. Y.	N. Y.	Commissioned February 11, 1892.
Solicitor ($3,500). Frank C. Partridge	Vt.	Vt.	Commissioned June 10, 1890.
Chief Clerk ($2,750). Sevellon A. Brown	N. Y.	N. Y.	Appointed temporary clerk December 21, 1864; clerk class one July 1, 1866; class two October 16, 1866; class four June 1, 1870; Chief of Bureau of Indexes and Archives July 1, 1873; member of Board of Civil Service Examiners for Department of State August 7, 1873; Chief Clerk August 7, 1873; resigned to take effect February 1, 1888; reappointed Chief Clerk February 11, 1890.
Chief of the Diplomatic Bureau ($2,100). Thomas W. Cridler	Va.	W. Va.	Appointed clerk of $900 class October 1, 1875; class one July 1, 1880; class three November 1, 1881; class four February 1, 1884; Chief of the Diplomatic Bureau July, 15, 1889.
Chief of the Consular Bureau ($2,100). Francis O. St. Clair	N. Y.	Md.	Appointed temporary clerk November 12, 1865; class two June 7, 1870; class three June 22, 1871; class four July 1, 1874; temporary Chief of the Consular Bureau June 7, 1881; permanent Chief of the Consular Bureau November 1, 1881.
Chief of the Bureau of Indexes and Archives ($2,100). John H. Haswell	N. Y.	N. Y.	Appointed temporary clerk January 23, 1865; class one August 1, 1867; class two March 22, 1869; class three June 1, 1870; class four June 22, 1871; Chief of the Bureau of Indexes and Archives August 7, 1873.
Chief of the Bureau of Accounts ($2,100). Francis J. Kieckhoefer	D. C.	D. C.	Appointed temporary clerk August 1, 1874; class one December 1, 1874; class three November 20, 1877; class two July 1, 1878; class three February 27, 1880; class four July 1, 1880; Chief of Bureau of Accounts and Disbursing Clerk January 28, 1884.

UNITED STATES CONSULAR SERVICE.

ITALY.

Place.	Name and Title.	Where born.	Whence appointed.	Date of commission or appointment.	Salary.	Fees for year ending June 30, 1892.
Castellammare	Alfred M. Wood . . . . C. A.	N. Y.	N. Y.	July 13, 1878	$1,500	
Do	Nestore Calvano . . V. C. A.			Sept. 30, 1891		
Catania	Carl Bailey Hurst * . . . C.	Germany	D. C.	July 22, 1892	1,500	$1,519.00
Do	Augustus Peratoner, V. & D. C.			Nov. 22, 1883		
Florence	James Verner Long . . . C.	Pa.	Pa.	Feb. 27, 1891	1,500	2,314.00
Do	Spirito Bernardi . V. & D. C.			Mar. 3, 1883		
Bologna	Carlo Gardini . . . . Agt.			June 2, 1881		529.00
Genoa	James Fletcher (n) . . . C.	Gt. Brit.	Iowa	May 14, 1883	1,500	3,296.50
Do	Frederick Scerni . . . V. C.			Dec. 10, 1883		
San Remo	Albert Aniceglio . . . Agt.			Nov. 27, 1883		40.00
Leghorn	Radcliffe H. Ford . . . C.	Me.	Me.	Jan. 6, 1892	1,500	3,272.50
Do	Emilio Masi . . V. & D. C.			Oct. 14, 1889		
Carrara	Ulisse Boccacci . . . Agt.			June 10, 1882		706.50
Messina	Darley R. Brush . . . C.	Iowa	S. Dak.	July 22, 1892	1,500	5,637.50
Do	. . . . V. & D. C.					
Gioja	L. Giffoni . . . . Agt.			Aug. 6, 1868		No fees.
Milazzo	Pietro Siracusa . . . Agt.			Mar. 12, 1880		55.00
Milan	George W. Pepper (n) . . C.	Ireland	Ohio	Jan. 30, 1890	1,500	2,059.50
Do	Anthony Richman . V. & D. C.			Mar. 11, 1885		
Naples	John S. Twells . . . . C.	Pa.	Pa.	Feb. 27, 1890	1,500	2,400.50
Do	Rob't O'N. Wickersham. V. C.			Nov. 7, 1883		
Do	Philip S. Twells . . . D. C.			July 1, 1890		
Bari	Nicholas Schuck . . . . Agt.			Feb. 8, 1892		455.50
Rodi	T. del Giudice . . . . Agt.			Mar. 6, 1878		125.00
Palermo	Horace C. Pugh . . . . C.	Ind.	Ind.	Oct. 16, 1890	2,000	8,028.50
Do	Carmelo G. Lagana . . V. C.			Dec. 22, 1884		
Girgenti	Francis Crotta . . . Agt.			Apr. 21, 1892		476.00
Licata	Arthur Verderame . . . Agt.			Apr. 27, 1888		171.00
Marsala	George Rayson . . . Agt.			Dec. 21, 1874		56.50
Trapani	Ignazio Marrone . . . Agt.			Oct. 24, 1890		308.00
Rome	Augustus O. Bourn . . C. G.	R. I.	R. I.	June 26, 1889	3,000	670.50
Do	Charles M. Wood V. & D. C. G.			Feb. 12, 1884		
Do	Charles M. Wood . . C. C.	Vt.	Vt.	Mar. 24, 1873	1,200	
Ancona	A. P. Tomassini . . . . Agt.			Mar. 19, 1875		74.50
Cagliari	Alphonse Dol . . . . Agt.			June 7, 1879		13.50
Civita Vecchia	G. Marsanich . . . . Agt.			June 14, 1862		83.00
Turin (b)	St. Leger A. Touhay (n) C. A.	France	D. C.	Jan. 7, 1892	Fees.	350.50
Do	Hugo Pizzotti . . . V. C. A.			Apr. 28, 1892		
Venice (b)	Henry A. Johnson . . . C.	D. C.	D. C.	Mar. 29, 1886	1,000	867.00
Do	Frederick Rechsteiner, V. & D. C.			June 8, 1891		

Let me give a few of them; they will show how our foreign service is conducted, and will serve as pictures of the beginnings of diplomatic and consular life.

CLASSES OF CONSULAR OFFICERS: THEIR POWERS AND DUTIES.

The Consular Service of the United States consists of agents and consuls-general, vice-consuls-general, deputy consuls-general; consuls, vice-consuls, deputy consuls; commercial agents, vice-commercial agents, deputy commercial agents; consular agents, consular clerks, interpreters, marshals, and clerks at consulates.

Consuls are of two classes: (1) Those who are not allowed to engage in business, and whose salaries exceed one thousand dollars per annum; (2) Those who are allowed to engage in business. The latter class of consuls is again subdivided into—(1) Those who are salaried (known as consuls in Schedule C), and, (2) Those who are compensated from the fees which they receive for their services.

These clerks, to the number of thirteen in all, are appointed by the President after examination, and can be removed only for cause stated in writing and submitted to Congress at the session first following such removal. Applicants must be over eighteen years of age, and citizens of the United States at the time of their appointment, and must pass examination before an examining board, who shall report to the Secretary of State that the applicant is qualified and fit for the duties of the office. They may be assigned to different consulates at the pleasure of the Secretary of State; and, when so assigned, they are subordinate to the principal consular officer, or the vice or deputy at the post, as the case may be.

If the applicant for the office of consular clerk is in a foreign country, he may be examined by a series of written questions by the Minister of the United States in that country, and two other competent persons to be named by him. The result of the examination, with the answers of the candidate in his own handwriting, will then be transmitted to the Secretary of State. Consular clerks are required to discharge such clerical and other duties of the consulate as may be assigned to them by the principal officer, whose instructions in all respects they are carefully to observe and obey. Punctual daily attendance at the consulate during office hours, diligence in the discharge of the consular duties, a cheerful obedience to the directions of their superiors, a courteous bearing toward all persons having business with the consulate, and uprightness of conduct in all respects will be expected from them. Disobedience, want of punctuality, neglect of duty, the abuse of their credit in pecuniary transactions, or exceptionable moral conduct will be followed by the revocation of their commissions.

The department is authorized by law to allow for the hire of clerks, when the money is actually expended therefor, as follows: To the consul at Liverpool, a sum not exceeding the rate of two thousand dollars for any one year; and to the consuls-general at London, Paris, Havana, and Rio de Janeiro, each a sum not exceeding the rate of one thousand six hundred dollars for any one year; to the consuls-general at Berlin, Frankfort, Montreal, Shanghai, Vienna, and Kanagawa, and for the consuls at Hamburg, Bremen, Manchester, Lyons, Hong-Kong, Havre, Crefeld, and Chemnitz, each a sum not exceeding the rate of one thousand two hundred dollars for any one year; and the consuls at Bradford, Marseilles, and Birmingham, each a sum not exceeding the rate of nine hundred and sixty dollars for any one year; to the consuls-general at Calcutta, Port au Prince, and Melbourne, and to the consuls at Leipsic, Sheffield, Sonneberg, Dresden, Nuremberg, Tunstall, Antwerp, Bordeaux, Colon (Aspinwall), Glasgow, Panama, and Singapore, each a sum not exceeding the rate of eight hundred dollars for any one year; to the consuls at Belfast, Barmen, Leith, Dundee, Victoria, and to the consuls-general at Matamoros and Halifax, each a sum not exceeding the rate of six hundred and forty dollars for any one year; to the consuls-general at Mexico and Berne and to the consuls at Beirut, Malaga, Genoa, Naples, Stuttgart, Florence, Manheim, Prague, Zurich, and Demerara, each a sum not exceeding the rate of four hundred and eighty dollars for any one year. The allowance to be made from this appropriation to the several consulates named being within the discretion of the Department of State, the amount of the allowance will be determined by the requirements of each office. No clerk will be employed without special instructions authorizing it, and the name and nationality, as well as the proposed amount of compensation of each clerk, will be reported to the department.

APPOINTMENT AND QUALIFICATION OF CONSULAR OFFICERS.

Consuls-general and consuls are appointed by the President, by and with the advice and consent of the Senate. They qualify by taking the prescribed oath (a copy of which is furnished by the department for the purpose), and by executing a bond to the United States in the form prescribed by the department.

Consuls-general and all consuls and commercial agents whose salaries exceed one thousand dollars a year are required, before receiving a commission, to execute a bond (Form No. 2) containing an express stipulation against engaging in business. Those whose salaries are at the rate of one thousand dollars or less, all of whom are entitled to the privilege of trading, execute the bond given in Form No. 3; and those who derive their compensation from fees (who may also engage in business) execute the bond prescribed in Form No. 4. The prohibition as to transacting business may, however, be extended, in the discretion of the President, to all consular officers, whether receiving salary or fees. All principal consular officers are required by law to take the oath in Form No. 1. For instructions respecting the sureties on the bond and the formalities of its execution see note to Form No. 2.

A consul-general or consul appointed to one consulate is prohibited from holding the office of consul-general or consul at any other consulate, or from exercising the duties thereof.

Commercial agents are appointed by the President. They qualify for their offices in the same manner in all respects as consuls-general and consuls.

Vice-consuls-general, deputy consuls-general, vice-consuls, deputy consuls, vice-commercial agents, deputy commercial agents, and consular agents are appointed by the Secretary of State, usually upon the nomination of the principal consular officer, approved by the consul-general (if the nomination relates to a consulate or commercial agency), or, if there be no consul-general, then by the diplomatic representative. If there be no consul-general or diplomatic representative, the nomination should be transmitted directly to the Department of State, as should also the nominations for subordinate officers in Mexico, British India, Manitoba, and British Columbia. The nominations for vice-consul-general and deputy consul-general must be submitted to the diplomatic representative for approval, if there be one resident in the country. The privilege of making the nominations for the foregoing subordinate officers must not be construed to limit the authority of the Secretary of State, as provided by law, to appoint these officers without such previous nomination by the principal officer. The statutory power in this respect is reserved, and it will be exercised in all cases in which the interests of the service or other public reasons may be deemed to require it.

Consular officers recommending appointments of this character must in all cases submit some evidence of the capacity, character, and fitness of the nominee for the office, and also information respecting his residence and the State or country of which he is a citizen or subject. A nomination failing to give these particulars will not be considered. The nomination must be made in a dispatch addressed to the Assistant Secretary of State, transmitted through the legation or consulate-general, or directly, as the case may be. A minor will not be approved for any subordinate consular office. All persons nominated for subordinate appointments must be able to speak and read the English language.

These pages may seem dull, yet they illustrate certain facts that American boys should know, as it should be a part of education to show how the departments of our own government are conducted.

Reader, when you are travelling, always visit the consulates, and also the stations of the missionaries of your own church. You will find more information in these places than anywhere else. It is the consul's business to answer your questions in regard to travel and to treat you well, and he will usually do these things with great pleasure to himself as well as to you. As for the missionary stations, they stand for progressive education, and you may make yourself a kind of missionary by bearing good reports of the progress that such places usually illustrate. Such visits will educate your heart as well as your head, and perhaps stimulate your conscience. Go!

Percy was delighted with the tales of the East. Let me give you from time to time some of the books that he read.

"Count Lucanor," a Spanish book, written a century before the invention of printing, was a favorite study. It had the charm of old Spain and Moorish places. Its author was Don Juan Manuel, the Spanish Chaucer. We will give you some tales from this curious book.

"Folk-Lore Legends, Russian and Polish," as published by W. W. Gibbings, 18 Bury Street, London, he also found rich in tales that were almost as charming to the fancy as the story of the days of "Good Haroun Alraschid."

We shall give you adaptions of the best stories from these pages, as they are still the delight of the Eastern ports.

Percy also liked those American stories that closely resemble those of the East.

The long twilights of the story-telling garden had the atmosphere for such curious tales and wonder-tales. His father's friends in the State Department and old consular friends would gather under the trees, and with them social travellers, and tell tales of many lands. After the story-telling they would leave the garden to see the dome of the Capitol gleaming over the city in the moonlight.

Let me give you some of these old stories by visitors from the New England port cities, that have the Oriental curiosity and flavor. There were two that particularly held Percy's fancy. The boy used to repeat them to new visitors, and they seemed to many to have an almost Eastern charm. The favorite of all these peculiar stories which he used to relate with sympathetic coloring, after the Eastern way, and which we reproduce in our own, was,—

THE SINGING MOUSE.

"GOOD-BY, Alice. It is a cold morning, and it seems hard to go away and leave you all alone in the dark; but I must work. We have to work to live. To-morrow will be Christmas. I wish I had something to give you; but I have n't. Never mind, Alice. I love you."

The old man opened the door to go, then looked back on his blind daughter, whom he was about to leave all alone for the day. He wished to say something more to comfort her in the long hours of loneliness that were to follow.

"Well, be good, Alice. Perhaps the good fairies will come to you; they come at Christmas-time, they say, to those who believe that the world is good."

He closed the door.

"The world." The words had a strange far-away meaning to Alice. She had never seen the world. She had felt the sunshine, she had heard distant bells ringing on Sundays, and happy birds singing in the cool green trees of the park on summer morns. She knew when the seasons came and changed, but she had never seen the springs light up the hills, and burst into flowers, or the summer dawns and groves and rivers and hay-fields, or the autumn fruits and burning leaves, or the fleecy fall of white snows. The winds of the seasons sang to her; she had listened to their music for sixteen years. When a young child she had had the scarlet-fever, and it had left her weak and helpless, and a slow darkness had come over her eyes, shutting out the light more and more day by day, until at last the bright world disappeared, and was lost. She was blind. She could now only dimly remember that she had ever seen the world. Only two things had left pictures on her mind; they were the face of her mother, who was now dead, and a canary-bird that had sung over her bed in her sickness. She loved to dream of them always, — the beautiful face and the golden bird.

Late in the morning an old woman named Lucy came into the room. She always visited the blind girl once a day, and in winter oftener.

"Can I do anything for you, Alice?" she asked kindly.

"Father says that to-morrow will be Christmas. It is the day of Christ, and I suppose that everything is beautiful. Shall I ever see Christmas? I wish I could!"

"Oh, Alice, believe that you will, and you will. How bright the snows glisten on the roof of the Perkins Institute for the Blind! I wish you could see the wings of the doves that fly among the chimneys over there. It always looks bright up there; all places look pleasant where people do good."

"For the blind? Did you say for the blind? Could I not go there? Perhaps they would help me."

"But you would have to leave your dear old father. That is an asylum, and your eyes are all grown over. But don't lose heart, child. Strange things happen to those that believe. The believing heart receiveth all things. Ask the Lord to send you the good fairies of Christmas, and the good fairies will come. I have always noticed that the good fairies come to those who expect them."

"Oh, Lucy, I do so wish I could see, like you! The bells will ring, but I shall not see the Day Beautiful. Don't you pity me, Lucy? Let me kiss you." The old woman clasped the girl to her bosom. "Lucy, I believe in you — and father."

The faith of the girl touched the old woman's heart. There are few sweeter words than these, "I believe in you." The confidence made old Lucy wish to help the sightless girl. Faith always has this influence. Lucy turned away, and a happy thought came into her mind, like an angel flying across the sky. She had a few pennies. She would buy some chestnuts from the grizzly old chestnut-roaster on the street, and would put them in Alice's stocking. So she stopped at the door as she was about to go, and said, —

"Alice, other girls hang their stockings under the shelf on Christmas Eve, and they do say that the good fairies come in the night and put things into them. You hang up yours to-night above the stove. You cannot tell what may happen. I see you have faith in your heart. It is a good thing to believe in God and everybody. If all people did this, what a happy world it would be!"

Alice did not comprehend all this homely philosophy, but she felt the spirit of it. She heard Lucy going. A new delight came into her heart, her face grew bright, and she said,—

"Oh, Lucy, I feel that everything is good around me and above me, and I believe in everything! I shall see Christmas — the Day Beautiful — some day. Yes, Lucy, I surely will. I feel it *here*. I shall see."

She crossed her white hands on her heart, and sat smiling. Old Lucy went away, but Alice sat there still, as lovely as a mute statue of Faith. She heard the footsteps hurrying by on the street, a rift of sunlight came into the room from the thinly parting snow clouds, and she felt the brightness of the light that she could not see.

There was a little noise in the room — a rustle. Something was there, — a tiny something. Was it a fairy's foot? It was now here, now there, airy, timid.

Alice listened. She heard nothing more for a time. She recalled the tales of Grimm, Anderson, Fouqué, Haupt, and Hoffmann that her mother used to tell her. Was it a fairy? It was not the wind, for the air was still.

Again an airy trip across the floor like a little wing. Was it the spirit of the dead canary that she could see still in the dim twilight of memory? Her heart beat. Again and again it sped across the floor, like a thing of air. Once it came near her feet. Oh, that she could see!

What was *that*? Music? Surely it was. In a corner of the room. Soft music like the summer wind among the high wires over the street, like a harp in the park, like the dead canary's remembered song, only not sharp like that — more light, more soft, more timid. Fairy music it might be. A fairy playing a harp.

It came again. It could not be a cricket. Crickets sometimes came to those tenement-houses in the dead world, but it was winter now. How it sang and sang! Alice listened with a thrilled and wonder-delighted heart. She moved her foot. The music was gone with a little rustle like a wing.

"Lucy!" she screamed.

Old Lucy came. "What, Alice, girl?"

"My old canary has come back, and has been singing to me. Something good is going to happen. Do dead birds sing?"

Lucy did not know. She saw nothing and heard nothing. She kissed

Alice, and only said, "You have been dreaming, child; but dreams of faith often come true."

That afternoon the street was all bells. Door-bells were ringing. There were bells on the horses, bells on the sleds of the children. The sun of the short day faded out of the room, and all the air became melodious and palpitating with chimes. At twilight all was music, — bells, bells, bells.

Then fell a hush between the twilight and the evening festivals. The street lamps were lit; one of them flashed into the window. There were a few still moments, a rustle, and the same sweet harp-like, cricket-like music filled the room again. Alice did not stir. It lasted long. There was a footfall on the stairs, another little rustle and an airy run, and the music was gone.

The door opened. "Oh, father, father, my dead canary has been here, and has been singing to me! Oh, it was like silver; so beautiful — beautiful! I wish that I could see!"

"Be patient, my little daughter. Perhaps it will all come by-and-by. I told you that the fairies of good came to those who believe in them. I have brought home a whole loaf of pound-cake and two oranges to-night because it is Christmas Eve, and I have been thinking so much of you to-day. We will eat them together."

Poor old Hugh Meadowcraft, the laborer at the docks where ships unloaded their freight, felt a new vitality in his weary limbs as he rattled the grate, and put the meat on the stove to fry, and poured out the coffee into the coffee-pot, and prepared the evening meal. His employer, the ship-master, had added two dollars to his simple wages for this week. He had paid his rent for his two rooms, and bought a pound-cake for *her*, and he was a happy man. He heard nothing but goodness in all the bells that were ringing near and far, and as he sat down to his tea with his blind child, he said, "I tell you what it is, Alice, this is a good world to live in; and I think that the next will be better still. There's nothing, child, like love and faith and hope; they are all the world of happiness. A king can have no more. Smell the coffee, and hear the kettle sing. The bells are all ringing yonder, everywhere."

They ate in happy silence. Suddenly there was a lute-like sound, like a harp of air.

"Listen, father."

"Fairies."

Old Hugh moved his chair. The music ceased.

"You have heard it, father — the canary?"

"It is very strange. It is nothing bad, Alice; it bodes no evil; only a good fairy ever sang like that."

THE SINGING MOUSE.

Night came, with the temples of the stars shining in the sky; the streets thronged; there were merry voices in the clear still air. Old Lucy came in, and laughed at Alice's fairy. Nine o'clock came, and Hugh went to his room, and Alice for the first time in her life hung up her stocking for Santa Claus, or the fairies, or the spirit of good that haunts the world's better self. She went to bed — it had been a thrilling day to her — and went to sleep to dream of the song of the golden bird.

She awoke early, or was awakened by a little noise. What was that? A nibbling sound under the shelf and over the stovepipe; in the very place where she had hung her stocking.

She rose softly, slowly. The nibbling sound continued, and there was a rustle as of nuts. Hush! The canary was singing again, — in the dark, under the shelf, over the stove-pipe, where she had hung her stocking.

She crept toward the place silently and listened. Could it be? Yes, the music was *in* her stocking, away down in her stocking toward the foot. How sweet and silvery and happy it was! She put out her trembling hand and grasped the top of the stocking; she felt a motion of some living thing in it. She pinched the toe; it was full of something. What had happened? She screamed.

Her father came to the door with a light. "What is it, Alice?"

"The canary in my stocking."

"No, no, girl. Here, let me see."

Old Hugh opened the top of the stocking. "Santa Claus has been to see you, Alice; and he has left a *mouse*, I do declare."

Old Lucy came, running. "See here, will wonders ever cease? Alice has found a mouse in her stocking."

"Kill it!" said old Lucy. "It is after the nuts that — "

"Oh, no, no; don't kill it!" said Alice. "I beg of you, don't kill it! It sings."

"Oh, no, girl, it don't sing; and it will eat up all the nuts. Let me call the cat."

"Oh, no; I tell you it sings like a canary. Let me have the stocking;" and Alice seized it, and threw herself upon the bed. "Let me have it — let me have it until day!" said she. "Let me be alone with it for a little while. Oh, please do! It means good to me. I feel it does. Let me have it a little while."

"Let her be," said old Hugh. "Perhaps it is a singing mouse — who knows? I have heard of them. They bring good luck. Likely it was that she heard yesterday, and that we heard at tea."

Morning came, — a splendor of billowy clouds, sunshine, and glistening snow. Old Hugh rose late, and came into the room.

"Oh, father, it has been singing again; and the stocking is half full of nuts, and I have touched *it* with my hand It is soft, and its heart makes its little body tremble all over. Did Santa Claus leave it, father?"

"I don't know; and it isn't much matter, I guess, as long as you are happy."

The mouse continued to nibble the nuts and to sing. Hugh began to be interested in it. He called old Lucy into the room to hear it sing.

"Just you be still and listen." said he.

The mouse began to nibble, then to sing.

The doctor called to see a sick woman who lived in the house.

"Doctor," said Lucy, "did you ever hear of such a thing as a singing mouse?"

"Yes."

"There's one in the other room, and I want you to hear it."

The doctor was in a hurry to go, but his curiosity was excited. He stepped into Alice's room, saw the little mouse in the trap cage, and presently heard it sing.

It looked so cunning standing there on its hind-feet, and moving its fore-feet as though playing on a tiny violin — so pretty, so toy-like, so comical — that the doctor was delighted, and he lingered there for nearly half an hour, notwithstanding his haste at first to go. Then his face turned to Alice — how happy and lovely she looked! — and he said, —

"What is the matter with your eyes, my girl?"

"I am blind. I cannot see you or father; I cannot see Christmas, the day that they call Beautiful; I cannot see the singing mouse. Oh, doctor, I wish I could see! I feel that some good influence is following me. Can't you help me?"

"Come to the window with me, my girl, and let me examine your eyes. You ought to be treated by an oculist," said he. "I declare, I must tell my friend Phillips about you. His wife is an invalid; she will want to see the singing mouse. *She* likes to meet everybody who has trouble and to make them happy. She feeds with coin all the organ-grinders in the street, and watches at her window for faces in distress. Here is a case for her. My girl, I have hopes that you may see again. There is a growth over your eyes; it may be removed. I will be your friend. What is your name?"

"Alice — Alice Meadowcraft."

He went away slowly, leading Alice back to her chair. And the mouse was singing.

"Will be your friend." Alice's face was a picture of happiness, and beautiful with hope. "Friend!" He might cause the heavens to lift again before her eyes full of sunrises, moonrises, sunsets, rainbows, and stars. He might cause the flowers to bloom again, the birds to come again, to her eyes. He might bring again the face of her father to hers, and she might yet see the Day Beautiful.

There lived on Essex Street at this time a tall, patriarchal man, with grand manners and a most beautiful face, whom the whole nation feared, but whom all the poor people of that neighborhood loved. He would face a political mob with perfect calmness, but he could never say "No" to an unfortunate man or a homeless child. He was of distinguished family, and had inherited wealth; a graduate of Harvard, and a correspondent of the greatest statesmen of the world, yet he lived in a simple way, and died poor, having given away all that he had. He sleeps now in a lot assigned him by friendly charity in the beautiful Milton (Massachusetts) burying-ground, near the old house of the "Suffolk Resolves," which "resolves" was the first Declaration of Independence.

This man, whose criticism even good President Lincoln declared that he dreaded more than any other, and whose white hand waved mobs backward like a prophet's, at this time towered through the streets near where the Old Colony and Albany depots now are, loved, feared, hated, carrying his own market basket in the morning, and at night thrilling assemblies with silver-tongued eloquence such as is not now heard in Boston. His wife was an invalid, and he was her nurse for a lifetime.

The next day the doctor came to the long rambling house where Alice lived, and he brought with him this statesman who scorned public office, but whose words moved the conscience of the people and led the struggles of the world.

How grand and noble he looked as he stood there in that poor room and took the hand of Alice, the blind girl!

"I have come to hear your little mouse sing," said he. Then he started back. He looked upon the blind eyes of that beautiful face. "I must let you go over and see Ann. She will send you to Mrs. Anagnos."

The little mouse was induced to sing after a time, and the two went away.

"I will call for you some day," said the patriarch.

"Mrs. Anagnos!" Who was Mrs. Anagnos? The name rang in Alice's mind. She asked the few that came into her room who was Mrs. Anagnos. None of them knew.

At last the grocer came with a simple parcel. Alice asked him the question that so haunted her.

"Oh, she is the daughter of Julia Ward Howe — she who wrote, —

'Mine eyes have seen the glory of the coming of the Lord.'"

And he hurried away. But the mouse was singing.

The line seemed a prophecy. Who wrote it, — Mrs. Julia Ward Howe or Mrs. Anagnos? She would ask the newsboy when he passed. She did. His answer was odd, but satisfactory: —

"She is the wife of Mr. Anagnos, who keeps the Blind Asylum over in South Boston, and helps blind people to read. He might make *you* see. Better go and see her. She is a great big woman, and she's just good to everybody, like *Mis'* Phillips. She'd make you see, like's not. I'd try her, anyway."

Alice went back to her room, her mind all roses, and the little mouse was singing again.

One day the patriarch came again, and he took Alice to the two-story brick house on Essex Street, to meet his invalid wife. How tenderly they talked to her! And "Ann" kissed her, and said, —

"We will see your father, and I think I will send a carriage for you some day, and you shall visit Mrs. Anagnos. I think, too, that Mrs. Anagnos will want you to stay with her a while, and I perhaps will take care of your mouse while you are gone. I love little animals, and I live in my room alone."

"Do you think that she will make me see?" said Alice, — "see father and the day that they call Beautiful?"

The high rooms of the Blind Asylum at South Boston overlook the city, the bowery suburbs, and the glorious harbor. The world of life, of spires, towers, ships, parks, and gardens, lies under them. In one of these rooms Alice found a new home. And here one day the doctors gave her a breath of ether, and she went away to dreamland; and when she came back again, Mrs. Anagnos stood over her, and kissed her, and a doctor said, —

"The operation has been successful. You will see again."

"When?" said Alice, whose eyes were in thick bandages. "Oh, when?"

"I will say on Christmas Day, — the day you call Beautiful. You must be kept in a dark room until then. If your eyes do well, I will let your friends come to see you next Christmas, and I will lift the curtain, and you shall see the world again."

Touchingly faithful were the visits of Mrs. Anagnos to the silent room of Alice. All the blind people loved this woman whom they could not see, but whose presence was a spiritual benediction. Her heart was always with them,

"'WAIT TILL THE SUN GOES INTO A CLOUD,' SAID THE DOCTOR."

and when she lay dying, her last request was, "Don't forget my poor blind children."

Christmas was drawing near; streets were crowded and bells were ringing again; the mellowness of autumn lingered, and there was an April blue in the December sky.

"I shall see the world to-morrow," said Alice.

"Yes, to-morrow," said the doctor; "and your father and friends will be here."

It was Christmas afternoon. Alice sat in a dim room, the bandages had long been removed from her eyes, and she had seen Mrs. Anagnos in the shadows, and had kissed her face. For a few days, indeed, she had sat in a room that was almost light. She had been tempted again and again to lift the curtain, and open the blind, and steal one glimpse of the new world.

Her father came. She looked upon his old hard hands — into his eyes. They were like her own. His hair was white — not like hers. Were other men's heads so white? One of the teachers had sent her a Christmas rose. How lovely it was! How pitiable it seemed that any one should be unable to see it! Dr. Howe came, his soul of love shining through his noble face. The doctor came — he who had promised to be her friend — and the patriarch. Shadow people were they all, but such glorious shadow people!

The doctor's hair was not white; it was like her own. His face was not white; it was olive, and a rose was on it. Alice was filled with wonder at the stately shadow people, but her heart went out to the doctor at once. Was it not he who had said, "I will be your friend"?

"Wait till the sun goes into a cloud," said the hospital doctor. A shadow passed over the glimmering window. "Now!"

The curtain was lifted.

There it lay — the Day Beautiful! The blue sky, with the sun curtained in a cloud; the broad city, with its dome; the long harbor, with its white sails; the streets full of people; the parks; the far horizons; there it lay, — the world, and she had come among the people of all this beautiful existence to be one of them.

"This is Christ's day," she said.

"Yes."

"Are other days like this?"

"Yes — all."

"And I shall see them? Oh, what a bliss it will be to live!"

She turned to her friend the doctor with streaming eyes, and said, "It was you that promised to be my friend. I owe this all to you."

"No," he said; "it was the mouse,— the singing mouse."

"It was not a common mouse. Do you think so?"

"No; it was a *singing* mouse."

"I did not mean that; it was all a finger of — something." She held out her hand and looked at her own finger. "I can't tell what I want to say. Don't you know, doctor?"

It was a wet day in February; I recall it well. It had rained and rained, and all the tall houses were dripping. It had been announced that a private

FANEUIL HALL.

citizen would that day lie in state in Faneuil Hall. The Shaw Guards were to escort the remains thither, and stand guard over them. He had never held an office; he had never led Senates or armies, or anything but the march of human thought. Yet the great square filled with people in the rain. Faneuil

Hall market-places were full of drenched people, — poor people, shivering people, teamsters, old farmers, Irishmen, Irishwomen, colored men, colored women, children, folk from out of town, men of the trades, an army of laborers. Social leaders were not there; politicians were not there, men who trade in the hopes of the poor were not there; nor any who, under any pretext, take from the poor their birthright. But the squares were full. There was a dirge in the rain, a procession of black faces, and then a stay in the pouring rain; after which the great tide of hearts was allowed to pour into the hall.

A man and a very beautiful woman came with the surging crowd, and as the woman bent over to kiss the white form of the dead, it seemed as if her heart was broken. The man was compelled to force her away that others might rain tears on the cold roses. That woman was Alice Meadowcraft Holly, and the man was her husband, the doctor. Then I thought of the singing mouse, of the Day Beautiful, and of the good Angel of Faith, whose hand, unseen, had been in it all.

Another of these stories which the American practical mind, unlike the Eastern, seeks to explain, was a mid-New-England fireside tale which has found many versions, of which the following is one.

THE VILLAGE MYSTERY.

ONE April morning in the early part of the present century, a very curious group of farmers might have been seen in an old blacksmith's shop near the village of Henniker, N. H., intent on discussing a remarkable event that had recently occurred in the neighborhood.

A common farm-horse, of no especial note, except it was white, had walked in the night across the deep torrents of Contoocook River at a point where the bridge had been lately washed away by a freshet, carrying a young woman on his back. The river at the time was swollen, and from twelve to fifteen feet deep. The night was dark and cloudy, and had followed an early spring tempest, which the farmers had called the "breaking-up of winter." The young woman was not aware that the bridge had been carried away until the day after this mysterious crossing of the swollen stream.

The event was regarded as well-nigh miraculous, and had caused great excitement in the usually quiet little village. The proof was positive that the horse had crossed the torrent, and people came daily to visit the old white animal in the stable; and the poor creature that had led an uneventful life of good and steady service among the roads, fields, and pastures of the Contoocook received the name of The Miraculous Horse.

How many people in Henniker many years ago were familiar with the story of The Enchanted Horse in the "Arabian Nights," or with the Magic Horse of Dan Chaucer's delightful fiction, we do not know. But many of them were proud that their town had produced a horse that could walk upon the water, even if he could not fly.

There were other people, in a very small minority, as is usual in such cases, or was at that time, who believed that some natural explanation could be found for the feat of the water-walking horse, and that time would bring to light some curious solution of the mystery.

Such was the state of the public mind on this blue April morning that found a gathering of rugged farmers at the old New Hampshire smithy.

The occasion of the extraordinay gathering was as follows: Smith Smart, the honest blacksmith, had been told the day before, by Samuel Samson, the owner of The Miraculous Horse, that the latter would ride over to the smithy the next morning, and have the white horse shod. The interesting animal had not been shod since he had walked upon the water on the cloudy night. Smith Smart therefore regarded the shoeing of the horse as a matter of no common concern, and he had told his friends to "come around" and see the shoes set on the miraculous roadster, and further discuss the mystery.

"What time did Samson say that he would be here?" asked old Judge Campbell, stamping the snow from his feet, and holding his great hands over the fire of the smithy.

"About nine, I guess," said the blacksmith, bearing down on the lever of the bellows, and so sending a red flame into the air which touched the judge's coat-sleeve.

"Cracky! don't you burn me!" said the judge. "I am not made of iron or steel, if I do sit upon the bench and administer justice. There he comes now, I do declare. I don't know how it may be with the rest of you, but I can't see anything peculiar about that old white horse. He is just a horse, a white horse, to me; and I would n't have given twenty dollars for him before he walked across the Contoocook on the water."

Farmer Samson came riding up to the smithy. He had often done so before, as now, on horseback, and neither he nor the horse had been objects of any special interest to anybody. But he came now gravely and silently, as though he were a prophet, and the heavens were about to fall; and the old farmers gaped at the horse with open mouths and wide eyes. The farmer dismounted, and left the horse standing in the April sun, that poured through the great doors of the smithy.

"Well," he said at last, "there he is. If you can shoe the air and the water, shoe him. These are solemn times, judge, — solemn times! Signs and wonders, wheels within wheels, like Ezekiel's vision; and I don't know what the world is a-comin' to. I sometimes think that the times of Cotton Mather and ghosts and flying women are about to return again to New England. It is a mystery why fate should set its sign on that old white horse, but so it is."

The horse stood there, very quiet and demure. He did not look as though he had been the medium of any special revelation. He did not so much as wink. He was worn with hard work of many years; had an intelligent, reliable look; did not fear the forge; and seemed to be glad that spring had come, and to enjoy the sunshine. No one would have taken him for an oracle.

"Samson, did you ever notice anything peculiar about that horse before that awful night?" asked the judge.

"No; only he is the most sure-footed animal I ever had. Whatever I set him to doin', he will do, — plough without a driver; furrow without lines; go home from mill all alone with a bag of meal on his back, and leave the grist at the door. He never had no antics nor capers, nor nothin' of that kind; but he has had the strongest horse-sense of any animal I ever knew. Seems as though sometimes he had a soul. I always thought that I would hate to kill him when he became old. He might haunt me.

"He carried me to be married, and bore away two of my children to their graves; and Martha would have been dead, too, if he had n't a-walked over the water like a spirit horse in the dead o' night, under the scudding clouds, and brought the doctor just in the nick o' time. Poor old Jack! there are not many more weddings and funerals for you to go to in my family. I do think, judge, that there ought to be some law to protect an old family horse, — a hospital, or somethin'."

Samson twined his fingers in the animal's mane.

"I always noticed that that animal had a kind of far-away look in his eye, as though he was sort of pryin' into futurity," said old Deacon Bonney. "It's a case like Balaam, you may depend. It ain't no use talkin'; your Martha is a good woman, and she was goin' to die without a doctor, and the powers above just let the good old white horse have his way; and he went over the river, waterfalls and all, dry shod, like the Israelites of old. He was uplifted."

"He never went over the Contoocook River dry shod, without there was somethin' under his feet," said the village schoolmaster, Ephraim Cole, who had come with the rest, as the day was Saturday and a holiday. "Even the Israelites had the winds to help them. There are no effects without causes, and that horse went across the river in some perfectly natural way, you may be sure. Wait and see. Time will tell the truth about all things."

"Samson," said the judge, "I want you to tell us the true story of that night, while Smart sets the shoes on that marvellous animal."

Smith Smart plied the lever again. The forge began to blaze. Some new shoes were dropped into the fire, and the blacksmith began to pare down the horse's hoofs with his steel scraper. The horse was quite used to these things, and did not move, except at the will of the smith.

"He is the patientest horse to be shod that ever I see," said Smart. "Always was. I noticed that years ago. I always thought that there was somethin' mysterious about him."

The men sat down on sooty benches and boxes, and Samson began his strange story.

"Well, this is how it was, this way, as I remember. It was early in March, of a Tuesday night. Wife began to feel sick in the evening; chills, and fever flashes. Then she began to have a difficulty of breathin', and I see that she was threatened with pneumonia, and says I to Minnie, my daughter, 'You bridle Jack and go for the doctor as quick as you can. 'T is a dark night, but Jack knows the way. He's been after the doctor in the night before. Wrap up warm, and don't mind the thunder. It will be cold when you cross the bridge, so wrap up warm.'

"I hadn't heard then that the bridge had been carried away by the freshet. Well, Minnie, she bridled up Jack and started. It was a troubled night; I could hear the wind in the branches of the trees, and see the clouds scud across the half-moon. The wind was keen, and Minnie drew the shawl over her head, and gave Jack the rein, and let him go.

"Well, when they came to the bridge, or the place where the bridge was, Minnie drew the shawl more closely about her ears, and dropped the rein; and Jack walked right across the river, carefully like, and Minnie never so much as thought that there was no bridge there, except once during a flash o' lightning. The water was pouring down from the hills in torrents. There hadn't been such a freshet for years. Minnie called the doctor, and returned in the same way.

"The doctor came late, and found wife very sick; and I incline to think that his comin' just saved her. After givin' her medicines, he said to me, said he, 'I should have been here before, but for the bridge being washed away. It is a bad road round.'

"'The bridge washed away?' said I.

"'No, doctor,' said Minnie, 'the bridge is not washed away. I went over it, and came back the same way.'

"'No, no,' said the doctor, said he, in surprise, 'there is no bridge over this part of the Contoocook. You must have been dreaming, Minnie. The horse went round.'

"'No, doctor, I crossed the bridge direct. You will find it so by the horse's tracks. There was a minute or two that seemed to me kind o' strange. There came a flash of lightning and all around me looked like water.'

"Wife was better in the mornin', and I had to go to the river. I followed the tracks of Jack goin' and comin'. The horse certainly went to the river, and as Minnie was gone but half an hour, and it would have been an hour's hard riding to have gone and returned the other way, the horse surely crossed the river.

"But to make the matter clear beyond a doubt, Minnie's scarf blew off while crossin' the river, and we saw it on the next day at the place that she crossed on a rock in the river. My hired man found the horse's tracks on the other side of the river. — No, sure as preachin', and the stars above us, that horse crossed the river with Minnie on his back. It was a supernatural event of some kind. The horse crossed the bridge, and there was no bridge to cross."

There was another confirmation to this amazing story, — a rheumatic old woman living near the river, who stood by her window that night, looking out on the breaking clouds. There came a flash of lightning, and she saw a white horse with a black rider, walking on the water in the middle of the river. She said that she had seen her " death fetch."

A long silence followed the emphatic " there! " of the blacksmith. It was broken by the mathematical schoolmaster.

"Will you let me ride the horse down to the river after he is shod? If Minnie could cross where there is no bridge, I can."

"You can?" exclaimed a chorus of voices.

"Just follow me," he continued. "I think I can show you all how a horse can walk upon the water. What has been done, can be done."

Mounting the horse, the schoolmaster rode to the edge of the swollen river, where the old bridge had been. But he did not stop there. Old Jack went on, not stepping far into the water, but seemingly walking upon it. Very carefully went the horse, but steadily, as though feeling his way. The men gazed in wonder.

"That stream is ten feet deep," said one.

"Was there ever such a sight before, — a horse walking upon the water?" said another.

When Jack reached the other side, the old schoolmaster turned his head.

and waved his hat. He then turned the horse's head, and the two came back again, like a general and his war-steed. It was noticed that before taking a step forward, Jack lifted high his right fore-foot and very carefully felt for a place on which to rest it, as though there were hard and reliable places in the gliding water.

As soon as the schoolmaster returned, he clasped the horse around the neck, and said,—

"Jack, you are a good animal, and know more than most other people do."

The farmers began to investigate. They walked into the river. They found that they, too, could walk upon the water. A line of posts covered by wide strips of board belonging to the old bridge, had not been carried away, but remained about half a foot under the surface, the foaming current passing over them.

"Time tells the truth about all things," repeated the schoolmaster, "and there are no effects without causes."

"That was risky business," said the judge.

It was a very thoughtful procession that followed the trustworthy old white horse back to the smithy. Then the old breadcart man came along, with a jingle of bells, and the judge bought five cakes of gingerbread and treated the company at the blacksmith's.

"Cracky!" continued the judge, philosophically, "fingers are fingers, and thumbs are thumbs. If we haven't a miraculous horse, we have a miraculous schoolmaster. Let us be thankful, deacon. What do you say?"

And the Deacon said, "Amen."

And the bluebirds sang, and the woodpeckers pecked, and flocks of robins chorused, "Cheer up, cheer up!" in the gnarled old apple-trees, and all the world went on happily, as before.

THE VALLEY OF MEXICO.

CHAPTER III.

A PLAN FOR A JOURNEY OF EDUCATIONAL TRAVEL

The Places to be visited: The City of Mexico; Caracas; a Zigzag Journey across the Sea from Pernambuco to Gibraltar; then all the Consular Ports of the Mediterranean.

HE journey began to Mexico and La Guayra. One day in the Garden Mr. Van der Palm said to Percy, "I have business which will take me to the city of Mexico for some months, and then to Caracas for a few weeks. I shall then go to Pernambuco, and thence sail on a Portuguese steamer directly for Lisbon, stopping for a short time at the Cape Verd Islands and the Canaries. Here is a map; let me trace the route with a pencil."

Mr. Van der Palm slowly traced the route to Mexico, South America, and Europe.

"I should think such a journey," said Percy, "would be one of the most delightful in all the world."

"It is. I know the route well. The valley of the City of Mexico is one of the most beautiful spots in North America, and there are few places in the world more beautiful than Caracas and Valentia in the Maritime Andes. The sea-route from Brazil to Portugal by way of the Southern Islands is unequalled at the right seasons of the year."

"You will be gone a year?"

"Yes."

"And I?"

"I shall take you with me. You will begin your studies in educational travel in the City of Mexico. You will find it a good place to commence Latin-America Spanish. You can continue the study in Caracas and Valentia; take Portuguese in Pernambuco, and Castilian Spanish at the port of Gibraltar and at Barcelona. You will be able to learn at these ports the commercial law and usages of Spain and Portugal, and to study the literature of those countries in the original language."

"Where shall we go from Lisbon and the ports of Spain?"

"To all the consular ports of the Mediterranean. It will be a zigzag journey, as I shall not follow the coast on either side, but pass from the port cities of one coast to the other, as my commission directs."

The journey thus planned was at once begun. In Monterey, Percy spoke his first *Buenos dias, Señor; Felizes trades, Señora; Como lo pasa, usted?* In the City of Mexico he began to hear, for the first time, those characteristic Spanish words, in which may be read the decline of the Latin empire in the New World, — *Hasta manana* (until to-morrow). Here he also began to be familiar with those terms of elegant and deferential politeness which form a part of all the dialogue of Spanish America *Con mucho gusta; A los pies de usted,* — At the feet of you (to ladies); and *Beso a usted los manos, Caballero,* — I kiss your hands (to gentlemen).

Here he was not rudely asked to sit down in cold business terms, but, "Be *pleased* to sit down;" and he received not *one thank* for any favor that he did, but a *thousand,* — *mil gracias.*

Here, too, instead of the old Washington garden, he used to go out to study on the Paseo, which we must describe and picture.

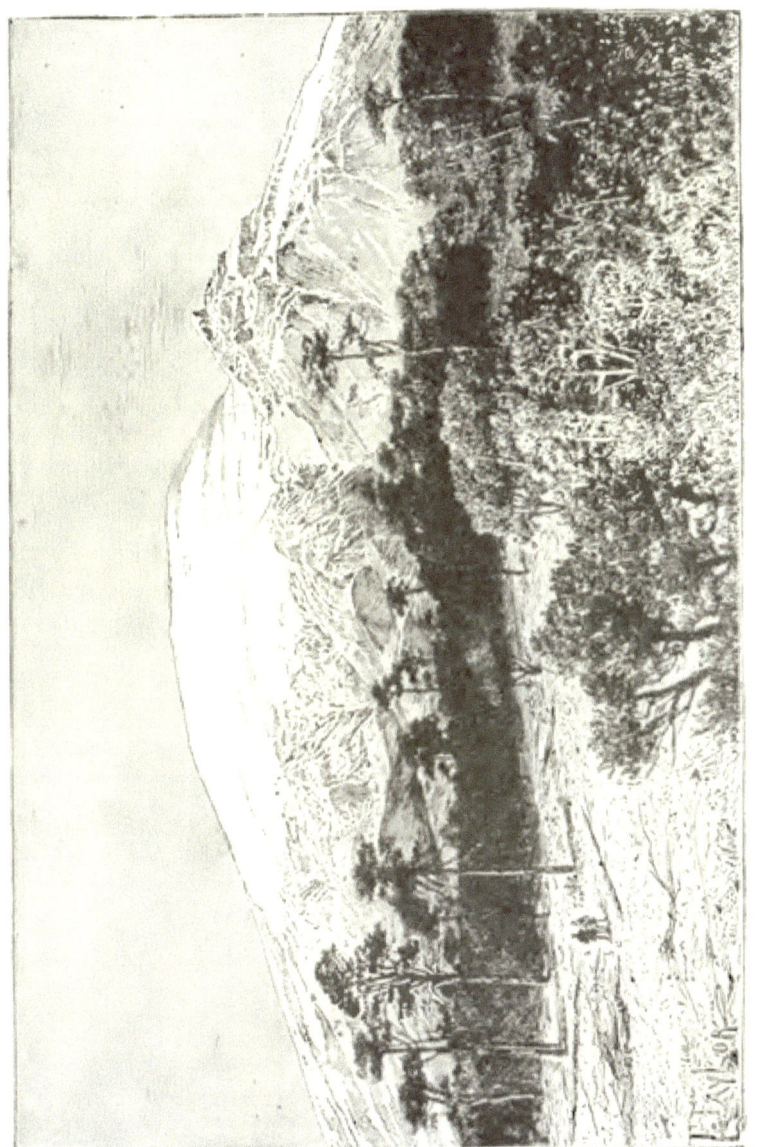

POPOCATEPETL.

THE GOD OF FIRE.

THE PASEO, THE MOST BEAUTIFUL STREET IN THE NEW WORLD.

The Paseo, from the plaza of the City of Mexico to the castle and gardens of Chapultepec, is probably the most beautiful street in the New World. It is certainly the most historic. It was trodden by ancient monarchs and priests of the Sun; by Montezumas, caciques, and Spanish viceroys; and now, at last, by the people's presidents. Its history and traditions cover a period of one thousand years, and no other street in the New World has such a record.

The street, or boulevard, or paseo, is some three miles long, and stretches from the place where the great Mexican pyramid once stood, but where now is the cathedral and official palace, to the Castle of Chapultepec, which was once the famous Halls of the Montezumas. It is one long procession of statuary. It might be called the boulevard of the Montezumas. One leaves the grand plaza, where once the great pyramid stood, passes the old palace of Iturbide (the first Mexican monarch after the overthrow of the Spanish power), the Alemada (a music park of enchanting beauty), and comes to two colossal statues of Montezumas. He is now in the Paseo proper. The vista before him is one of the most beautiful in the world. The highway is lined with Spanish cypress and eucalyptus trees, and is sentinelled, as it were, with statues of heroes. Around it stretch meadows of flowers and alfalfa grass. Clarinas sing in the air, and at the end rise the white porticos of Chapultepec, over gigantic trees and beautiful gardens, and shine down on the city like things of life and joy.

But this is not all; over the white castle and the gardens of giant cypresses, gray with mosses and crumbling with the shadows of centu-

THE PRESIDENT'S PALACE.

ries, loom Popocatapetl and Istaccihuatl like white clouds in the sky, a pearly splendor of glistening snow. The first of these dead volcanoes is higher than Mount Blanc, or any mountains in Europe. One may here gather oranges and one hundred varieties of Mexican roses, and tread the alfalfa meadows, and then glance upward to crystal winters of the sky.

THE SACRIFICIAL STONE.

THE PASEO.   61

The tourist who would see the glory and grandeur of this historic highway would do well to devote to it a day, and to make his first visit to the National Museum, which joins the palace in the plaza. Here he will see Chac Mool, the Aztec god of fire, and the stone statue of

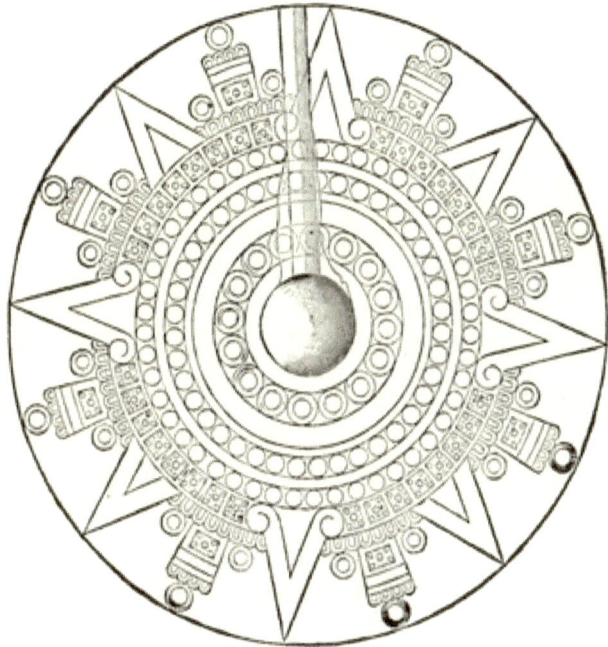

TOP OF SACRIFICIAL STONE.

Death. The Aztec sacrificial stone is here, and the Calendar Stone. A study of the latter great stone puzzle will give to his mind the proper historical mood and coloring for the three-mile journey to Chapultepec, over which he is to pass.

What is the meaning of this mysterious Calendar Stone? The view in Mexico follows a famous lecture by Philip G. G. Valentini, published by F. P. Hoeck, that it was an altar for human sacrifices. The learned archæologist thus interprets it: —

"I will, in the first place, inform you in what year, by whose order, and upon what particular festival occasion this stone disk was first made.

"It was, according to our reckoning, about the year 1478, or nearly four hundred years ago, and only two years before the death of the then reigning king of Mexico, Axayacatl, that he was reminded by the high priest of the State of a vow that he had once made, who spoke as follows (I will give the long text of the Indian writer, Tezozomoc, in the fewest words): '" The building of the large sacrificial

SCULPTURE ON THE SIDE OF THE SACRIFICIAL STONE.

pyramid which you have undertaken approaches its end. You vowed to decorate it with a beautiful work, in which the preserver of mankind, Huitzilopochtli, could take pleasure. Time presses; do not delay the work any longer." "I think," said the king, "to replace the sacrificial stone which my father once devoted to the god of the sun, with a new one. Let that be laid aside, but carefully preserved. I will give the laborers provisions and clothing that they may select the most proper stone from the quarries, and I will send the sculptor gold, cocoa, and colored cloth, that he may engrave a picture of the sun as it is surrounded by our other great gods." So the workmen went out and quarried the stone, laying it upon rollers, and fifty thousand strong men rolled it along. But as it was upon the bridge of

Xoloc, the beams gave way, the bridge broke in pieces, the stone fell into the water, and no one dared to remove it from the bottom of the lake. Then the king was angry and said, "Let them build a new bridge, with double beams and planks, and bring a new stone from the quarries of Cuyoacan. Let them bring a second stone here, out of which a trough may be made to receive the blood which flows as expiation from the sacrificial stone." When the stone had been

THE CATHEDRAL.

quarried and prepared, and had been rolled over the bridge in good condition, there was a feast of joy. Then was the question asked, How should the immense stone be placed on the pyramid? After it was placed in position, we read that it was sunk in the surface of an altar. The altar is of stone, of the height of eight men, and of the length of twenty cubits. Before it the trough was placed. A bloody festival was held for the dedication of this sacrificial slab, and upon it thousands of victims were slain. The king, as chief sacrificer, on the first day killed a hundred of victims with his own hand, drank of their blood, and ate of their flesh; and so arduous was his labor, and so much did he eat, that he became sick, and soon after died. He had only time to have his portrait sculptured upon the surface of the rock of Chapultepec, according to the custom of Mexican kings.' So much for Tezozomoc's report.

"That the sacrificial stone here mentioned is the one still extant, I will, in addition to the description, bring a still further proof. No doubt this stone served for all their bloody sacrifices up to the year 1521. In that year the Spaniards captured the city; and Cortez ordered the destruction of the entire pyramid, and that the canals of the city be filled with its fragments. Neither Cortez nor Bernal Diaz, nor any of the chroniclers of the conquerors, make mention of the existence of any such monument as the afore-described stone. They did not undertake its destruction; nay, they even placed it in the market-place, on exhibition, where the pyramid once stood. This we have from a missionary chronicler named Duran, between the years 1551 and 1569, who says he has always seen it in the same place, and that there has been so much talk about it, among Spaniards and natives, that finally his eminence, the Bishop of Montufar, took umbrage, and ordered its burial in the place where it stood, in order that the memory of the infamous actions that had been perpetrated upon it might be blotted out. Until the year 1790 no one of the many writers on Mexican antiquities has made the least mention of it. In that year the repair of the pavement of the market-place was undertaken. In a deep excavation the laborers struck a slab of stone which gave such a hollow sound from the stroke of the iron that they thought a treasure-vault might be concealed under it. When they lifted the slab they found no treasure-vault, but were astonished when they beheld on one side, the spectacle of this incomparable treasure of ancient Mexican art. The clergy wished it to be again buried, but the art-loving and liberal viceroy, Revillagigedo, ordered it to be exposed. He caused it to be built in on the southerly side of the cathedral, in the ashlar work of one of its towers, so that all could see it. Here it remained until the year 1885, when it was removed to the National Museum, where it now stands.

"No one had then the least idea that such a stone had ever existed, or for what purpose it might have served. The archæologists said at once that it must have some connection with the worship of the sun. They thought the shield in the centre represented the ancient sun-god; and as they found the always well-known twenty pictures of the days of the Mexican month engraved about in a circle, they gave to the disk the name by which it is still known, — the Mexican Calendar Stone.

"The ancient Mexicans had a superstition that the sun-god would destroy the world in the last night of the fifty-second year, and that he would never come back. To prevail on him to remain, they offered to him of their own free will the greatest sacrifices; not a human life only, but also on all their hearths, and in all their dwellings and temples, they extinguished their fires. They left it to the goodness of the god to give them back this element so necessary to mankind. They broke all their household furniture; they hung black masks before their faces; they prayed and fasted; and on the evening of the last night they formed a great procession to a neighboring mountain. Arriving, there is found a man lying on a circular stone, who gives himself voluntarily as a sacrifice to the god. Exactly at the midnight hour a priest thrust a knife into his breast, tore out the heart, and raised it toward the starry heavens with uplifted hands, while another priest laid a small round block of dry soft wood upon the open wound, and a third priest, springing on the stone and kneeling over the body, placed a hard stick perpendicularly on the block, which he then with his hands caused to revolve. This violent friction produced a spark, which was caught up, and was immediately carried to a neighboring funeral pile, whose rising flame proclaimed to the people the promise of the god to delay for a season the destruction of the world, and to grant to mankind a new lease of fifty-two years of existence."

This is thrilling history. The tourist may now go out into the open air, under the blue sky, pass the palace, the cathedral, the flower and bird market, and enter San Francisco Street on his way to the wonderful Paseo.

The great cathedral shines like the sun, holding its great bells in air. The palace where the great pyramid once stood throngs with bright, happy faces. The bazaars are gay with color. Women with-

THE TOMB OF JUAREZ.

out bonnets, or any head covering, mingle with the gayly dressed *señors;* and lazy, happy *peons,* as the poorer classes of Mexicans are called, sit in the sun along the crowded way.

Passing the old palace of Iturbide, now a grand hotel, one pauses at the Alemada, and rests among the statues and fountains in the deep cool shadows of cathedral-like trees. Or perhaps he crosses a

MAIN PLAZA.   MONTEREY.   BISHOP'S PALACE.

street or two beyond the Alemada, and visits the Mexican garden of the dead, called the Pantheon, in the shadows of the crumbling church of San Fernando. Here is the pyramidal tomb of Juarez, hung with wreaths of immortelles from all the Mexican States, and bright with living flowers. In the chamber of the pyramid is the effigy of

STATUE OF CUITAAHUAC.

the emancipator of Mexico in white marble. It represents Juarez as lying dead on the lap of Mexico, the face of the goddess nation being turned to the sun. It is one of the most beautiful works of art in America. Iturbide was the first monarch of Mexico. He threw off the Spanish yoke; but it was Juarez who made the Indian races free and gave them the rights of men.

Entering the Paseo between the statues of the Montezumas, the charm of the wonderful highway begins. Before the tourist rises a most beautiful statue of Columbus, surrounded, as it were, by a court of Montezumas and later heroes. One of these monuments is very painful, but long holds the eye. It represents two Aztec kings, chained to blocks of stone, and being tortured by the Spaniards, who have lighted slow fires under their feet to make them disclose their treasures of gold.

On one side of the Paseo is the ruin of a gigantic aqueduct man-

THE PLAZA AND LA MITRA, MONTEREY.

tled with vines. The way is lined with heavy stone seats. Cool trees wave above them. Out of these shadowy vistas one sees the houses of Mexican officials and foreign ministers,— prison-like looking structures on the outside, but beautiful within, where *patios* or open courts, surrounded by *zulas* or halls, stand open to the sky.

Chapultepec glimmers in the distance, — a pile of simple beauty that haunts one forever.

The castle and gardens of Chapultepec! Who can describe them? Their charm is overwhelming, and yet money did not nor could not create them. There is poetry and sentiment in the air. The birds sing of the spirit of the place. One sits down under the ancient cypresses, some of which are fifty feet in circumference, and pictures the past. Here were the halls of the Montezumas; here a romantic viceroy, Galvez, lifted his white palace out of the ruins of the past; here Carlotta saw a few happy days; and here come the cantering presidents of the last republic to spend their summers! One wonders how the American soldiers ever scaled the walls of rock-ribbed elevation.

From the airy porticos one looks down upon the white city burning in pure, clear sunlight, and up to the mountains that glimmer in the cerulean splendor of the far sky, and feels that this is the throne of beauty in the New World. Below are the old baths of the Montezumas, and close at hand is the military academy. Clarinas sing; soldiers without occupation march to and fro; glittering officers on slick ponies and gay saddles disappear in the winding ways of the ancient cypresses; children play about the cages of native wild animals in the cool gardens below, and afar the air is a melody of bells.

But the present vanishes from the mind. Here the tourist, be he a poet or not, dreams. The visions of Prescott's history rise before him. The vanished courts of the Montezumas glitter around him, and in fancy he sees the *tocalli* smoking where the melodious city now stands.

As he returns past the orange sellers, the flower-girls, and the pulque dealers, he is perhaps glad that the native Indian races are again masters of their own country. Juarez was an Indian; President

Diaz has native blood. The Indian races in all Spanish-American countries are retrieving their ancient rights, and are seeking to put education in the place of ignorance. The influence of the Latin conquerors is failing and departing, and the halls of the viceroys are being changed into seats of learning. In this movement, the Mexican President leads, and the twentieth century will be likely to find the beautiful Paseo of Mexico more glorious than in all the eventful and picturesque centuries of the past.

After six months' studies in Mexico, under a Spanish teacher, Percy accompanied his father to Caracas, whose port is La Guayra. At this port he made the acquaintance of genial Consul Hanna; and at the window of the consulate that looked out on a narrow street, he listened to many stories of the Spanish Main, one of which we give here, — our first story of a consulate: —

AN ESCAPE FROM PIRATES.[1]

IF a feeling of superstition with regard to unlucky vessels were ever pardonable, it must surely have been so in the case of the brig "Crawford," owned first at Freetown, Mass., and afterwards for many years at Warren, R. I.

It would seem as if no nervous person, acquainted with her history, could have trod her decks in the still midnight watches upon the ocean, without a creeping sensation of dread.

The writer has a distinct recollection of this little full-rigged brig, as a vessel which figured prominently among the notable craft of his boyhood. There were dark stains on her deck which had the appearance of iron rust, but which all knew were not iron rust. She had been the scene of a tragedy that, with its associations, was one of the most remarkable upon record.

Her whaling voyages from Warren, of which she made a number, were all unfortunate in a pecuniary sense. From one of them, after an absence of fourteen months, she returned without having taken a drop of oil, — her captain having actually been obliged to purchase a supply for the binnacle lamp at some foreign port.

[1] By Geo. H. Coomer, in the "Household," by permission.

But the one dreadful event of her history had occurred while she belonged to Freetown. In fact, it was chiefly in consequence of this that she was sold to her purchasers in Warren, — her original owners feeling that they could no longer bear to look upon her.

It was, I think, about 1829, that the "Crawford" sailed for the West Indies, under the command of a Captain Brightman, whose crew consisted of his two mates, a cook, and three foremast hands.

Her outward cargo was disposed of at Havana, and she was nearly ready for the homeward voyage when four Spaniards came on board, seeking for a passage to the United States. They were villanous-looking fellows, with swarthy faces and flashing black eyes.

The mate advised Captain Brightman not to accept them, and urged his objections with some force. The captain himself hesitated at first; but the thought of the passage-money was too tempting, and he finally consented to take the strangers on board.

One of the four passengers could speak English, but his companions knew only Spanish. After the brig had been at sea a few days, the cook detected this man, whose name was Tardy, in the act of sprinkling some white substance on a quantity of food in the galley. Tardy explained that the article was a kind of seasoning well known in Cuba, and that he wished the officers and crew to try its flavor.

The cook scraped off as much of it as he could; but, although the fact of his doing so shows that he must have had a suspicion of foul play, he unfortunately did not make known the incident until too late. He may have thought that his knife had removed all danger.

Immediately after eating, the captain and chief mate were taken violently ill. The foremast hands also felt some bad effects from their meal, though in a less degree; but the second mate escaped, as his duties on deck had kept him from eating with the captain. As to the four passengers, they, of course, had taken care not to touch the food on which the white powder had been sprinkled.

It was now that the terrified cook told the mate what had occurred in the galley. But in a few moments his voice was silenced forever. He was struck down by the murderous pirates, who, seeing that their work was but half accomplished by the poison, at once proceeded to complete it with their knives.

The captain and chief mate they killed in the cabin; the cook and one of the foremast hands were murdered close by the windlass, on the forward part of the deck; while another sailor was killed as he stood at the wheel.

Meanwhile, the second mate, whose name was Durfee, and a man named

Allen Bicknell, of Barrington, R. I., who were now the only survivors, ran aloft, in the forlorn hope of thus saving their lives. The pirates fired at Bicknell with pistols, wounding him as he stood in the foretop.

Tardy now hailed the second mate, promising to spare his life if he would come down, as they required him to navigate the vessel. He accordingly decended, and was not harmed. Seeing the officer in present safety, Bicknell, the poor sailor, already wounded, asked if they would spare him also. Upon receiving a reply in the affirmative, he came painfully down the rigging; but the moment he reached the deck he was killed.

The vessel was now entirely in the possession of these monsters, and the feelings of Durfee must have been indescribable, as he realized the extent of the tragedy and his own dreadful situation.

He knew, of course, that the pirates would never, if they could help it, permit him to leave the vessel alive. It might serve their purpose to spare him for a time, but unless he should be able to hit upon some manner of deliverance, the fate of his shipmates must at last be his.

The bodies of the victims were thrown into the sea, and the four murderous scoundrels then commenced searching the cabin, being apparently aware that she had on board a considerable amount of money. This they brought on deck and divided, all the while talking rapidly in Spanish.

Tardy now informed the second mate that the brig must be taken to South America. Durfee well knew that should he carry the wretches to that part of the world, his own doom would be sealed the moment they reached its shores. He sought for some excuse to land elsewhere and fortunately found one.

"I can take you to South America," he said, "but for such a voyage we must have more water. We have only enough to last for a short time, and we may be sixty or seventy days on the passage."

Tardy uttered a Spanish oath or two, and then asked if a supply could not be obtained by entering some inlet of the coast where there would be no danger of capture.

"Yes," replied Durfee, glad that the pirate had anticipated a proposition which he himself had intended to make. "We could run in at night and get out before morning. Then we should be all ready for a voyage to South America or anywhere else."

Tardy flourished his knife fiercely before the face of his helpless prisoner, thus indicating what would be done in case of the least attempt at deception. Durfee's nerves had already suffered terribly, and it was only by the greatest effort that he could maintain anything like an appearance of calmness.

Hastily running over in his thoughts the various inlets of the coast, he

STATUE OF COLUMBUS, MEXICO.

resolved upon making for Chesapeake Bay. He was far, however, from telling the pirates of his decision, but led them to suppose that the destination was some obscure nook among islands and promontories. It was fortunate for him that they knew nothing whatever of the coast, and were ignorant even of the existence of the wide water sheet which he had in mind.

He used to relate that while the vessel was running on the course he had chosen, and he was filled with the most dreadful anxiety lest his plans should, after all, miscarry, Tardy would come to him, and with oaths, boast of the murders he had committed.

Great was Durfee's anxiety as the brig made the land. Soon his fate would be decided. He thought with a sickening sensation of the pirates' threats, but he thought, too, of the fort at Old Point Comfort; and upon this his hope rested. It must, of course, be approached at night; and luckily the Spaniards were as anxious for the cover of darkness as was he himself, so that he was permitted to keep off shore until past sunset.

Then the little brig stood in under all sail. With a fine breeze she passed Cape Henry, and continued her course up the bay. It was for Durfee an hour of unspeakable suspense. At any moment the pirates might take alarm, and he felt almost a surprise to find that they did not do so. Here and there could be seen distant lights, but the shores were hidden in darkness, and the evil-eyed wretches, wary as they were, seemed not to suspect treachery.

Being for the time in command, as navigator and pilot, the anxious officer was at the wheel, while his unwelcome companions stood ready to shorten sail and let go the anchor at his bidding. It may well be imagined that he measured with every nerve alert each inch of the way.

The brig's yawl hung at the stern davits. He had made sure that its tackles were in running order. How near to the fort would he dare to approach before bringing the brig to?

Presently he directed his dangerous crew to take in the light sails and the courses. Tardy repeated the order in Spanish, and it was obeyed.

"Let go the topsail halyards," was the next command; and down came the top-sail yards upon the caps.

Clearing his throat for another effort, Durfee felt that his heart-throbs were almost suffocating. Nevertheless, he was able to command his voice.

"Stand by to let go anchor!" he cried, feeling that in another moment he would know his fate. The four pirates ran to the windlass.

"Let go!"

There was a splash under the bow, and a swift paying out of the cable. Just then Durfee sprang over the taffrail and into the boat, lowering it instantly and with a violent push sent it spinning from under the brig's counter; then, seizing an oar, he commenced sculling with all his might. As he did so, he heard the Spaniards rushing aft, but they were too late to get more than a glimpse of him in the darkness.

The grim fortress at Old Point Comfort was not a quarter of a mile distant. Durfee's calls drew the attention of the sentries, and in a few minutes there were lights gleaming from a row of port-holes, with the black muzzles of cannon looking threateningly forth into the darkness, and a dozen soldiers were at once ordered to board the vessel. On reaching her, they found only three of the pirates on deck. These were at once made prisoners. Hurrying into the cabin, they found Tardy lying dead upon the floor. Struck with despair at the impossibility of escape, he had chosen to die by his own hand rather than to await the inevitable halter.

His three accomplices were tried and hanged at Norfolk. They died protesting their innocence, and declaring that the entire guilt rested upon their dead confederate.

As to poor Durfee, the second mate, after the dreadful scenes he had passed through, he was never really himself. His nervous system had been thoroughly shattered.

Who can wonder that painful thoughts were always associated with the "Crawford," or that a gloom should seem to invest even the old Warren wharf where she used to lie?

CHAPTER IV.

CARACAS ON THE FIRST DAY OF THE REVOLUTION, 1892. — AMUSEMENTS AT SEA.

PERCY was in Caracas on the first day of the last revolution, when President Palacio issued his proclamation that made the revolution inevitable. Percy will never forget that scene as he stood in the plaza of Bolivar.

It was a bright March day, and the circle of hills — a part of the "thousand hills" of the Caraci — shone serenely in the clear purple sky. It is eternal springtime here. The port of Caracas, La Guayra, three thousand feet below, is one of the hottest cities in the three Americas, but the capital is cooled by its altitude. Caracas stands on a plateau or valley in the maritime range of the Andes, which here rise to a height of nearly ten thousand feet; and the city itself is three thousand feet above its port and the sea. It has a most romantic history, being associated with the names of the early discoverers, — with Drake, Raleigh, and the poetic cavalier, Ponce de Leon.

Percy and his father had been wandering about the beautiful city, among the crowds that stood telling each other with terribly serious faces that great political events were at hand. They had seen the solitary church that survived the great earthquake nearly a hundred years ago, and had wondered how the worshippers in that church must have felt on that eventful Saint's day, when they rushed to the doors, to find that all the other churches and houses had gone down, and twelve thousand people had perished! Every tourist who is familiar with history sees in fancy that scene. They had been to Calvario, or Calvary Hill, where Guzman Blanco, Venezuela's ambitious ex-president, had made a park, as it were, in the sky, and placed his own statue upon it, — which was erected too soon, for the people forced him into exile and tore it down.

BOLIVAR.

On returning from the long walk they found the plaza and all the public squares filled with excited people. They sat down in the plaza near the statue of Bolivar.

The statue is a wonder, and commemorates the deeds of a most

LA GUAYRA.

wonderful man. It was made in Germany, is equestrian, and to the imagination, the horse of brass seems to have leaped proudly into the air, leaving the hero in a most gracious attitude in his saddle to face the people he had liberated. It is the pride of Caracas, as well it may be, and one of the marvellous creations of art in the world.

STATUE OF BOLIVAR, CARACAS.

The guards came out of the military palace in front of the plaza. The press began to issue copies of the President's manifesto, and the newsboys to sell them on the street. Every one knew what it was, but desired to read it with his own eyes. His own life and destiny might be involved in it.

Every copy was eagerly seized as it came out from the press, and was read with staring eyes, and passed on to others.

"*It means war*," was the one short sentence that passed from lip to lip. In many cases those three words covered the thought, "It means me!" The Venezuelan well knows the meaning of a revolution.

The political situation may be briefly stated. President Palacio desired a re-election by the House of Deputies. He saw that he would fail to secure it, and imprisoned certain of the deputies for political reasons; but it was popularly believed it was a subterfuge that there might be left no quorum, and that he might thus have an excuse for continuing in office, in default of an election. He thus assumed dictatorial powers, in the name and in the interest of the liberal party which had done so much for Venezuela. The Supreme Court declared his course illegal, and he imprisoned the judges. The country rose against him; and Caracas, the capital, found itself in a state of siege.

The shadows of the high Andes

A YOUTHFUL BEGGAR OF CARACAS.

began to fall upon the valleys and the green palms and coffee plantations of La Guayra. The top of Calvary Hill flashed in the paling sun. The plaza and streets were black with men, each holding in his hand the white sheet of the manifesto.

The bells rang, — it was Lent, — and half-veiled women pushed their way through the excited crowds to the golden churches.

It was not a noisy, but a silent crowd. There was an expression of inquiry in every dark face. It was like those days of our own war, when President Lincoln's proclamation made the pulses of great cities to stand still. There was an awful silence in those crowds, and the same was here.

A Venezuelan was with our travellers. He owned an estate in the interior, twenty-four miles square, as large as a province. His

ANCIENT HOUSE IN CARACAS.

brother had been killed in a former revolution, and he had lived much in Europe and could speak English well.

He turned his face toward the grand statue of Bolivar, that looked like a thing of life in the sunset of the Andes. He did not talk politics. No one did. He simply said, " They offered Simon Bolivar the crown, and he answered them : ' I have achieved the liberation of five countries. That is all the honor I desire!' His heart is in the cathedral of Santa Martha, and his dust is in yonder Parthenon. I would that his *spirit* were here!"

From Caracas, Percy sailed for Pernambuco. He was now in the seas of the great American discoverers.

"The years roll back — we see again
Thy fleet, Columbus, dare the main,
Upborne by Faith, till rises fair
The new world in prophetic air !
The mighty waves yield to thy prow;
The stormy heavens before thee bow,
The sun stands still, and earth appears
A wheeling star 'mid circling spheres !

"Then Science rose ; then Learning woke ;
And Freedom's voice to heroes spoke ;
And Progress broke the chains of time,
And upward marched to heights sublime.
No day like this 'neath purple skies
E'er met expectant prophets' eyes ;
The drums of peace the roll-call beat,
And nations pass on children's feet !

"O Star of Faith, that led afar
Columbus, 'neath the Hesperian Star,
Shine on the world's new march, and light
Hope's aspirations for the right !
Achievement waits yet bolder keels
Than broke the waves of old Antilles,
The unattained to find and prove
In virtue, brotherhood, and love !"

THE CONSULAR FLAG.

"I keep the flag of my country always waving," said Consul Hanna of La Guayra. Percy looked upon that flag as one of the most beautiful objects in the narrow streets. It is one of the most beautiful objects in the world.

"Do all consuls fly the American flag daily?" asked Percy of his father at the beginning of his voyage towards the islands of the Canary birds.

"Consuls," said his father, "have no claim to any foreign ceremonial, but they may glory in the flag. The consular regulations as issued from the State Department are something like this: —

"'The consuls have a right to the private use of the flag, and the right to place the national arms and the name of the consulate on the offices is given by treaties with Austria-Hungary, Italy, and the Netherlands (and colonies), on

GRAND OPERA HOUSE, CARACAS.

their offices or dwellings by treaty with Belgium and Germany; the right to place the national flag on their dwellings, except where there is a legation, by treaties with Austria-Hungary, Belgium, Germany, Roumania, and Serbia; the right to place the arms, name, and flag on their offices or dwellings by treaties with France and Salvador; and the right to place the name and flag on their dwellings by treaty with Colombia.'

"And," added Mr. Van der Palm, "the consular office in some countries, like the old Hebrew cities of refuge, is practically inviolable.

"To quote the instructions: —

"'This inviolability of office and dwelling is secured by treaties with Belgium, Bolivia, Corea, France, Germany (of consuls not citizens), Italy, Morocco, Muscat, Roumania, Salvador, and Serbia; but the dwelling cannot be used as

A DONKEY CAR, CARACAS.

an asylum. It is agreed with Colombia that the persons and dwellings of consuls are to be subject to the laws of the country, except as specially exempted by treaty. The consulates in Germany are not to be made asylums for the subjects of other powers.'"

He added, still quoting the consular instructions of the State Department: —

"'By convention with Belgium, Germany, Netherlands, Roumania, Serbia and Italy, the consul is exempted from arrest, except for crimes. By treaty with Turkey he is entitled to suitable distinction and necessary aid and protection. In Muscat he enjoys the inviolability of a diplomatic officer. In Austria-

Hungary and France he is to enjoy personal immunities; but in France, if a citizen of France, or owning property there, or engaged in commerce, he can claim only the immunities granted to other citizens of the country who own property, or to merchants. In Austria-Hungary and Roumania, if engaged in business, he can be detained only for commercial debts. In Colombia, the fourteen consuls of the United States have no diplomatic character. In Great Britain, Liberia, Netherlands (as to colonies), Nicaragua, and Paraguay they are regarded as appointed for the protection of trade.'

"So you see that a consul in his little office somewhat resembles the old Roman officer of that name. He has a little republic of his own."

Percy began to study Portuguese stories and poems on the ship, which belonged to Lisbon. One of these stories, which we quote, we found very curious. We give the version that we find in English Folk-Lore: —

THE SEVEN IRON SLIPPERS.

(FROM PORTUGUESE FOLK-TALES, BY CONSIGLIERI PEDROSO.)

THERE lived once together a king and a queen, and a princess who was their daughter. The princess had worn out every evening seven pair of slippers made of iron; and the king could not make out how that could be, though he was always trying to find out. The king at last issued a decree that whosoever should be able to find out how the princess managed to wear out seven pairs of slippers made of iron in the short space of time between morning and evening, he would give the princess in marriage if he were a man, and if a woman he would marry her to a prince.

It happened that a soldier was walking along an open country road, carrying on his back a sack of oranges, and he saw two men fighting and giving each other great blows.

The soldier went up to them and asked them, "O men, why are you giving each other such blows?"

"Why, indeed should it be!" they replied. "Because our father is dead; and he has left us this cap, and we both wish to possess it."

"Is it possible that for the sake of a cap you should be fighting?" inquired the soldier.

The men then said, "The reason is that this cap has a charm, and if any one puts it on and says, 'Cap, cover me so that no one shall see me!' no one can see us."

The soldier upon hearing this said to them, "I'll tell you what I can do for you; you let me remain here with the cap whilst I throw this orange to a great distance, and you run after it, and the one that shall pick it up first shall be the possessor of the cap."

The men agreed to this, and the soldier threw the orange to a great distance, as far as he possibly could, whilst the men both ran to pick it up. Here the soldier, without loss of time, put on the cap, saying, "Cap, make me invisible!"

When the men returned with the orange they could see nothing and nobody. The soldier went away with the cap, and further on he met on his road two other men fighting, and he said to them, "O foolish men, why do you give each other such blows?"

The men replied, "Indeed, you may well ask why, if it were not that father died and left us this pair of boots, and we each of us wish to be the sole possessor of them."

The soldier replied, "Is it possible that for the matter of a pair of boots you should be fighting thus?"

And they replying said, "It is because these boots are charmed, and when one wishes to go any distance he has only to say, 'Boots, take me here or there,' wherever one should wish to go, and instantly they convey one to any place."

The soldier said to them, "I will tell you what to do; I will throw an orange to a great distance, and you give me the boots to keep. You run for the orange, and the first that shall pick it up shall have the pair of boots."

He threw the orange to a great distance, and both men ran to catch it. Upon this the soldier said, "Cap, make me invisible, boots take me to the city;" and when the men returned they missed the boots and the soldier, for he had gone away.

He arrived at the capital and heard the decree read which the king had promulgated, and he began to consider what he had better do in this case. "With this cap, and with these boots, I can surely find out what the princess does to wear out seven pairs of slippers made of iron in one night."

He went and presented himself at the palace. When the king saw him he said, "Do you really know a way of finding out how the princess, my daughter, can wear out seven pairs of slippers in one night?"

The soldier replied, "I only ask you to let me try —"

"But you must remember," said the king, "that if at the end of three days you have not found out the mystery, I shall order you to be put to death."

The soldier to this replied that he was prepared to take the consequences. The king ordered him to remain in the palace. Every attention was paid to all his wants and wishes; he had his meals with the king at the same table, and slept in the princess's room.

But what did the princess do? She took him a beverage to his bedside and gave it to him to drink. This beverage was a sleeping-draught, which she gave him to make him sleep all night.

Next morning the soldier had not seen the princess do anything, for he had slept very soundly the whole night. When he appeared at breakfast the king asked him, "Well, did you see anything?"

"Your Majesty must know that I have seen nothing whatever."

The king said, "Look well what you are at, for now there only remains two days more for you, or else you die!"

The soldier replied, "I have not the least misgivings."

Night came on and the princess acted as before. Next morning the king asked him again at breakfast, "Well, did you see anything last night?"

The soldier replied, "Your Majesty must know that I have seen nothing whatever."

"Be careful, then, what you do. Only one day more, and you die!"

The soldier replied, "I have no misgivings."

He then began to think it over. "It is very curious that I should sleep all night. It cannot be from anything else but from drinking the beverage which the princess gives me. Leave me alone! I know what I will do. When the princess brings me the cup I shall pretend to drink, but shall throw away the beverage."

The night came, and the princess did not fail to bring him the beverage to drink to his bedside. The soldier made a pretence to drink it, but instead threw it away, and feigned sleep though he was awake.

In the middle of the night he saw the princess rise up, prepare to go out, and advance towards the door to leave. What did he do then? He put on the cap, drew on the boots, and said, "Cap, make me invisible; boots, take me wherever the princess goes."

The princess entered a carriage, and the soldier followed her into the carriage and accompanied her. He saw the carriage stop at the seashore. The princess then embarked on board a vessel decked with flags. The soldier on seeing this, said, "Cap, cover me, that I may be invisible," and embarked with the princess. She reached the lands of giants; and when on passing the first sentinel, he challenged her with, "Who's there?" "The Princess of Harmony," she replied. The sentinel rejoined, "Pass with your suite."

The princess looked behind her, and not seeing any one following her, she said to herself, "The sentinel cannot be in his sound mind; he said 'Pass with your suite;' I do not see any one."

She reached the second sentinel, who cried out at the top of his voice, "Who's there?" "The Princess of Harmony," replied the princess. "Pass with your suite," said the sentinel. The princess was each time more and more astonished.

She came to the third sentinel, who challenged her as the others had done, "Who's there?" "The Princess of Harmony." "Pass on with your suite," rejoined the sentinel. The princess, as before, wondered what the man could mean.

After journeying for a long time the soldier, who followed her closely, saw the princess arrive at a beautiful palace, enter in, and go into a hall for dancing, where he saw many giants.

The princess sat upon a seat by the side of her lover who was a giant. The soldier hid himself under their seat. The band struck up, and she rose to dance with the giant, and when she finished the dance she had her iron slippers all in pieces. She took them off and pushed them under her seat. The soldier immediately took possession of them and put them inside his sack. The princess again sat down to converse with her lover. The band again struck up some dance music, and the princess rose to dance. When she finished this dance another pair of her slippers had worn out. She took them off and left them under her seat. The soldier put these also into his sack.

Finally, she danced seven times, and each time she danced she tore a pair of slippers made of iron. The soldier kept them all in his sack.

After the ball the princess sat down to converse with her lover; and what did the soldier do? He turned their chairs over and threw them both on the middle of the floor. They were very much surprised, and they searched everywhere and through all the houses and could find no one. The giants then looked out for a book of facts they had, wherein could be seen the course of the winds and other agencies peculiar to their race. They called in a black servant to read in the book and find out what was the matter.

The soldier rose up from where he was and said, "Cap, make me invisible." He then gave the negro a slap on the face; the negro fell to the ground, while he took possession of the book and kept it. The time was approaching when the princess must depart and return home; and not being able to stay longer, she went away.

The soldier followed her, and she returned by the same way she came. She went on board; and when she reached the city, the carriage was already waiting for her. The soldier then said, "Boots, take me to the palace;" and he arrived there, took off his clothes, and went to bed.

When the princess arrived she found everything in her chamber just as she left it, and even found the soldier fast asleep. In the morning the king said, "Well, soldier, did you see anything remarkable last night?"

"Be it known to your Majesty that I saw nothing whatever last night," replied the soldier.

The king then said, "According to what you say, I do not know if you are aware that you must die to-day."

The soldier replied, "If it is so I must have patience, what else can I do?"

When the princess heard this she rejoiced much. The king then ordered that everything for the execution should be prepared before the palace windows.

When the soldier was proceeding to execution he asked the king to grant him a favor for the last time, and to send for the princess so that she should be present.

The king gave the desired permission, and the princess was present when he said to her, "Is it not true to say that the princess went out at midnight?"

"It is not true," replied the princess.

"Is it true to say," again asked the soldier, "that the princess entered a carriage, and afterwards went on board a vessel and proceeded to a ball given in the kingdom of the giants?"

"It is not true."

The soldier yet asked her another question, "Is it true that the princess wore out seven pairs of iron slippers during the seven times she danced?" Then he shewed her the slippers.

"There is no truth in all this," replied the princess.

The soldier at last said to her, "Is it true to say that the princess at the end of the ball fell on the floor from her seat, and the giants had a book brought to them to see what bewitchery and magic pervaded and had taken possession of the house, and which book is here?"

The princess now said, "It is so."

The king was delighted at the discovery and happy ending of this affair, and the soldier came to live in the palace and married the princess.

The voyage to the volcanic Cape Verd Islands was a delightful one, over the smooth waters of tropical seas. The stars of the Southern Cross gleamed over the waters; the nights were clear, cool, and refreshing; the days, long splendors.

There were on board English, Spanish, and Portuguese, some forty in number. Time at last hung heavily, and Percy was sought for diversions. He found himself able to speak Spanish well, and he introduced to the passengers the simple educational amusements of his old Washington life. Among these were " Daft Day," in which each one was expected to act the most simple character, like Simple Simon. People were easily imposed upon and cheated. The origin of this play is very odd, and Mr. Van der Palm, one evening on board, gave the following history of it:—

HOGMANAY.

Perhaps no poet has ever presented such a pleasing picture of the old Yule Days, in the halls of the barons, as Sir Walter Scott. Who does not love to recall it during mid-winter holidays, even now?

> "On Christmas eve the bells were rung,
> On Christmas eve the mass was sung,
> Then opened wide the Baron's hall,
> To vassal, tenant, serf and all."

When the white towers of Abbotsford rose over the Tweed, and became Sir Walter Scott's home, its master delighted to reproduce the old Christmas games and customs of the time of the barons. The songs of the old minstrels of the camp and court were sung; the bagpipes were played, and the old legends of England and Scotland were told.

The stories have entered into Scott's prose works, and the songs of the old harpers and minstrels, which he loved to revive on such occasions, have been made familiar to the world through his poems.

especially through the "Lay of the Last Minstrel" and the "Lady of the Lake." The Christmas days at Abbotsford were a picture of the past. Scott wrote the "Bonnets of Bonny Dundee" on Christmas days.

Christmas *days*, we say, for the old-time Christmas was not a single day, but a season. It often lasted from Christmas Eve until Twelfth Night, the sixth of January, and at Abbotsford, from Christmas Eve until Hogmanay.

"Hogmanay?" What is that? It is a lost holiday of old provincial France and England and Scotland. It meant "on to the mistletoe!" a cry of the minstrels and the children in the old provinces of France on that merry day. It really means "the last day of the year," or the end of the Christmas season.

"Daft Day" it was called in Scotland, because on that day the people were at liberty to act as foolishly as they pleased. It became, in Sir Walter Scott's time, a children's day, and Hogmanay was the crowning event of the Abbotsford's Christmas holidays.

Scott was, at this time, at the prime of life, and was writing "The Tales of the Crusaders." He was concealing the authorship of his works, and was spoken of as "The Great Unknown." Every one believed him to be the real author of the Waverley Novels, but none of his guests could ever discover how or when he did his literary work.

Captain Hall thus speaks of an evening at Abbotsford during the holidays: "In the evening we had a great feast indeed. Sir Walter asked us if we had ever read 'Christabel,' and upon some of us admitting with shame that we never had seen it, he offered to read it, and took a chair in the midst of all the party in the library. . . . He also read to us the famous poem on 'Thomas the Rhymer's Adventure with the Queen of the Fairies.' There was also much pleasing singing; many old ballads, and many ballads pretending to be old, were sung to the harp and piano-forte."

We note this programme, for it is suggestive. The reading and singing of old historic ballads is a worthy entertainment for the evenings of the Christmas holidays.

The mood of Scott, at this time, is thus pictured by Hall, in the description of a breakfast after the holidays: "At breakfast, to-day, we had, as usual, many stories.

"I quite forget all these stories but one. 'My cousin, Walter Scott,' said he, 'was a midshipman some forty years ago, in a ship at Portsmouth. He and two companions had gone ashore, and had overstayed their leave, and spent their money, and run up an immense bill at the tavern on the Point.

"'The ship made a signal for sailing, but the landlady said, —

"'"No, gentlemen, you shall not go without paying your reckoning."

"'But they had nothing wherewith to pay.

"'"I'll give you one chance," said she. "I am so circumstanced here that I cannot carry on my business as a single woman, and I must contrive, somehow, to have a husband. You may go, if one of you will marry me. I do not care which it is, but one of you shall have me, or you shall all go to jail, and the ship sail without you."

"'They agreed to comply. The marriage ceremony was performed, and the three sailed away, including the husband. Some months after, at Jamaica, a file of papers reached the husband, and looking them over carelessly, he suddenly jumped up, and exclaimed in ecstasy, "Thank heaven, my wife has been hanged!"'"

We give this story with slight abridgment.

"Yesterday being Hogmanay," says Hall, in his Journal, January 1, 1825, "there was a constant succession of Guisards, — that is, boys dressed up in fantastic caps, with their shirts over their jackets, and with wooden swords in their hands." About one hundred boys, in fools' costumes, used to visit Sir Walter on this Daft Day. They sometimes acted a masque or pantomime.

Sir Walter used to give each boy and girl who visited him on Hogmanay a "penny apiece" and an oaken cake.

The memories of the Christmases at Abbotsford were a delight to the people of Melrose for many years. There are some yet living who remember them, with their celebration of the old lost holiday of Hogmanay.

"A Christmas gambol oft would cheer
A poor man's heart for half the year."

The picture of the gracious face of Sir Walter Scott at the doors of Abbotsford, with his dogs, the hills showing above the clustered towers of the great mansion, and the Tweed rolling below; the pipers with their bagpipes; the gathering children on the grounds, with their harlequin caps, and shirts over their jackets, and wooden swords; the funny play, the distribution of the pennies and oaken cakes is one worthy of a poet or artist, and one in which any reader will love to remember the Wizard of the North.

The spirit of it, too, has a Christmas lesson for all, — the happiness that makes happiness, and the equality of love that the herald angels sang, —

"Centuries ago."

Among the diversions that Percy used to entertain his English friends were: —

BOOK PARTIES.

The book party consists of a reading family, or several families, who hold a meeting once a week, or at stated periods, to rehearse to each other the contents of books that each member has lately read.

Each member of the circle presents a title of a book, new or old, gives an analysis of its contents, perhaps reads a few selections from it as an illustration, and criticises it and gives his view of its literary value and moral worth.

A general discussion may follow the presentation of this subject-matter.

It will be better that the books shall not be presented in a topical way, — as, for instance, scientific books on one evening, fiction on another, or travel, art, or poetry, at stated times. It is more interesting if the analysis is made miscellaneous; there should be variety and contrasts.

Parties of this kind stimulate good reading and educate the mind to an acquaintance with the best thought. The social feature is healthy, and the discussions are sure to be animating and entertaining.

A very pleasant amusement of this order is the play which we may call "Animated Book Titles." A party is given in which each guest is to appear as the representative of a title of a book, or as a character of a popular and well-known book. A young man who comes with a hoe may represent "Ivanhoe" (I've an hoe). The "dude" who appears in contortions may be "Oliver Twist" (all-of-a-twist). We have seen "Lucille" puzzle a company by being acted as a scene in a shoemaker's shop, — *Loose heel*.

Such titles as "The Ring and the Book," "We are Seven," "Never too Late to Mend" (a seamstress), are sufficiently suggestive.

The word *Eurydice* will admit of carefully prepared classical tableaux. The word may be used as a sentence, as "You-ride-I-see," in a mock dialogue between two persons of fortunate and unfortunate social standing. The conductor of the entertainment may say, "My whole is one word, and represents a character of classical fiction. The whole word will first be acted as a sentence, in the form of a dialogue between a poor debtor, who has to go on foot, and an equestrian, who has just alighted from a fine horse. The second scene will represent the character in tableau."

The second scene will be Orpheus and his lyre (the music may be played on a piano) at the door of a darkened room, and an appearance of the shade of Eurydice. She follows Orpheus as he beckons over his shoulder until she comes to a place near the door, when he, contrary to the commands of the gods, looks around, and she vanishes after the manner of the old mythological story, which should be carefully studied by the leader of such an entertainment. The tableau can be made very beautiful.

In the Orange Party everything is supposed to assume the colors of Lord Baltimore. The dresses of the ladies must be orange, or orange and white, or orange and black. The orange color in them is to be made conspicuous or to predominate. The gentlemen will wear orange neckties, perhaps orange sashes or vests. The rooms or halls are to be trimmed with orange colors, as festoons of orange cloth, or green boughs to which oranges are attached.

If possible, decorate the dining-room with the Spanish moss of Florida. Your fruit dealer, or any friends that you may have in Florida, will secure the moss for you. The rooms, in which we attended the party, were so trimmed.

Provide orange shades for the lights, which is easily done by covering the globes with orange silk or tissue paper.

The refreshments are to be oranges of all kinds. It is not so expensive to provide these as it might seem. Tangerine, Musketine, Navel, Blood, and Indian River oranges, together with Florida grape-fruit, are to be found in the cool seasons in nearly every large market, as are also Havana oranges and the Sicilian varieties.

These all should be picturesquely piled upon a long table, and the pyramids decorated with leaves, evergreens, Spanish moss, or flowers.

In serving the oranges there should be a lecturer, whose office it is to describe each variety, as it is quartered and laid upon the plates. Let many varieties be laid cut upon each plate, so that the eating and the testing of the flavors will furnish a very pleasant theme for conversation.

Sugar will be served with the oranges for the sour varieties and grape-fruit. Orange cake may also be served.

The music will be plantation songs to the accompaniment of the guitar or banjo. American negro melodies and Spanish *boleros* were sung at Percy's arrangement of such a party, to which his father added a lecture on oranges.

The Question Class is a very entertaining and educational home amusement. The game consists of presenting the names of obscure places for guessing, and "throwing light" on them by description and history.

For example: "Where is Zag-a-zig?" A long pause. "Shall I throw light?" The one who has given out the word may begin to give the history of the Suez Canal.

The geography of obscure names in poems may be used in this way; also obscure names of battle-fields, *Belgrade;* and Indian names and their meanings.

An odd question has sometimes been asked at such parties, which is usually difficult to answer, but very stimulating to thought: "Who would you choose to be if you could not be yourself?" To which last one of the passengers made answer, "The next best man in all the world."

The ship was so steady in the afternoons that these refined amusements answered well. When the ship was unsteady, new games of pitching quoits were favorites. The men played and the women laughed at their miscalculations.

In the evenings songs were sung, — songs of many lands, — among them, "Songs of the Pyrenees," "Songs of Caracas," and the "Mexican National Hymn," that in Mexico announces the President, and is only played when the President is present.

Percy composed a student's song to the air of the "Red, White, and Blue." He sung it daily at the meetings for diversions.

The ship touched at the Cape Verd Islands, and again at the "blue Canaries." Percy saw the native canary birds, which here were gray. These islands were among the earliest discoveries of navigators who ventured beyond the Pillars of Hercules, as Gibraltar was once called.

Percy could imagine how the Peak of Teneriffe, twelve thousand feet high, must have looked to the crews of Columbus as it blazed over the sea. From these sea volcanoes, chimneys of the sea, the ship sailed directly to Lisbon. Thence Mr. Van der Palm and Percy took passage for Gibraltar.

During the voyage the passengers and officers amused themselves at times by repeating proverbs. A prize was offered to the person who could collect and repeat the largest number of Proverbs of the Sea. Percy was something of a student of this kind of literature, and having the assistance of a popular book of sea literature, presented at the end of the voyage the longest list, and was voted a Solomon and the purse.

PROVERBS OF THE SEA.

1. The sea is like sorrow, — one never sees the end.
2. My good-will toward you is as great as the sea, and my love as its depth.
3. A bad reputation spreads even to the sea. A good reputation remains at the threshold of the door.
4. Patience is grander than the ocean.
5. One can look into the bosom of the sea, but one cannot see what is in the heart of man.
6. We shall pass away; the land and the sea will remain.
7. As rich as the sea.
8. Rich as the sea, or rich as Saint Peter, are expressions used of a man who possesses a large fortune. To the Breton sailor, all which falls to the sea belongs by right to Saint Peter.
9. Give yourself a pond when you wish the sea; it is insatiable.
10. Nothing is richer than the sea.
11. There are many things in the field, but there are more in the sea.
12. Avarice is like the sea; it takes all and gives nothing.

13. Not for all the treasures of the ocean, would I place its limits to my existence.

14. Avarice is a sea without bottom, and rarely does a man fall therein and save himself.

15. Hell, the sea, and avarice never have enough.

16. Three things are insatiable; priests, monks, and the sea.

17. The sea complains it wants water.

18. He measures the waters of the sea in his fist (he attempts an impossibility).

19. He is building a bridge over the sea.

20. To carry water to the sea (to carry something to a place where there is a great abundance).

21. To turn water into the sea; to give to the rich.

22. He gives of the water of the ocean (to obtain from the aid of another or to draw from an abundant source, but to give nothing from his own heart).

23. To throw water into the sea; to do good to the rabble.

24. No sea without water, no God without wisdom.

25. A drop of water does not make the sea.

26. Can the sea be filled with the falling dew?

27. The sea is in want of water (when a woman has no reply to make on the spot.)

28. To demand of avarice is to dig into the sea.

29. Drop by drop the sea is drained.

30. Water always runs into the sea.

31. All water goes to the sea, and all money passes through the hand of the rich.

32. All the waters go to the sea, and yet it is not more full.

33. The sea receives into its bosom sweet waters, and that which it gives is salt.

34. Rivers run to the sea.

35. All rivers do what they can for the sea.

36. The sea refuses no river.
37. Follow the river, and you'll get to the sea.
38. He drinks the sea and the fishes.
39. To drink the sea is a difficult task.
40. When one has drunk the sea, he can well eat the fishes (when one has suffered a great outrage, one can well endure others).
41. I am so very thirsty, I could drink the sea.
42. It is as though he attempted to count the sands of the desert or to drink the ocean.
43. One cannot dry the sea with sponges.
44. Can a dog lapping water diminish the ocean?
45. He went to the sea and he found it dry. (He who proceeds without courage would do well to turn back, for he will fail in his enterprise.)
46. He could not find water in the sea.
47. To be in the ocean and to return to one's home thirsty.
48. Salt as the sea.
49. To salt the sea and the fishes (to salt too much).
50. A merchandise is salt when it has been paid for dear.
51. There is more water to drink in wells than in the sea.
52. There is more to drink in a bottle than in the sea.
53. In the water of the sea, one can see his (visage) face (changeableness).
54. To till the shore of the sea (to take useless trouble).
55. I have only learned to till upon the sea and to reap upon the rocks.
56. Could he who cannot leap over a canal, jump over the sea?
57. He desires to cross the ocean, but cannot cross a little stream.
58. A tenacious man is like the sea upon the rock.
59. The trident of Neptune is the sceptre of the world.
60. He who is master of the sea is master of the earth.
61. The seas make the soul of man. The waves give him intelligence.

62. A fool throws a stone into the sea. One hundred wise men could not draw it out.

63. If you are not happy, you can throw yourself into the sea.

64. Treacherous as the ocean.

65. He that would sail without danger, must never go on the sea.

66. He that would learn to pray, let him go to sea.

67. When starting for war, make one prayer; when going upon the sea, make two prayers; do you wish to marry, make three prayers.

68. He who would learn to pray should go to sea; and he who would know how to sleep should go to church.

69. Sailors have no need of books to learn to think of God; the sea and the heavens speak clearly enough to them.

70. The sea is a beautiful sight from the shore.

71. Praise the sea, (but) a in foreign country.

72. Praise the sea, but hold yourself on the shore.

73. It is much better to trust one's self to men on land than to sails on the sea.

74. It is safer to live poor on land than rich on sea.

75. Nothing is more subject to changes than the sea.

76. Every man who wishes to be reduced to misery and to beggary has only to trust his life and fortune to the sea.

77. One sou earned upon land is worth more than ten earned on the sea; one can possess a sou earned on the land, but he can see the ten earned on the sea drown themselves.

78. There are two things of which we demand something without ceasing; they give without reserve and without spite, — the sea and the land.

79. I encompass the land with all the coasts. I am agitated with frequent tempests; it is I who go where the water has the most space in which to move (the sea).

80. What is the most impossible thing? To dip the sea with a sieve.

81. What is that which carries easily a cartload of hay but which cannot carry a sou? The sea.
82. In the salt sea fresh fish are born.
83. Do not sell the fish which are yet in the sea.
84. To fish well, it is necessary to go to the sea.
85. The sea does not complain of the fishes.
86. Do good, and throw it to the sea; whether the fishes swallow it or men forget it, God will remember it.
87. A straw can remain in the sea, but a secret cannot remain in the soul.
88. If the sea boiled, plenty of fish would be cooked.
89. If the ocean became clouds, the universe would be submerged.
90. The sea does not buy fish.
91. The sea is a good paymaster.
92. The sea belongs to the whole world.
93. The sea does not burn; there is nothing which crowds.
94. Man is like the sea; if he does not move to-day he will to-morrow.
95. Man is like the sea, what he does to-day he will do to-morrow.
96. Not the sea, but the wind, makes vessels perish.
97. To mix heaven and earth (deep trouble).
98. The sea even, which is so great (grand), becomes calm.
99. The virtues which have not been tried by danger are not in honor either in empty ships or among men.
100. To search by land or sea.
101. Fortune is like the sea, sometimes high and sometimes low.
102. The world resembles the sea: we see those drown who do not know how to swim.
103. He sails on a full sea.
104. To sail in great waters.
105. Being on the sea, sail; being on the land, settle.
106. "The sea tires," said the man who had already eaten his provisions after sailing the first quarter of a league.

107. Some one said that his great-grandfather, grandfather, and his father died on the sea. "If I were you," said one to him, "I would never go upon the sea." "Why," he replied; "where did your great-grandfather, grandfather, and father die?" "Where, if not in their beds?" "If I were in your place, I would never go to bed."

108. I have seen a man who has seen another man who has seen the sea.

109. A mariner ought never to laugh till he has reached port.

110. A Sicilian who carried figs in his ship was wrecked and saved. One day, when he was on the shore and the sea was calm, he said, "I see what you would have; you wanted my figs!"

The steamer passed over a part of the sea through which Columbus made his outward voyage, and the red peak of Teneriffe recalled to Percy the terror of the crews of the caravels of the discovery. He also remembered the old tale of the kraken, or the sea-monster which was supposed to inhabit the western seas, and to uplift its gigantic head and seize the adventurous ships. There was on board the ship a number of books entitled, "The Fisheries Exhibition Literature," and from one of these volumes he obtained a very interesting account of the early Northern legends of this fabulous monster, which we quote.

THE KRAKEN.

In the legends and traditions of northern nations, stories of the existence of a marine animal of such enormous size that it more resembled an island than an organized being frequently found a place. It is thus described in an ancient manuscript (about A. D. 1180), attributed to the Norwegian King Sverre, and the belief in it has been alluded to by other Scandinavian writers from an early period to the present day. It was an obscure and mysterious sea-monster, known as the kraken, whose form and nature were imperfectly understood, and it was peculiarly the object of popular wonder and superstitious dread.

Eric Pontoppidan, the younger, Bishop of Bergen, and member of the Royal Academy of Sciences at Copenhagen, is generally, but unjustly, regarded as the

OLD MISSION NEAR CARACAS.

inventor of the semi-fabulous kraken, and is constantly misquoted by authors who have never read his work ("Natural History of Norway"), and who, one after another, have copied from their predecessors erroneous statements concerning him. More than half a century before him, Christian Francis Paullinus, a physician and naturalist of Eisenach, who evinced in his writings an admiration of the marvellous rather than of the useful, had described as resembling Gesner's "Heracleoticon," a monstrous animal which occasionally rose from the sea on the coasts of Lapland and Finmark, and which was of such enormous dimensions that a regiment of soldiers could conveniently manœuvre on its back. About the same date, but a little earlier, Bartholinus, a learned Dane, told how, on a certain occasion, the Bishop of Midaros found the kraken quietly reposing on the shore, and mistaking the enormous creature for a huge rock, erected an altar upon it and performed Mass. The kraken respectfully waited till the ceremony was concluded, and the reverend prelate safe on shore, and then sank beneath the waves.

And a hundred and fifty years before Bartholinus and Paullinus wrote, Olaus Magnus, Archbishop of Upsala, in Sweden, had related many wondrous narratives of sea-monsters,—tales which had gathered and accumulated marvels as they had been passed on from generation to generation in oral history, and which he took care to bequeath to his successors undeprived of any of their fascination. According to him, the kraken was not so polite to the laity as to the bishop, for when some fishermen lighted a fire on its back, it sank beneath their feet, and overwhelmed them in the waters.

Pontoppidan was not a fabricator of falsehoods; but, in collecting evidence relating to the "great beasts" living in "the great and wide sea," was influenced, as he tells us, by "a desire to extend the popular knowledge of the glorious works of a beneficent Creator." He gave too much credence to contemporary narratives and old traditions of floating islands and sea-monsters, and to the superstitious beliefs and exaggerated statements of ignorant fishermen. But if those who ridicule him had lived in his day and amongst his people, they would probably have done the same; for even Linnæus was led to believe in the kraken, and catalogued it in the first edition of his "Systema Naturæ," as "Sepia Microcosmos." He seems to have afterwards had cause to discredit his information respecting it, for he omitted it in the next edition. The Norwegian bishop was a conscientious and painstaking investigator, and the tone of his writings is neither that of an intentional deceiver nor of an incautious dupe. He diligently endeavored to separate the truth from the cloud of error and fiction by which it was obscured; and in this he was to a great extent successful, for he correctly identifies, from the vague and perplexing descriptions submitted to him, the animal whose habits and structure had given rise to so many terror-laden narratives and extravagant traditions.

The following are some of his remarks on the subject of this gigantic and ill-defined animal. Although I have greatly abbreviated them, I have thought it right to quote them at considerable length, that the modest and candid spirit in which they were written may be understood: —

"Amongst the many things," he says, "which are in the ocean, and concealed from our eyes, or only presented to our view for a few minutes, is the kraken. This creature is the largest and most surprising of all the animal creation, and consequently well deserves such an account as the nature of the thing, according to the Creator's wise ordinances, will admit of. Such I shall give at present, and perhaps much greater light on this subject may be reserved for posterity.

"Our fishermen unanimously affirm, and without the least variation in their accounts, that when they row out several miles to sea, particularly in the hot summer days, and by their situation (which they know by taking a view of different points of land) expect to find eighty or a hundred fathoms of water, it often happens that they do not find above twenty or thirty, and sometimes less. At these places they generally find the greatest plenty of fish, especially cod and ling. Their lines, they say, are no sooner out than they may draw them up with the hooks all full of fish. By this they know that the kraken is at the bottom. They say this creature causes these unnatural shallows mentioned above, and prevents their sounding. These the fishermen are always glad to find, looking upon them as a means of their taking abundance of fish.

"There are sometimes twenty boats or more got together and throwing out their lines at a moderate distance from each other; and the only thing they then have to observe is whether the depth continues the same which they know by their lines, or whether it grows shallower, by their seeming to have less water. If this last be the case they know that the kraken is raising himself nearer the surface, and then it is not time for them to stay any longer; they immediately leave off fishing, take to their oars, and get away as fast as they can.

"When they have reached the usual depth of the place, and find themselves out of danger, they lie upon their oars, and in a few minutes after they see this enormous monster come up to the surface of the water. He there shows himself sufficiently, though his whole body does not appear, which in all likelihood no human eye ever beheld.

"Its back or upper part, which seems to be in appearance about an English mile and a half in circumference (some say more, but I choose the least for greater certainty), looks at first like a number of small islands surrounded with something that floats and fluctuates like sea-weeds. Here and there a larger rising is observed like sand-banks, on which various kinds of small fishes are seen continually leaping about till they roll off into the water from the sides of it; at last several bright points or horns appear, which grow thicker and thicker the higher they rise above the surface of the water, and sometimes they stand up as high and as large as the masts of middle-sized vessels. It seems these are the creature's arms; and it is said if they were to lay hold of the largest man-of-war they would pull it down to the bottom. After this monster has been on the surface of the water a short time it begins to slowly sink again, and then the danger is as great as before; because the motion of his sinking causes such a swell in the sea, and such an eddy or whirlpool, that it draws everything down with it, like the current of the river Male.

"As this enormous sea animal in all probability may be reckoned of the polype, or of the starfish kind, as shall hereafter be more fully proved, it seems that the parts which are seen rising at its pleasure, and are called arms, are properly the tentacula, or feeling instruments, called horns as well as arms. With these they move themselves, and likewise gather in their food.

"Besides these, for this last purpose the great Creator has also given this creature a strong and peculiar scent, which it can emit at certain times, and by means of which it beguiles and draws other fish to come in heaps about it. This animal has another strange property, known by the experience of many old fishermen. They observe that for some months the kraken or krabben is continually eating, and in other months he always voids his excrements. During this evacuation the surface of the water is colored with the excrement, and appears quite thick and turbid. This muddiness is said to be so very agreeable to the smell or taste of other fishes, or to both, that they gather together from all parts to it, and keep for that purpose directly over the kraken; he then opens his arms or horns, seizes and swallows his welcome guests and converts them after due time, by digestion, into a bait for other fish of the same kind. I relate what is affirmed by many; but I cannot give so certain assurances of this particular as I can of the existence of this surprising creature, though I do not find anything in it absolutely contrary to Nature. As we can hardly expect to examine this enormous sea animal alive, I am the more concerned that nobody embraced that opportunity which, according to an account once did, and perhaps never more may, offer, of seeing it entire when dead."

CHAPTER V.

GIBRALTAR.

HE Port of Gibraltar to a lover of stories is one of the most interesting in the world.

Gibraltar is a rocky promontory, some three miles in length, and is connected with the mainland of Spain, although it does not seem so to be as seen from the sea. The town of Gibraltar has some seventeen thousand inhabitants, and a changing population, and is connected with a garrison of some five thousand men. This town of twenty thousand or more people is a picture of the types of the world. English, Spaniards, Jews and Moors, sailors from all lands, commercial agents, travellers, and adventurers, are to be found here, and the consular rooms are nowhere more interesting.

The rock of Gibraltar is the world's greatest fortress,—the pride of England, and the humiliation of Spain, from which it was wrested. It is composed of gray marble and covered with moss and dwarf vegetation. Birds and little animals find a secure home on the sides of the defiant sea mountain, as they are protected by local law. The peak has an elevation of about 1440 feet. He who goes up to the top to see the Bay of Gibraltar, the coasts of Spain and Africa, "the Pillars of Hercules," and the sea, passes grassy glens where grow capers, palmitas, aloes and cacti, where live pigeons, woodcocks, and Barbary apes.

The wars of Gibraltar would fill volumes, that of 1872 being the most remarkable, when red hot shot, or rains of liquid fire brought

THE ROCK OF GIBRALTAR.

the fortress securely and for all time, it is probable, under the English dominion. The fortress is one mountain of protected batteries. Nothing but some new art of scientific discovery could ever wrest it from the English flag.

Gibraltar may be said to be the port of all ports, the capital port of the world. The Mediterranean is the sea of the world. From it the ships of discovery sailed. Its shores are the ruins of empires, and the seats of eastern powers.

All nations have their representatives at times in the old commercial houses here that line the narrow streets, where children of many colors play together, pet apes gibber, and parrots scream. Here many flags, a *congress* of flags, daily float in the sea winds.

Curiosities abound in the streets, — ships, commercial houses, and consulates. Gibraltar is the curiosity shop of the world.

TALES OF THE CONSULATES OF GIBRALTAR.

"THE GRINDING OVER YOUNG."

In one of the old consular rooms of Gibraltar, Percy discovered a very old and curious picture. Among all the curiosities of the place, nothing more haunted his imagination than this odd print. He used to return to it as often as he went to that consulate, and stand before it with a stimulated imagination.

The picture represented a number of old men in various stages of decrepitude going up an inclined plane to a funnel to be ground over young. There was one man gleefully sinking down into the funnel-shaped hopper to be ground over. A young woman had charge of this wonderful mill, and a priest was praying on his knees during the miraculous grinding. The old man who was to be ground over used some kind of magic medicine to assist the progress, and an expectant group of fair young ladies were waiting to receive the young men as fast as they were ground out. These young ladies were seen going happily away with the ground-over men, who came out young and handsome, and full of good spirits.

The picture was droll, rude, and incongruous, and yet it held the fancy like Ponce de Leon's dream of the Fountain of Youth.

"What history has that picture?" asked Percy of the French consul.

"None; none at all, my American boy. It is tavern print, and may be found in many old taverns on the Continent. It is very droll and popular. This one always excites the curiosity of you Americans."

"It would be better if the funnel were larger, and there was a box for mill-stones. How could a man be ground over in that way? The passage is too small."

"*Quien sabe*," said the consul, in the Spanish term of the place, "I do not wonder that you look at it. The world all wants to be ground over, and most of us need to be. But no day ever returns again; the days go, and go, and leave us the products of the past. There is something in that picture that makes me serious, as curious as it is. No one over fifty years of age could look upon it without a regret in his laugh. I sometimes find myself dreaming over it. It is a thing that sets one's fancy flying."

The consulates of Gibraltar were indeed story-telling places. The stories of many lands were to be heard here, most of them either tragic or humorous. Here Percy made a study of the tales of the Spanish Chaucer, and gathered into the note-book of his memory some of the most curious happenings and fancies of the world.

THE GRINDING OVER YOUNG.

WHAT HAPPENED TO A MOORISH KING, WHO HAD THREE SONS, AND WHO DESIRED TO KNOW WHICH WOULD BECOME THE BEST MAN.

FROM COUNT LUCANOR;

OR, THE FIFTY PLEASANT STORIES OF PATRONIO, WRITTEN BY THE PRINCE DON JUAN MANUEL, A. D. 1335–1347. FIRST DONE INTO ENGLISH FROM THE SPANISH BY JAMES POLK, M. D., 1868.

COUNT Lucanor, being one day in conversation with Patronio, said as follows: —

"Patronio, there are many young men who are being brought up at my court. Some are of high birth, some are not. Now, I find their manners and dispositions so various that I am perplexed; and, knowing the strength of your judgment, I pray you to tell me how I may be able to form an opinion as to which of them will become the best man."

"My lord," said Patronio, "the question which you place before me is very difficult to answer, for we cannot speak with certainty of that which is to come; and as what you demand is hidden in the future, so must some uncertainty rest upon my opinion.

"But we may be able to form some idea by particularly observing their development internally as well as externally. As regards this latter, there is the form of the features, the grace of movement, the complexion, as also the growth of the body and development of its members; by the principal members I mean those essential to good health, — the heart, the brain, and the liver. Yet though all the signs may appear satisfactory, we can speak with no certainty as to the ultimate result, for seldom do they all accord long, one deraignment influencing all the functions, or the contrary. But for the most part, according to the indications above named, may we judge of the future. Notice the form of the features, and particularly the eyes, with the grace of movement; these signs seldom deceive. Do not, however, suppose that gracefulness is dependent upon beauty or ugliness, for there are many men who are handsome and well-formed, but without grace: while again, others, decidedly ill-made, have that gracefulness which entitles them to be called fine men. Nevertheless, the development of the body and limbs should be taken as indications of valor and activity, although it may not be always so. It is, therefore, as I said before, very difficult to speak with certainty; for what appears favorable now may, by the force of circumstances, be entirely changed. Again, the condition of the mind is still more difficult to understand, when you seek through it for indications of what the young man is to become. You required that I should give you some certain signs whereby you can form an opinion of which of your young men will become the most manly. It will much please me to be permitted to recount to you how, upon a similar occasion, a Moorish king proved his three sons, to ascertain which of them would become the bravest man."

"Relate to me," said the count, "what that was."

"My lord," said Patronio, "there was a Moorish king who had three sons. Now, he having the power to appoint which of them he pleased to reign after him, when he had arrived at a good old age, the leading men of his kingdom waited upon him, praying to be informed which of his sons he would please to name as his successor. The king replied that in one month he would give them an answer.

"After eight or ten days the king said to his eldest son, 'I shall ride out to-morrow, and I wish you to accompany me.'

"The son waited upon the king as desired, but not so early as the time appointed. When he arrived, the king said he wished to dress, and requested him to bring him his garments. His son went to the Lord of the Bedchamber, and requested him to take the king his garments. The attendant inquired what suit it was he wished for; and the son returned to ask his father, who replied, his state robe. The young man went and told the attendant to bring the state robe.

"Now, for every article of the king's attire it was necessary to go backwards and forwards, carrying questions and answers, till at length the attendant came to dress and boot the king. The same repetition goes on when the king called for his horse, spurs, bridle, saddle, sword, and so forth. Now, all being prepared, with some trouble and difficulty, the king changed his mind, and said he would not ride out; but desired the prince, his son, to go through the city, carefully observing everything worth notice, and that on his return he should come to give his father his opinion of what he had seen.

"The prince set out, accompanied by the royal suite and the chief nobility. Trumpets, cymbals, and other instruments preceded this brilliant cavalcade. After traversing a part of the city only, he returned to the palace, when the king desired him to relate what most arrested his attention.

"'I observed nothing, sire,' said he, 'but the great noise caused by the cymbals and trumpets, which confounded me.'

"A few days later the king sent for his second son, and commanded him to attend very early the next day, when he subjected him to the same ordeal as his brother, but with a somewhat more favorable result.

"Again, after some days, he called for his youngest son's attendance. Now, this young man came to the palace very early, long before his father was awake, and waited patiently till the king arose, when he entered his chamber with that respectful humiliation which became him. The king then desired him to bring his clothes that he might dress. The young prince begged the king to specify which clothes, boots, and so forth; the same with all the other things he desired, so that he could bring all at the same time, neither would he permit the attendant to assist him, saying, if the king permitted him he would feel highly honored, and was willing to do all that was required.

"When the king was dressed, he requested his son to bring him his horse. Again the son asked what horse, saddle, spurs, sword, and other requisites he desired to have; and as he commanded, so it was done without trouble or further annoyance.

"Now, when all was ready, the king, as before, declined going. He, however, requested his son to go, and to take notice of what he saw, so that on his return he might relate to him what he thought worthy of notice.

"In obedience to his father's commands, the young prince rode through the city, attended by the same escort as his brothers; but they knew nothing, neither did the younger son, nor indeed any one else, of the object the king had in view. As he rode along, he desired that they would show him the interior of the city, the streets, and where the king kept his treasures, and what was supposed to be the amount thereof; he inquired where the nobility and the people of importance in the city lived; after this, he desired that they should present to him all the cavalry and infantry, and these he made go through their evolutions; he afterwards visited the walls, towers, and fortresses of the city, so that when he returned to the king it was very late.

"The king desired him to tell him what he had seen. The young prince replied that he feared giving offence if he stated all he felt at what he had seen and observed. Now the king commanded him relate everything, as he hoped for his blessing. The young man replied that although he was sure his father was a very good king, yet it seemed to him he had not done as much good as he might, having such good troops, so much power, and such great resources; for, had he wished it, he might have made himself master of the world.

"Now, the king felt much pleased at this judicious remark of his son. So when the time arrived that he had to give his decision to the people, he told them that he should appoint his youngest son for their king, from the indications he had given him of his ability, by certain proofs of fitness to govern, to which he had subjected all his sons: although he would have desired to appoint his eldest son as his successor, yet he felt it a duty to select the one who appeared best qualified for the station.

"And you, Count Lucanor, if you desire to know which of the young men is the most promising, you must reflect on what I have related to you, and, by the adoption of similar means, you will be enabled to form your opinion."

The count was much pleased with what Patronio had said; and as Don Juan found this to be a good example, he ordered it to be written in this book, and with the following lines which say: —

<blockquote>
By ways and works thou mayest know
Which youths to worthiest men will grow.
</blockquote>

NOTE. — This interesting narrative, evidently of Arabic origin, recalls to us the heroic tale related in the history of Rodrigo Diaz de Vivan, commonly called the Cid Campeador. This interesting tale is immortalized by Corneille in one of his best plays. The story is as follows: The old Count Diego de Vivan, after the gross insult he received from Count D'Orgaz, called his three sons to him, and forcibly pressed their hands within his own. Now, the two elder ones, Fernando and Bermuda, shrieked out as if they had been seized by the gripe of a lion, whilst Rodrigo, the younger, gave no indication of pain, but uttered an exclamation, and said, "If you were not my father, I would strike you!" To which the count replied, "It would not be the first blow I have received. You now know the offence; see, here is the sword; I have nothing further to add. With my white hairs I go to weep over my insulted honor, leaving you, my son, the duty to avenge it."

The sentence uttered by the old count, addressing his son, as written by Corneille, is truly beautiful, when with impassioned dignity he exclaims, "Rodrique, as-tu du cœur?" ("Rodrigo, have you a heart?")

With more discernment, Don Manuel, who has probably taken this historical fact as the foundation of his own story, with this difference, however, that in his recital he relies, not as the Cid upon physical indications, but after due investigation, as is shown in his narrative, places his reliance more upon the reasoning powers and mental development of, as in the case of Diego, the younger son.

WHAT HAPPENED TO A KING WITH A MAN WHO CALLED HIMSELF AN ALCHEMIST.

FROM COUNT LUCANOR.

ONE day Count Lucanor conversed with Patronio in the following manner: —

"Patronio, a man came and told me he possessed a secret which would enable me to acquire great riches and honor, but that to begin the work certain sums of money would be required; and this being furnished, he promised

THE CITY OF MOROCCO.

to return me tenfold on my outlay. Now, since God has blessed you with a good understanding, tell me what you think most desirable to be done under such circumstances."

"My lord," said Patronio, "in order that you may know how to act, having regard for your own interest, under such circumstances, I should like to inform you what happened to a king with a man who called himself an alchemist."

The count desired him to relate it.

"There was once," said he, "a man who, being a great adventurer, desired by some means or other to enrich himself, and rise out of the miserable situation in which he then was. Knowing of a certain king who taxed his people heavily, and was very anxious to acquire a knowledge of alchemy, he procured a hundred doublas and filed them down, mixing the gold dust so procured with other metals, and from this alloy he made a hundred false coins, each weighing as much as a doubla. He then took a supply of these spurious coins, dressed himself as a quiet and respectable man, and went to the city where the king dwelt, and, entering the shop of a grocer, sold to him the whole of his counterfeits for about two or three doublas. The purchaser inquired the name and use of these coins, to which he replied, 'They are essential to the practice of alchemy, and are called *tabardit*.'

"Now, our adventurer continued to reside in this city for some time as a respectable and well-dressed man, and it became circulated as a secret that he knew the science of alchemy. When this news reached the king, he sent for him, and asked if he were an alchemist.

"He, however, appeared as if anxious to conceal his knowledge, and replied that he was not, but ultimately admitted that he was, at the same time telling the king that no great outlay was required; but that if his Majesty desired it, he could furnish him with a little of the ingredients, and then show him all he knew of the science. This pleased the king very much, as it appeared, according to the alchemist's representation, that he would incur no risk. Our adventurer now sends, in the king's name, for the things required, among them being the tabardit, which were easily procured at a cost of not more than three dineros, and when they were bought and melted down before the king, there was produced the weight of a doubla of fine gold. The king seeing that these materials which cost so little produced a doubla, was delighted, and told the alchemist that he considered him to be a most worthy man, giving him an order to make more.

"Our adventurer replied, as if he had no more information to give, 'Sire, all that I know I have shown to you, and henceforth you will be able to do it as well as myself. Nevertheless, should any of the ingredients be wanting, it will be quite impossible to produce gold.' Saying this, he departed for his own house.

"The king now procured some of the material himself, and made gold. He then doubled the quantity, and produced the weight of two doublas; again doubling this quantity, he produced four doublas of gold; and so, in proportion, as he measured the weight of the ingredients, he produced an increase of gold. When the king saw that he could make any quantity of gold he desired, he ordered as much of the material to be brought him as would produce a hundred doublas. So the quantity was brought him as he desired, with the exception of the tarbardit, which could not be got. The king, seeing that the tabardit was wanting, and that without it he could not make gold, sent for the alchemist and told him he was unable to make gold as he had been accustomed to do.

"On this the alchemist begged to know if he had all the ingredients the same as hitherto.

"The king replied, 'Yes, all except the tabardit.'

"'Then,' said the alchemist, 'although you have all the other things, yet, failing this one, you cannot, as I told you at first, expect to make gold.'

"The king then asked if he knew where to procure the tabardit, and he was answered in the affirmative; the king then requested that he should procure for him a sufficient quantity to make as much gold as he might desire.

"The alchemist now replied that any other person could obtain it as well as himself, and perhaps, better; but, if the king particularly wished it, he would return for some to his own country, where he could procure any amount. The king then counted, and found that, including all expenses, it would cost a large sum to procure this one ingredient; but he furnished our adventurer with the sum required, and sent him on this service.

"As soon as the alchemist had received the money, he went away in great haste, never to return.

"When the king found that his alchemist remained away longer than he ought, he sent his servants to his house to know if there had been any tidings of him, but they found none whatever; but at his house was left a small chest which was locked; this they opened, and in it they found a paper on which was written, 'I know well there is no such thing in the world as tabardit, but be assured that your Majesty has been deceived. When I came to you and said that I could enrich you, you ought to have said to me, "First enrich thyself, and then I will believe thee."

"Some days after this, some men were laughing and amusing themselves by writing the names and characters of their friends and acquaintances, saying, such and such were foolish, and of others in like manner, good and bad.

NEMOURS.

Amongst those classed as imprudent was found the name of the king. When the king heard of it, he sent for the authors of this writing, and having assured them that no harm should come to them, demanded why they had placed his name among those of imprudent men. They then answered him, 'Because you have entrusted so much treasure to a stranger of whom you had not the least knowledge.'

"The king replied that they were mistaken, for should the man return he would bring with him much gold.

"'Then,' said they, 'our opinion would lose nothing; for should he return, we will erase your name and insert his.'

"And you, Count Lucanor, if you do not wish to be considered a man of weak understanding, must not risk so much of your property for a thing that is uncertain; otherwise you may have to repent sacrificing the certain for the uncertain."

This advice pleased the count much, so he acted upon it, and found the result good.

And Don Juan, seeing this to be a good example, ordered it to be written in this book with these following lines: —

> "To venture much of thy wealth refuse
> On the faith of a man who has nought to lose."

This tale, so full of point and humor, is, as we see in the paper found in the alchemist's trunk, not without its bearing on the caution required in daily life to avoid impositions, as also the dangers to which cupidity exposes men who grasp at every delusive project to gratify their passion for gain.

It may be, also, that Don Manuel desired in his narrative to ridicule the follies of alchemy, to which his learned uncle, Alfonso XI., was much addicted, and the belief in which was so universal in the Middle Ages.

CHAPTER VI.

ALGERIA.—TUNIS.—THE HOLIEST PLACE IN AFRICA.

CARAVAN TALES.

LGIERS, crowned by the ancient fortress of the deys, five hundred feet high, has a romantic history of a thousand years, and is now the Paris of Africa,—a charming French city. The old town of Algiers is on high ground; the new town is a coast habitation of government houses, squares, and gay streets, in which the Place Royale, with its shadows of orange and lime trees, invite a gay population, and where life flows at full tide under the hill of the mosques and old Moorish houses.

In the lower town, Arabs, Moors, Jews, French, Spaniards, Germans, and Englishmen gather on the charming promenades which are flanked by airy colonnades. The city has a hundred or more mosques, and is Orientally famous for its marabouts, or tombs of the saints.

The street that leads up to the old fortress of the deys is called the *casbah*. The houses of the upper town are flat-roofed, and without windows, except iron gratings. The people of these ancient houses spend their evenings on the flat roofs, the bright stars above, the sea before, and the cool sea-breeze constantly blowing.

In 1830, the long despotism of the deys came to an end in the Mahometan town, by the occupation of the French. The Turks withdrew in large numbers to Tunis.

The French had an ambition to make Algiers beautiful, and the city began to change into gay bazaars, and to wear a Parisian appearance. It is a resort of wealth and fashion, the civilization of the East having arisen amid the vanishing crescents. The city has a population of some fifty thousand people.

The country of Algeria is now a French colony, and the possession of it is said to have cost France the lives of 150,000 men. It has about

TRAVELLING IN ALGERIA.

2,505,000 inhabitants, including some 250,000 Europeans. Behind Algeria lies the desert of Sahara.

Algeria at the close of the last century and the beginning of the present, became a terror to all Christian nations by its corsairs or sea-robbers. The American flag having been insulted, the best ships of the navy were sent to the Mediterranean. The fleet attacked the Algerian pirates on the 20th of June, 1815, and compelled the Dey to respect American shipping. The contest is called the Algerian War.

CONSULAR COURTS AND THEIR POWER.

While in Algeria Mr. Van der Palm and Percy visited Tunis While there a very curious case came to Percy's notice. An American sailor was brought before the consul, accused of the crime of murder on the sea.

"He will be tried before the consul," said his father.

"Do consuls try cases?" asked Percy.

"Yes, on the coasts of the Mediterranean in several port cities."

"Like the old Roman consuls?"

"Yes, their power resembles that of old Roman officers."

"How much power do the consuls of such places really have?"

Mr. Van der Palm again quoted the consular instructions, with which he was familiar, after his long service.

"Consuls have exclusive jurisdiction over crimes and offences committed by citizens of the United States in Borneo, China, Corea, Japan, Madagascar, and Siam. In Morocco, Tripoli, and Tunis, the consuls are empowered to assist in the trials of citizens of the United States accused of murder or assault. In Persia, citizens of the United States committing offences are to be tried and judged in the same manner as are the subjects or citizens of the most favored nation. Americans committing offences in Turkey should be tried by their minister or consul, and are to be punished according to their offence, following in this respect the usage observed toward other Franks; but, in consequence of a disagreement as to the true text of the treaty, consuls in the Ottoman Dominions are instructed to take the directions of the minister of the United States at Constantinople in all cases before assuming to exercise jurisdiction over criminal offences.

"In China and Japan the judicial authority of the consuls of the United States will be considered as extending over all persons, duly shipped and enrolled upon the articles of any merchant vessel of the United States, whatever be the nationality of such person. And all offences which would be justiciable by the consular courts of the United States, where the persons so offending are native born or naturalized citizens of the United States employed in the merchant service thereof are equally justiciable by the same consular courts in the case of seamen of foreign nationality.

"Seamen serving on board public vessels of the United States, who have committed offences on shore in Japan and China, are held to be subject to the jurisdiction of the consuls of the United States in those countries."

What became of this particular case, Percy never learned, as he left Algeria in a few days for Tunis. The incident gave him a clear view of the workings of these little vice-republics, called consular offices.

KAIRWAN.

At Algeria, Percy began the study of French. But here the reader may ask "How came this ancient country in Northern Africa under the French rule?" The answer may be brief:—

Through a slight offered to a consul. In the reign of that powerful monarch, Louis Philippe, the Dey, a pasha of the Turkish school, owed the French government a considerable sum of money. The creditors asked the French consul to demand payment. The proud old Dey in indignation poked his fan spitefully at the consul, or some like movement, and the French government collected the whole country in payment of the debts. The Turks fled on the arrival of the French army, and since that date, deys and like rulers have been very polite to consuls.

There is a railway that runs from Algiers to Tunis; and an ancient road from Tunis leads the traveller to Kairwan, the so-called "Holiest spot in Africa." Mr. Van der Palm wished to visit Kairwan, and the two started for Tunis, and thence made their way to the holy Moslem city in a caravan.

The city is fabled to contain five hundred mosques. The real number is less than a hundred, unless the shrines or marabouts are to be so regarded. Kairwan is one of the strangest sights of the world, and the legend of its founding is very queer.

The great mosque of Kairwan is the history of the city. According to the legend, when the founder of Kairwan was at a loss to know where to lay the corner-stone of the mosque he heard a voice from heaven which gave him directions. The country was full of wild beasts at the time, and these all gathered themselves together, and in honor of the Prophet (Mahomet) marched away in a miraculous army, to the wonder of the faithful.

With a consul from Tunis, Mr. Van der Palm and Percy entered this wonderful mosque. Over the walls of the prayer-chamber, the consul translated the following inscription from Arabic.

"Cursed is he who shall count these pillars, for verily he shall lose his sight."

The pillars are the products of the spoils of Africa. There were two most splendid ones very near together, and it is claimed that if one squeeze through these, he may enter Paradise. Percy passed through, but his father and the fat consul were unable to secure the Mahometan promise.

"Fat people do not go to paradise," said the consul.

Percy's eyes roamed about the forest of pillars. His mind seemed engaged in some mathematical calculation.

"Well, my son, how many pillars *are there?*" asked his father, as the three travellers put on their shoes at the door.

"Just one hundred and ninety-four," was the prompt reply.

"But your eyes?"

"They smart!"

"So do mine," answered his father.

But nothing worse than this happened to Percy. Perhaps he did not count the pillars correctly. It is claimed that there are two hundred and ninety-six.

AN ALGERIAN ANTELOPE-HUNTER.

THE WIND-RIDER.

(FROM FOLK-LORE AND LEGENDS, RUSSIAN AND POLISH.)

A MAGICIAN was once upon a time much put out with a young countryman; and being in a great rage, he went to the man's hut and stuck a new sharp knife under the threshold. While he did so he cursed the man, saying, —

"May this fellow ride for seven years on the fleet storm-wind, until he has gone all around the world."

Now, when the peasant went into the meadows in order to carry the hay, there came suddenly a gust of wind. It quickly scattered the hay, and then seized the peasant. He endeavored in vain to resist; in vain he sought to cling to the hedges and trees with his hands. Do what he would, the invisible power hurried him forwards.

He flew on the wings of the wind like a wild pigeon, and his feet no more touched the ground. At length the sun set, and the poor fellow looked with hungry eyes upon the smoke which curled up from the chimney in his village. He could almost touch them with his feet, but he called and screamed in vain, and all his wailing and complaints were useless. No one heard his lamentation, no one saw his tears.

So he went on for three months, and what with thirst and hunger he was dried up and almost a skeleton. He had gone over a good deal of ground by that time, but the wind most often carried him over his native village.

He wept when he saw the hut in which dwelt his sweetheart. He could see her busied about the house. Sometimes she would bring out some dinner in a basket. Then he would stretch out his dried-up hands to her, and vainly call her name. His voice would die away; and the girl, not hearing him, would not look up.

He fled on. The magician came to the door of his hut, and seeing the man, cried to him, mockingly, —

"You have to ride for seven years yet, flying over this village. You shall go on suffering, and shall not die."

"O my father," said the man, "if I ever offended you, forgive me! Look! my lips are quite hard; my face, my hands, look at them! I am nothing but bone. Have pity upon me."

The magician muttered a few words, and the man stopped in his course. He stayed in one place, but did not yet stand on the ground.

"Well, you ask me to pity you," said the magician. "And what do you mean to give me if I put a stop to your torment?"

"All you wish," said the peasant, and he clasped his hands, and knelt down in the air.

"Will you give me your sweetheart," asked the magician, "so that I may have her for my wife? If you will give her up, you shall come to earth again."

The man thought for a moment, and said to himself, "If I once get on the earth again, I may see if I cannot do something." So he said to the magician, "Indeed, you ask me to make a great sacrifice, but if it must be so, it must."

The magician then blew at him, and the man came to the ground. He was very pleased to find the earth once more under his feet, and to have escaped from the power of the wind. Off he hurried to his hut, and at the threshold he met his sweetheart. She cried aloud with amazement when she saw the long-lost peasant whom she had so long lamented and wept for. With his skinny hands the man put her gently aside, and went into the house, where he found the farmer who had employed him, sitting down, and said to him as he commenced to weep, —

"I can no longer stay in your service, and I cannot marry your daughter. I love her very much, — as much as the apple of my eye, — but I cannot marry her."

The old farmer wondered to see him; and when he saw his white pinched face and the traces of his suffering, he asked him why he did not wish for the hand of his daughter.

The man told him all about his ride in the air, and the bargain he had made with the magician. When the farmer had listened to it all, he told the poor fellow to keep a good heart, and putting some money in his pocket, went out to consult a sorceress.

Toward evening he returned very merry, and taking the peasant aside, said to him, —

"To-morrow morning before day, go to the witch, and you will find all will be well."

The wearied peasant, who had not slept for three months, went to bed, but he woke before it was day, and went off to the witch. He found her sitting beside the hearth boiling herbs over a fire. She told him to stand by her, and, suddenly, although it was a calm day, such a storm of wind arose that the hut shook again.

The sorceress then took the peasant outside into the yard and told him to look up. He lifted up his eyes, and — oh, wonder! — saw the evil magician whirling round and round in the air.

"There is your enemy," said the woman; "he will trouble you no more. If you would like to see him at your wedding, I will tell you what to do; but he must suffer the torment that he meant to put you to."

The peasant was delighted, and ran back to the house; and a month later he was married. While the wedding-folk were dancing, the peasant went out into the yard, looked up, and saw right over the hut the magician, turning round and round. Then the peasant took a new knife, and throwing it with all his force, stuck it in the magician's foot.

He fell at once to the ground, and the knife held him to the earth so that he could only stand at the window and see how merry the peasant and his friends were.

The next day he had disappeared, but he was afterwards seen flying in the air over a lake. Before him and behind him were flocks of ravens and crows; and these, with their hoarse cries heralded the wicked magician's endless ride on the wind.

THE LEGEND OF THE TERRESTRIAL PARADISE OF SHEDDÁD, THE SON OF 'A'D.

A Tale of the Moorish Quarters of Eastern Coast Cities.

It is related that 'Abd Allah, the son of Aboo Kilábeh, went forth to seek a camel that had run away, and while he was proceeding over the deserts of El-Yeman and the district of Seba, he chanced to arrive at a vast city encompassed by enormous fortifications, around the circuit of which were pavilions rising high into the sky. So when he approached it he imagined that there must be inhabitants within it, of whom he might inquire for his camel; and accordingly he advanced, but on coming to it he found that it was desolate, without any one to cheer its solitude.

"I alighted," says he, "from my she-camel, and tied up her foot; and then, composing my mind, entered the city. On approaching the fortifications I found that they had two enormous gates, the like of which, for size and height, have never been seen elsewhere in the world, set with a variety of jewels and jacinths, white and red, and yellow and green; and when I beheld this, I was struck with the utmost wonder at it, and the sight astonished me. I entered the fortifications in a state of terror and with a wandering mind, and saw them to be of the same large extent as the city, and to comprise elevated pavilions, every one of these containing lofty chambers, and all of them constructed of gold and silver, and adorned with rubies and chrysolites and pearls and various-colored jewels. The folding-doors of these pavilions were like those of the fortifications in beauty, and the floors were overlaid with large pearls, and with balls like hazel-nuts, composed of musk and ambergris and saffron. And when I came into the midst of the city, I saw not in it a created being of the sons of Adam; and I almost died of terror. I then looked down from the summits of the lofty chambers and pavilions, and saw rivers running beneath them; and in the great thoroughfare-streets of the city were fruit-bearing trees and tall palm-trees. And the construction of the city was of alternate bricks of gold and silver; so I said within myself, no doubt this is the paradise promised in the world to come.

"I carried away of the jewels, which were as its gravel, and the musk that was as its dust, as much as I could bear, and returned to my district, where I acquainted the people with the occurrence. And the news reached Mo'áwiyeh, the son of Aboo Sufyán (who was then caliph), in the Hejáz; so he wrote to his lieutenant in San'a of El-Yemen, saying, 'Summon that man, and inquire of him the truth of the matter!' His lieutenant therefore caused me to be brought, and demanded of me an account of my adventure, and of what had befallen me; and I informed him of what I had seen. He then sent me to Mo'áwiyeh, and I acquainted him also with that which I had seen, but he disbelieved it; so I produced to him some of those pearls and the little balls of ambergris and musk and saffron. The latter retained somewhat of their sweet scent; but the pearls had become yellow and discoloured.

"At the sight of these Mo'áwiyeh wondered, and he sent and caused Kaab el-Ahbár to be brought before him, and said to him, 'O Kaab el-Ahbár, I have called thee on account of a matter of which I desire to know the truth, and I hope that thou mayest be able to certify me of it.'

"'And what is it, O Prince of the Faithful?' asked Kaab el-Ahbár.

"Mo'áwiyeh said, 'Hast thou any knowledge of the existence of a city constructed of gold and silver, the pillars whereof are of chrysolite and ruby, and the gravel of which is of pearls, and of balls like hazel-nuts, composed of musk and ambergris and saffron?'

"He answered, 'Yes, O Prince of the Faithful! It is Irem Zat-el-'Emád, the like of which hath never been constructed in the regions of the earth; and Sheddád, the son of 'A'd the Greater, built it.'

"'Relate to us,' said Mo'áwiyeh, 'somewhat of its history.'

"And Kaab el-Ahbár replied thus:—

"''A'd the Greater had two sons, Shedeed and Sheddád; and when their father perished they reigned conjointly over the countries after him, and there was no one of the kings of the earth who was not subject to them. And She-

AN ALGERIAN BEAUTY.

deed the son of 'A'd died, so his brother Sheddád ruled alone over the earth after him. He was fond of reading the ancient books; and when he met with the description of the world to come, and of paradise, with its pavilions and lofty chambers, and its trees and fruits, and of the other things in paradise, his heart enticed him to construct its like on the earth, after this manner which hath been above mentioned. He had under his authority a hundred thousand kings, under each of whom were a hundred thousand valiant chieftains; and under each of these were a hundred thousand soldiers. And he summoned them all before him, and said to them, " I find in the ancient books and histories the description of the paradise that is in the other world, and I desire to make its like upon the earth. Depart ye therefore to the most pleasant and most spacious vacant tract in the earth, and build for me in it a city of gold and silver, and spread, as its gravel, chrysolites and rubies and pearls, and as the supports of the vaulted roofs of that city make columns of chrysolite and fill it with pavilions, and over the pavilions construct lofty chambers, and beneath them plant, in the by-streets and great thoroughfare streets, varieties of trees bearing different kinds of ripe fruits, and make rivers to run beneath them in channels of gold and silver.'

" To this they all replied, ' How can we accomplish that which thou hast described to us, and how can we procure the chrysolites and rubies and pearls that thou hast mentioned? '

" But he said, ' Know ye not that the kings of the world are obedient to me and under my authority, and that no one who is in it disobeyeth my command? '

" They answered, ' Yes, we know that.'

" ' Depart then,' said he, ' to the mines of chrysolite and ruby, and to the places where pearls are found, and gold and silver, and take forth and collect their contents from the earth, and spare no exertions. Take also for me, from the hands of mine, such of those things as ye find, and spare none, nor let any escape you; and beware of disobedience!'

" He then wrote a letter to each of the kings in the regions of the earth, commanding them to collect all the articles of the kinds above mentioned that their subjects possessed, and to repair to the mines in which these things were found, and extract the precious stones that they contained, even from the beds of the seas. And they collected the things that he required in the space of twenty years; after which he sent forth the geometricians and sages, and laborers and artificers, from all the countries and regions, and they dispersed themselves through the deserts and wastes, and tracts and districts, until they came to a desert wherein was a vast open plain, clear from hills and mountains, and in it were springs gushing forth, and rivers running. So they said, 'This is the kind of place which the king commanded us to seek, and called us to find.'

"They then busied themselves in building the city according to the directions of the King Sheddád, king of the whole earth, in its length and breath; and they made through it the channels for the rivers, and laid the foundations conformably with the prescribed extent. The kings of the various districts of the earth sent thither the jewels and stones, and large and small pearls, and carnelian and pure gold, upon camels over the deserts and wastes, and sent great ships with them over the seas; and a quantity of those things, such as cannot be described, nor calculated, nor defined, was brought to the workmen, who laboured in the construction of this city three hundred years. And when they had finished it, they came to the king and acquainted him with the completion; and he said to them, 'Depart, and make around it impregnable fortifications of great height, and construct around the circuit of the fortifications a thousand pavilions, each with a thousand pillars beneath it, in order that there may be in each pavilion a vizier.'

"So they went immediately, and did this in twenty years; after which they presented themselves before Sheddád, and informed him of the accomplishment of his desire.

"He therefore ordered his viziers, who were a thousand in number, and his chief officers, and such of his troops and others as he confided in, to make themselves ready for departure, and to prepare themselves for removal to Irem Zat-el-'Emád, in attendance upon the king of the world, Sheddád, the son of 'A'd. And they passed twenty years in equipping themselves. Then Sheddád proceeded with his troops, rejoiced at the accomplishment of his desire, until there remained between him and Irem Zat-el-'Emád one day's journey, when God sent down upon him and upon the obstinate infidels who accompained him a loud cry from the heaven of His power, and it destroyed them all by the vehemence of its sound. Neither Sheddád nor any of those who were with him arrived at the city, or came in sight of it, and God obliterated the traces of the road that led to it; but the city remaineth as it was in its place until the hour of the judgment!'

"At this narrative, related by Kaab el-Ahbár, Mo'awiyeh wondered, and he said to him, 'Can any one of mankind arrive at that city?'

"'Yes,' answered Kaab el-Ahbár; 'a man of the companions of Mahomet (upon whom be blessing and peace!), in appearance like this man who is sitting here, without any doubt.' Esh-Shaabee also saith, 'It is related, on the authority of the learned men of Hemyer, in El-Yemen, that when Sheddád and those who were with him were destroyed by the loud cry, his son Sheddád the Less reigned after him; for his father, Sheddád the Greater, had left him as successor to his kingdom, in the land of Hadramot and Seba, on his departure with the troops who accompanied him to Irem Zat-el-'Emád. And as soon as the news reached him of the death of his father, on the way before his arrival at the city of Irem, he gave orders to carry his father's body from those desert tracts to Hadramot, and to excavate the sepulchre for him in a cavern.

"And when they had done this, he placed his body in it, upon a couch of gold, and covered the corpse with seventy robes, interwoven with gold and adorned with precious jewels; and he placed at his head a tablet of gold, whereon were inscribed these verses: —

> "'Be admonished, O thou who art deceived by a prolonged life!
> I am Sheddád, the son of 'A'd, the lord of a strong fortress,
> The lord of power and might, and of excessive valor.
> The inhabitants of the earth obeyed me, fearing my severity and threats;
> And I held the East and West under a strong dominion.
> And a preacher of the true religion invited us to the right way;
> But we opposed him, and said, Is there no refuge from it?
> And a loud cry assaulted us from a tract of the distant horizon;
> Whereupon we fell down like corn in the midst of a plain at harvest;
> And now, beneath the earth, we await the threatened day.'

"Eth-Tha'álibee also saith, 'It happened that two men entered this cavern, and found at its upper end some steps, and having descended these, they found an excavation, the length whereof was a hundred cubits and its breadth forty cubits, and its height a hundred cubits. And in the midst of this excavation was a couch of gold, upon which was a man of enormous bulk, occupying its whole length and breadth, covered with ornaments and with robes interwoven with gold and silver; and at his head was a tablet of gold, whereon was an inscription. And they took that tablet, and carried away from the place as much as they could of bars of gold and silver and other things.'"

CHAPTER VII.

MARSEILLES.

ARSEILLES is the French port of the world. The winding ways of its harbor are something of a zigzag journey. It is said that there are but three safe ports on the Mediterranean: "Carthagena, *June*, and *July*." To these safe ports may perhaps be added Marseilles. The city is very ancient, and its modern history is associated with patriotism. It was the soldiers from Marseilles who first voiced that great trumpet tone of liberty, "The Marseilles Hymn."

Percy learned many things in the consular offices at Marseilles which gave him clear views of marine law in case of injustice at sea. He became a pupil here of a French consular clerk, and was now in full training as a *consular pupil*. He saw here for the first time marriages performed in the presence of consuls, and the dead bodies and the effects of those dying while travelling cared for by the consuls of the parts of the world to which the deceased belonged.

There came a case before the American consulate in which a sailor claimed that he had been defrauded by his captain at sea. What would the consul?

While the case was pending, Percy went to his father to have him explain consular jurisdictions in cases of the ill-usage of sailors.

"The ship is the consul's territory," said his father. "So you may see how wide his power is, and how closely his office resembles that of the consuls of old Roman republican days. In cases of abusive

PUBLIC GARDEN, MARSEILLES.

treatment it is the sailor's right and privilege to see the consul as soon as he comes to port. No captain has a right to forbid him from laying his case before the consul. The law runs like this:—

"'The right of the seaman to lay his complaint before the consular officer in a foreign port is one of great importance to him, and is carefully protected by the courts. When a seaman files a libel in a court of admiralty and maritime jurisdiction, alleging that the master had maltreated him while in the service of the ship, and his allegations are proved, the court decrees damages in accordance with the facts. And if it appears that the master denied the seaman liberty to lay his complaints before the consular officer in a foreign port, such denial is an aggravation of his offence and enhances the amount of the decree. And in particular instances, by act of Congress, a penalty is imposed upon a master who refuses his crew the right to lay their complaints before the consul.

"'The consular officer is regarded as the adviser and counsel of the seamen, and it is enjoined upon him to see that the latter is unrestricted in the privilege to submit his complaint. If there is reason to believe that a seaman is restrained in any way from appearing at the consulate, in order to prevent his application to the consular officer, the latter will not wait for the complaint, but will at once proceed on board or take the proper steps to secure his appearance before him. The investigation of these cases is often tedious, the evidence is apt to be conflicting, and the consular officer will require the use of all his good judgment, forbearance, discretion, and good temper.'"

A volume of stories might be written on the consular mails. Letters to sailors are directed in the care of the consuls: these letters, when uncalled for, are kept one year, then sent to Washington.

It is with an anxious face that the sailor usually asks the consul for letters. The memories of mothers, fathers, wives, children, sweethearts, of old roof-trees, or some holy and tender memories rush in upon the mind of the inquirer.

"Are there *anywhere* for me?" asked a sailor of the English consul at Marseilles.

"Your name?"

"Henry Moore."

"No — nothing — none."

"The world is nothing to me, or I am nothing to the world. I am one of the *none*. I sail."

While at Marseilles, there came to the American consul some poor travellers for letters, but there were none. Their means were exhausted and the consul is not allowed to furnish money to travellers at the government charge, whatever may be their condition. It was found on inquiry that the people were from the Canadian maritime provinces, and so their case was referred to the English consul. He could do nothing for them officially, but it was resolved to give a concert for them in the English quarters, and to sing the songs and read the poems of the sea. A call was made for amateur singers, and Percy responded.

"What will you give us?" asked the English consul.

"Two poems that relate to the hardships of the sea," was the answer.

The concert was successful. It brought the travellers money enough to take them third class to London. One of Percy's selections for reading was as follows: —

THE CASTAWAY.

[Edwin, the half brother of Athelstan, King of the Saxons, was the rightful heir to the throne. On the accession of Athelstan he was a mere boy, and his claim caused much dissension among the nobles. Athelstan wished to get rid of him without committing palpable murder, and at last, in a moment of passion, ordered that he should be pushed out to sea in a leaky boat without oars. The rest of the story is told in the poem.]

>THE Saxon monarch from his throne
> Looked through the light pavilion
>Upon the level sea, that shone
> Beneath the sky vermilion.
>"Go, bring the captive boy!" he said.
> They brought him, bound and bleeding,
>With moistened cheek and bended head,
> And lips for mercy pleading.

>Then said a chief of high renown,
> The monarch on him frowning,

"To whom in right belongs the crown
  The sun himself is crowning."
And Edwin, there on bending knee,
  The sun shone brightly over;
While Athelstan gazed on the sea, —
  The foaming sea of Dover.

The twilight sunshine dimmed; and far
  The moon, her disk uplifting,
Came goddess-like, her silver car
  Along the waters drifting.
And as on high she moved and shone
  The great pavilion over,
Athelstan, from his shadowed throne,
  Looked on the sea of Dover.

"Go, take the boy!" at last he cried,
  Half from the order shrinking;
" And when outgoes the evening tide,
  And low the moon is sinking,
Put him in yonder boat hard by
  Upon the ocean border,
And loose it! He shall live or die,
  As God himself shall order!"

Next morn a hundred anxious eyes
  Were strained the waters over,
As rose the sun in stormless skies
  Upon the sea of Dover.
There lightly, near the troubled land,
  The boat was seaward drifting.
And beckoned there a little hand,
  In vain for help uplifting.

Far, far to sea it drifts, it drifts,
  All, all that summer morning;
And, lo! a sudden cloud uplifts
  Its shadow like a warning.
Far, far to sea, the wind-swept waves
  Grow dark and deep and dreary;
And hard the rocks the ocean laves
  Where stand the watchers weary.

To him no more the nobles fair
  The tribute due will render,
Nor sunset leave upon his hair
  Her coronet of splendor.

Night o'er the sobbing billows crept,
  And stilled their wild commotion:
But ere the morn young Edwin slept
  Beneath the foaming ocean.

And once, when summers four had rolled
  The solemn convent over,
Old Whitesand's shaded peaks of gold,
  And silvered peaks of Dover.
The minstrels playing sweet and low,
  A tender strain awaking,
Athelstan's tears were seen to flow
  As though his heart was breaking.

"Four times to yonder convent lone
  The birds have crossed the seas,
And wandering airs of gentle tone
  Have breathed 'mid blooming trees.
Four times on yonder convent towers
  The snows have fallen deep
Since maidens strewed the place with flowers
  Where Edwin's ashes sleep.

"I sit and muse beside the sea
  When hangs the moon above:
The silvered tide comes back to me,
  But not a brother's love.
A vanished life still haunts my dreams
  When minstrel harps attune,
And on the shadowy convent gleams
  The solitary moon.

"'Gone! Gone!' it murmurs in the wood,
  It sobs amid the seas;
And lonely hours and solitude
  Are terrible to me.
I call my minstrels, and they sing,
  But when the strains depart,
I feel I am a crownless king,
  Discrowned of joy at heart.

"The years will come, the years will go,
  But never at my door
The fair-haired boy I used to meet
  Will smile upon me more;

> But memory long will hear the fall
>   Of steps at eventide,
> And in each saddened hour recall
>   The year when Edwin died.
>
> "I cleave the serried walls of shields,
>   The nobles' standards true;
> I strew with dead the Northern fields,
>   The Scottish chiefs subdue;
> Yet when the moon — a silver sun —
>   Rolls o'er the Tweed and Dee,
> The evening song for victory won
>   Returns no joy to me.
>
> "Oh, I would give a crown to view
>   The face of heaven again.
> And walk the fruited earth anew,
>   Unstained 'mid stainless men.
> The years will come, the years will go,
>   The birds will cross the sea,
> But calm delights that others know
>   Will ne'er return to me."

THE CONSULAR PRISONER.

At the English consulate at Marseilles Percy heard many curious stories told. Among them there was one that was so remarkable as to long haunt his memory.

"What is the strangest incident that ever happened in your consular experience?" asked an English consular clerk of an old English consul, who was smoking leisurely in the office.

"It was the escape of a consular prisoner named Wombut or Wombetta. They called him Wombat.

"I shall never forget that night. I can see the scene now. Wombetta was accused of robbery, and I had detained him under guard in the consular office. The ship's crew to which he belonged were still at the dock, waiting to sail. The ship, the "Victoria," had received her papers.

"I was sitting alone in my private room, reading, when there suddenly came a loud knocking at the door.

"'Come in,' I said.

"A stout man entered wearing a great cloak.

"'Please, your honor, may I see Wombat before we sail?'

"'Have you any particular business with him?'

"'Yes, your honor.'

"'Cannot you leave the matter with me?'

"'No, your honor; it is confidential. It is only a word with him.'

"The guard stood outside of the door. I was in an easy, good-humored mood, and somewhat preoccupied, and I said to the guard:

"'Let him pass.'

"The man in the cloak passed in and closed the door. I heard some strange movements, when I was suddenly brought to my feet by the report of a pistol.

"The guard threw open the door, and a stranger sight never met my eyes. The man in the great cloak apparently stood before me with Wombat on his shoulders. I saw Wombat's boots projecting forward, *so*; his hat tilted back, *so*; and the stranger's cloak was thrown, or seemed to be thrown, over his body.

"There came a muffled voice from this strange figure.

"'I've shot him; let me carry him into the air.'

"I thought it was the voice of the stranger.

"The guard opened his mouth, and stood like one petrified.

"The figure moved out of the room. I saw Wombat's boots distinctly, and I did not dream that they were not on his legs. I saw Wombat's old felt hat, and I thought it was on the head of the dying man.

"'Hold!' said I.

"'Let go into the air!' said the figure in an awful voice.

"I lost my senses, and opened the door.

"What followed was marvellous indeed. I would never trust my own eyes again.

"The cloak fell, and beside it a pair of boots. The figure all dropped to pieces and out of it emerged a man, hatless and bootless, who ran down the street crying 'Murder!'

"I started to follow him, and the guard to follow me, when a second man came flying out of the guard room into the court, leaped over a fence and was lost in the darkness.

"I looked before me and behind me. So did the guard.

"'What!' said I.

"'Wha-a-at!' said he.

"'Were there *three* of them?' said I.

"'Heaven defend us!' said he.

"'What has happened?' asked I.

"'Heaven only knows,' said he.

"'Where is the prisoner?' asked I.

"'*You* let him escape,' said he.

"'Which?' asked I.

"'You may ask your own eyes,' said he.

"'He has escaped!' said I.

"'Where?' said he.

"'Who?' said I.

"'You will never see any of them again,' said he. 'Ah, but and he was a slick one!'

"'Which?' asked I.

"'All three of them!' said he.

"'How many were there?' asked I.

"'Three — two — one,' said he.

"I accepted the report. The ship sailed that night, and I never saw Wombat or *any of them* again!"

CHAPTER VIII.

CONSULAR PETS AND PARROTS.

"VERY consul's office has a pet, and that pet is commonly a parrot," said Percy to his father one day at Marseilles.

"No, not every consul's office. I seldom kept pets when I was a consul. But what you say is, in a sense, true."

"Are consuls, as a class, lovers of natural history?"

"I do not know that they are when they are first appointed. But as a rule they come to be so. The pets and parrots that one finds in many consular offices are usually gifts from the people of the countries in which the consuls reside. A generous consul makes many friends among the people of his foster country, and these are likely to make him presents of any curious animals or birds in which he may show an interest. Many consuls lead a kind of bachelor life, and pets are company; so consuls come to be not only story-tellers but amateur naturalists. They may be presented with guinea pigs, marmosets, curious dogs, brilliant macaws, cockatoos, and parrots that can say odd things, or sing snatches of patriotic songs. In the East he may even be offered a camel or an elephant; in South America, a boa.

"The consuls' offices at Gibraltar were full of little animals and strange birds. Here they are museums of natural history; one finds in them all sorts of things. I think consular offices are among the most interesting places in the world.

"Let me tell you of some of the strange pets that I have known to be given to consuls; I doubt that you ever so much as heard of many of them: —

"A chimpanzee, a chinchilla, a chrysochloris capensus, a didelphys, a dormouse, an edensate, an echidna, ferrets, foxes, flying squirrels, guinea pigs, martens, lemmings, lynex, a gacchus, a lemur, a maki, otters, pebas, porcupines, sables, a silky tamarine, wombats, turtles, shells, queer fishes, and birds of many kinds and voices."

"They would fill a story book," said Percy. "I can form no idea of many of them. I have noticed that consuls like to tell stories of their pets."

"Especially of their parrots," said Mr. Van der Palm. "Almost every consul has had some wonderful parrot."

"That said strange things?" said Percy.

"Yes, like the parrots of the old sailors from the Spanish main."

"Did you have your parrot story when you were a consul?"

"Yes, although it was not about one of my own parrots, but one that lived in an old New-England town in the days of the whalers. I once related it to a story-writer, and he published it in verse, with some good pictures. You shall see it."

THE PARROT FROM THE SPANISH MAIN; OR, THE OLD RED SETTLE BY THE FIRE.

On Dorchester Bay the hills were blue,
And the Milton meadows were green and red;
There the bobolinks toppled at morn in the dew,
And high in the air the ospreys flew,
And the killdees screamed, and the lone sea-mew,
In the dusky eves o'er-head.
There were violets blue in the frosts of spring,
And gentians blue in the frosts of fall.
There the church bells rung with a mellow tone;
And the Quaker meeting-house, shy and lone,
Hid in the by-ways walled with stone,
Where rang no bell at all.
There the farmer's corn fields turned to gold,

And the blue-jays laughed his cribs to see;
And his heart and hearth were never cold,
When the north winds came, and they stories told
  On the old red settle by the fire,
  In the old Thanksgiving Days.

  That old red settle each night was brought
  Before the winter hearth. Ah me!
  'T was there my youthful mind was taught
  My A B ABS and the Rule of Three.
  What wondrous things that settle knew!
  Were ever elsewhere such stories told
  Since the caliphs' halls of airy gold?
  Of the Northmen's bark of the silver wing
  That, dragon-headed, came into the bay
  A thousand years ago, one day,
  From the moonless fiords of Norroway,
  And brought the bride of a king;
  Of Francis Drake and his golden ship,
  Of Captain Kidd and his bloody whip,
  And Mrs. Dunstan's awful fate,
And Peter Rugg, and Nix's mate;
Of the Judge's Cave: of the witches that flew
Through the hole in the sky where the rain came through.

I would not be so scared again
For all the apples they roasted there,
Or all the logs that used to flare
On the drying pumpkins and peppers red,
And the Almanac of Fate that said
'T would surely snow in March and *blow*.
How could "Poor Richard" such wise things know!

The waves were blue on Dorchester Bay:
The birds, the flowers, the shells, were blue;
Blue lay the grapes upon the walls;
Blue smoked the chimneys on the Charles;
And when the still nights longer grew,
The fire upon the hearth burned blue.
Then on the settle we all would sit,
With Grandma in her gown of gray,
And gaze on Grandpa's silhouette,
The mourning piece, and sampler gay, —
Rare works of art, they said, were they.
And there, while Grandma's eyes grew wet,
We 'd plan for the great Thanksgiving Day.
"I wish they 'd *all* come back," said she,
"And pass one hour again with me,
And be just as they used to be.
Ruth sleeps beneath the sod; and Ben —"
We never spoke of Ben, for he
Was the one black sheep of the family.
He owed a note that he could not pay,
And they sued him, and he ran away
And went to sea; and wicked arts
He learned, no doubt, in foreign parts.
So Grandpa willed his lands to the others:
And they met each year, — four prosperous brothers, —
And the family legends proudly told
On the old red settle by the fire
In the old Thanksgiving Days.

Ben's parrot was there, — an awful bird!
"Hey, Betty Martin!" in meeting he sung,
To the shame and scandal of all who heard:
And the children laughed, because they were young;
And Grandma, speaking not a word,
Poor Polly hid in the gay valance
That Ben had brought from the port of Nantes.
She knew that the bird was true to Ben,
And that only one other heart was true;

And her love for the bird with her sad years grew,
And they both wished the boy would come home again

A wonder came, — town-meeting day,
In the great March storm, and the Federals won!
Men went to the folkmote in the sleigh,
And Grandpa went in his dashaway:
And lieutenant-governor they made of John.
(He was Grandpa Jarvis's likeliest son.)
Oh, then the old man powdered his wig
And shod his cane, — there were grand times then, —
And he rode to town in his Sunday gig
On a *Monday* morning, and said with delight,
To all that he met, to the left and right,
That John had atoned for the shame of Ben.

A grand Thanksgiving they planned that year,
And John, in the turnpike coach, came down
From the General Court in Boston town.
What times were those! You should have seen
The roasted pig and the basted geese,
The succotash and pumpkin bread,
The great clam chowder with pepper red.

CONSULAR PETS AND PARROTS. 161

The apple-dumplings, bounteous ones,
With potato crusts! the pies, the buns,
The cranberry-tarts and gingerbread,
The quartered quince, the pickles green!
They herring-boned the chamber floors,
And open set the parlor doors.
I never knew a year like that!
The harvest air was full of jays.
The red woodpecker went rat-a-tat,
And the Quaker smiled 'neath his Sunday hat,
And they set the settle by the fire.
Oh, those good Thanksgiving Days!

What know the birds? I cannot tell.
They once were augurs thought to be, —
The prophets of the air and sea.
Now, when that fall the neep-tides fell,
And scallops came, and airs were mild,
Polly would scream the name of Ben,
Then listen strangely like a child.
Was Ben's ship coming home again?

Thanksgiving came, — a perfect day
On Milton Hills and Dorchester Bay.
The chimneys smoked that morning brown,
The tables smoked that afternoon.
And after church the sun went down,
And rose above the sea the moon.
The mighty meal was brought, and there
Grandpa arose with silver hair,
And spread his hands to offer prayer.
Four brothers knelt there in a row,
Grandchildren eight, and uncles three.
The back-log set the room aglow,
And all was still; the clock ticked slow.
"God of all mercies, thee we praise!"
So, in a deep voice, Grandpa spoke.
The sea upon the shingle broke,
And made us think of other days.
"Thou makest thy sun to rise on all;
On all thou makest the rain to fall.
Our mercies fail; thine faileth not;
None of thy children are forgot."
I heard a step; the gate latch fell.
The bucket rattled at the well;
Then some one passed the latticed pane,
Then to the lattice came again.

And listened to the rolling prayer.
I saw the parrot shake and stare.
It seemed a spirit-haunted place.
The face close to the window drew.
The bird's neck long and longer grew,
And burned her eyes; and then — oh, then —
Who could of such a wonder dreamed?
She three times flapped her wings, and screamed,
"Hey, Betty Martin, tiptoe fine!
Ho, Dandy Jim, o' Caroline!
Ho! ho! high-oh! 'T is Ben! 't is Ben!
Grandma, Grandma, 't is Ben! 't is Ben!"
Who ever saw a scene like that?
Right in the prayer a scene like that?
Grandpa forgot, and shouted, "Scat!"
And Deacon Brown, who'd come from town,
Rolled up his eyes in pious wonder;
And John said, "Hippographs and thunder!"
And the children hid the table under.
But Grandma softly rose, and took
The cage into the porch. And there —
There came *another* mystery.
A dark man met her from the sea.
"Do you know Ben?" he whispered low.
"He was my boy; and who are you?"
"Where'er the winds for me may blow,
My heart is to my mother true,
And I will always pray for you.
Take that, and pay Ben's debts," said he.
"My boat is waiting on the shore.
God bless you all for evermore!
I've longed that sight once more to see.
I'll go away, and thankful be
You've such a happy family.
Ask father to give thanks for me."
Then he was gone, and Grandma old
Came in, and brought a purse of gold.
Lord! how we stared! The cat was scared,
And ran and hid. And Grandpa said,
"Where is that bird?" They searched the shed.
They searched the wood-house, searched the green,
The well, the barn, the orchard ways.
But Polly nevermore was seen.

Then Grandma rose — her face was calm;
Her look uplifted was a psalm —

And said, with quivering lip and chin,
And one hand lifted, white and thin:
"So near the grave we all are living,
So near God's doors, let's be forgiving.
The best of all our days of praise,
God knows, are our forgiving days."

'T was strange, but Grandpa said, "Amen!"
And Silas the bass-viol strung,
And gave a twang, and then we sung
As if the gabled roof to raise:
"Sweet is the work, my God, my King,
To praise thy name, give thanks, and sing,
Oh, may my heart in tune be found,
Like David's harp of solemn sound!"
And these last lines a dozen times
We turned around and turned around
Sweet are all homes where love has been,
And only good lips utter praise:
But such a psalm I never knew

In all the homes of Milton blue,
When 'mid the frosts the gentians grew,
And set the settle by the fire.
In the old Thanksgiving Days.
On Dorchester Bay the hills are blue,
But the purple swallows come no more
To haunt the house that once I knew;
The mossy grave-stones on the shore,
That sink into the violets' floor,
Are all that's left of that old home

Whose virtues found so much to praise.
There Grandma sleeps beneath the yews;
Ben sleeps afar in Barbadoes.
Yet Milton's hills are fair to see;
And Grandma's plea for charity
Brings back life's sweetest thoughts to me,
That come as came the gentians blue
To frosty meadows by the bays
When stood the settle by the fire.
So near God's open doors we're living,
So near the heartache for forgiving,
We offer up our best thanksgiving.
And gain from Heaven our best desire.
On our Forgiving Days.

CHAPTER IX.

VENICE.

ENICE, the Bride of the Sea! The traveller may hardly know when he arrives at Venice from the Adriatic. The city seems to float upon the sea. In the old days of the doges, she used to be wedded to it by yearly ceremonies. The city of the lagoons seems at a little distance to be rising from the sea: —

"From out the wave her structures rise
As from the stroke of the enchanted wand."

The Grand Canal is her principal water-street, over which hangs the great bridge of the Rialto. On a "hundred isles," if poetry were history, stands Venice, or rather, "sits in state." The streets are narrow alleys, paved with flag-stones and overhung with glowing balconies. Her bridges are airy structures of life and light.

Her carriages are "water ponies," or gondolas; and in other days these were painted black by law, and many of them to-day still follow the color of the days of romance and story. They are usually propelled by a single gondolier. Four persons, as a rule, may ride in each. These sit in a little apartment of windows, blinds, and divans. The fare is about a shilling an hour for a passenger.

The state entrance to Venice from the sea is the piazza of the church of St. Mark, with its piazette. Here rise the granite columns, each of a single block, one of which is crowned with the winged lion of Saint Mark in bronze. Between these two columns criminals were executed in the dark days of the doges.

The square of St. Mark is almost the only open ground in Venice. It is usually thronged with people. Napoleon is said to have called it the most beautiful spot on earth.

THE GREAT BRIDGE OF RIALTO.

The famous church of St. Mark, which is the reputed tomb of the bones of Saint Mark, the writer of the second Gospel, gathered to itself every known form of beauty in the architecture of all lands. It is Byzantine, Roman, Greek, and Gothic, — a pantheon of art. It rose more than a thousand years ago, under the architects of Constantine. Over its doors stand the famous bronze horses of St.

VENICE.

Mark, once carried to Constantinople by Theodosius, once the spoil of France, but always a marvel of human art.

The church is a forest of pillars, and marbles of all the East, of jasper, agate, and gems. Over all rises the campanile, a square tower three hundred feet high. Here Galileo made sure of his wonderful discoveries.

The old ducal palace is the wonder tale of the East. Here was the Hall of the Council of Ten. Here are the portraits of the doges of forgotten glory.

The palaces of Venice are built on piles. They are usually constructed of marble, and are four stories high.

Venice has been called the paradise of the sea. It has for centuries been regarded as a most delightful place of residence. The salt water and the movement of the tides keep it healthy.

The port, or consular part of Venice, consists of islands of the shallows. Merchant vessels move in sight of the old palace, and sometimes come into the Grand Canal. The harbor is protected by a mole, constructed of a peculiar stone resembling marble. The harbor of Venice is one of the most picturesque in the world.

PIGEONS OF ST. MARK'S.

St. Mark's Place, Venice, has been a story-telling pleasure ground for a thousand years. Here people of all eastern nations congregate, and relate the marvels of their own lands, in the cool breezes of the sea. English and French people love to loiter here, and the Turk and Mahometan as well. It is a park common to all the ports of the Adriatic.

VENETIAN GLASS.

In Venice, Percy, for the first time, saw money paid for the relief of some American seamen who had been brought to the port on an Italian vessel.

"How are consuls provided with money to meet such wants?" he asked his father one evening on St. Mark's Place.

"By special appropriations by Congress. For example, among the latest provisions to meet the expenses of consulates, I may quote: —

FOOT OF FLAGSTAFF IN FRONT OF SAINT MARKS, VENICE.

Relief and Protection of American Seamen.

Relief and protection of American seamen in foreign countries, or so much thereof as may be necessary, fifty thousand dollars.

Foreign Hospitals at Panama.

Annual contributions toward the support of foreign hospitals at Panama, to be paid by the Secretary of State upon the assurance that suffering seamen and citizens of the United States will be admitted to the privileges of said hospitals, five hundred dollars.

Publication of Consular and Commercial Reports.

Preparation, printing, publication, and distribution, by the Department of State, of the consular and other commercial reports, including circular letters to chambers of commerce, twenty thousand dollars.

Contingent Expenses of United States Consulates.

Expenses of providing all such stationery, blanks, record and other books, seals, presses, flags, signs, rent, postage, furniture, statistics, newspapers, freight (foreign and domestic), telegrams, advertising, messenger service, travelling expenses of consular clerks, Chinese writers, and such other miscellaneous expenses as the President may think necessary for the several consulates and commercial agencies in the transaction of their business, one hundred and fifty thousand dollars.

Percy saw the manner of providing funds, which he might have learned from the consular book. He now, as a consular pupil, began to study the forms of consular book-keeping.

TALES OF ORIENTALS AT VENICE.

THE MAN WHO NEVER LAUGHED.

THERE was a man, of those possessed of houses and riches, who had wealth and servants and slaves and other possessions; and he departed from the world to receive the mercy of God (whose name be exalted!), leaving a young son. And when the son grew up, he took to eating and drinking, and the hearing of instruments of music and songs, and was liberal and gave gifts, and expended the riches that his father had left to him until all the wealth had gone. He then took himself to the sale of the male black slaves, and the female slaves, and other possessions, and expended all that he had of his father's wealth and other things, and became so poor that he worked with the laborers. In this state he remained for a period of years. While he was sitting one day beneath a wall, waiting to see who would hire him, lo! a man of comely countenance and apparel drew near to him and saluted him.

So the youth said to him, "O uncle, hast thou known me before now?"

The man answered him, "I have not known thee, O my son, at all; but I see the traces of affluence upon thee, though thou art in this condition."

The young man replied, "O uncle, what fate and destiny have ordained have come to pass. But hast thou, O uncle, O comely-faced, any business in which to employ me?"

The man said to him, "O my son, I desire to employ thee in an easy business."

The youth asked, "And what is it, O uncle?"

And the man answered him, "I have with me ten sheykhs in one abode, and we have no one to perform our wants. Thou shalt receive from us, of food and clothing, what will suffice thee, and shalt serve us, and thou shalt receive of us thy portion of benefits and money. Perhaps, also, God will restore to thee thine affluence by our means."

The youth therefore replied, "I hear and obey."

The sheykh then said to him, "I have a condition to impose upon thee."

"And what is thy condition, O uncle?" asked the youth.

He answered him, "O my son, it is that thou keep our secret with respect to the things that thou shalt see us do; and when thou seest us weep, that thou ask us not respecting the cause of our weeping."

And the young man replied, "Well, O uncle."

So the sheykh said to him, "O my son, come with us, relying on the blessing of God (whose name be exalted!)."

And the young man followed the sheykh until the latter conducted him to the bath; after which he sent a man, who brought him a comely garment of linen, and he clad him with it, and went with him to his abode and his associates. And when the young man entered, he found it to be a high mansion, with lofty angles, ample, with chambers facing one another, and saloons; and in each saloon was a fountain of water, and birds were warbling over it, and there were windows overlooking, on every side, a beautiful garden within the mansion. The sheykh conducted him into one of the chambers, and he found it decorated with colored marbles, and its ceiling ornamented with blue and brilliant gold, and it was spread with carpets of silk ; and he found in it ten sheykhs sitting facing one another, wearing the garments of mourning, weeping and wailing. So the young man wondered at their case, and was about to ques-

MASQUERADING IN VENICE.

tion the sheykh who had brought him, but he remembered the condition, and therefore withheld his tongue. Then the sheykh committed to the young man a chest containing thirty thousand pieces of gold, saying to him, "O my son, expend upon us out of this chest, and upon thyself, according to what is just, and be thou faithful, and take care of that wherewith I have intrusted thee."

And the young man replied, "I hear and obey."

He continued to expend upon them for a period of days and nights, after which one of them died; whereupon his companions took him, and washed him and shrouded him, and buried him in a garden behind the mansion. And death ceased not to take them one after another, until there remained only the sheykh who had hired the young man. So he remained with the young man in that mansion, and there was not with them a third, and they remained thus for a period of years.

Then the sheykh fell sick; and when the young man despaired of his life, he addressed him with courtesy, and was grieved for him, and said to him, "O uncle, I have served you, and not failed in your service one hour for a period of twelve years, but have acted faithfully to you, and served you according to my power and ability."

The sheykh replied, "Yes, O my son, thou hast served us until these sheykhs have been taken unto God, (to whom be ascribed might and glory!) and we must inevitably die."

And the young man said, "O my master, thou art in a state of peril, and I desire of thee that thou inform me what hath been the cause of your weeping and the continuance of your wailing and your mourning and your sorrow."

He replied, "O my son, thou hast no concern with that, and require me not to do what I am unable; for I have begged God (whose name be exalted!) not to afflict any one with my affliction. Now, if thou desire to be safe from that into which we have fallen, open not that door," and he pointed to it with his hand, and cautioned him against it; "and if thou desire that what hath befallen us should befall thee, open it, and thou wilt know the cause of that which thou hast beheld in our conduct; but thou wilt repent, when repentance will not avail thee."

Then the illness increased upon the sheykh, and he died; and the young man washed him with his own hands, and shrouded him, and buried him by his companions.

He remained in that place, possessing it and all the treasure; but notwithstanding this, he was uneasy, reflecting upon the conduct of the sheykhs. And while he was meditating one day upon the words of the sheykh and his charge to him not to open the door, it occurred to his mind that he might look at it. So he went in that direction, and searched until he saw an elegant door, over which the spider had woven its web, and upon it were four locks of steel.

When he beheld it, he remembered how the sheykh had cautioned him, and

CA D'ORO, VENICE.

he departed from it. His soul desired him to open the door, and he restrained it during a period of seven days; but on the eighth day his soul overcame him, and he said, "I must open that door, and see what will happen to me in consequence; for nothing will repel what God (whose name be exalted!) decreeth and predestineth, and no event will happen but by His will."

Accordingly he arose and opened the door, after he had broken the locks. And when he had opened the door he saw a narrow passage, along which he walked for the space of three hours; and lo! he came forth upon the bank of a great river. At this the young man wondered. And he walked along the bank, looking to the right and left; and behold! a great eagle descended from the sky, and taking up the young man with its talons, it flew with him, between heaven and earth, until it conveyed him to an island in the midst of the sea. There it threw him down, and departed from him.

So the young man was perplexed at his case, not knowing whither to go; but while he was sitting one day, lo! the sail of a vessel appeared to him upon the sea, like the star in the sky; wherefore the heart of the young man became intent upon the vessel, in the hope that his escape might be effected in it.

He continued looking at it until it came near unto him; and when it arrived, he beheld a bark of ivory and ebony, the oars of which were of sandal-wood and aloes-wood, and the whole of it was encased with plates of brilliant gold. There were also in it ten damsels, virgins, like moons.

When the damsels saw him, they landed to him from the bark, and kissed his hands, saying to him, "Thou art the king, the bridegroom." Then there advanced to him a damsel who was like the shining sun in the clear sky, having in her hand a kerchief of silk, in which were a royal robe, and a crown of gold set with varieties of jacinths. Having advanced to him, she clad him and crowned him; after which the damsels carried him in their arms to the bark, and he found in it varieties of carpets of silk of divers colors. They then spread the sails, and proceeded over the depths of the sea.

"Now when I proceeded with them," says the young man, "I felt sure that this was a dream, and knew not whither they were going with me. And when they came in sight of land, I beheld it filled with troops, the number of which none knew but God, (whose perfection be extolled, and whose name be exalted!) clad in coats of mail. They brought forward to me five marked horses, with saddles of gold, set with varieties of pearls and precious stones; and I took a horse from among these and mounted it. The four others proceeded with me; and when I mounted, the ensigns and banners were set up over my head, the drums and the cymbals were beaten, and the troops disposed themselves in two divisions, right and left.

"I wavered in opinion as to whether I were asleep or awake, and ceased not to advance, not believing in the reality of my stately procession, but imagining that it was the result of confused dreams, until we came in sight of a verdant meadow, in which were palaces and gardens and trees and rivers and flowers, and birds proclaiming the perfection of God, the One, the Omnipotent.

"And now there came forth an army from among those palaces and gardens, like the torrent when it poureth down, until it filled the meadow. When the troops drew near to me, they hailed, and lo! a king advanced from among them, riding alone, preceded by some of his chief officers walking."

The king, on approaching the young man, alighted from his courser; and the young man, seeing him do so, alighted also; and they saluted each other with the most courteous salutation. Then they mounted their horses again, and the king said to the young man, "Accompany us; for thou art my guest." So the young man proceeded with him, and they conversed together, while the stately trains in orderly disposition went on before them to the palace of the king, when they alighted, and all of them entered, together with the king and the young man, the young man's hand being in the hand of the king, who thereupon seated him on the throne of gold, and seated himself beside him. When the king removed the litham from his face, lo! this supposed king was a damsel, like the shining sun in the clear sky, a lady of beauty and loveliness, and elegance and perfection, and conceit, and amorous dissimulation. The young man beheld vast affluence and great prosperity, and wondered at the beauty and loveliness of the damsel.

Then the damsel said to him, "Know, O king, that I am the queen of this land, and all these troops that thou hast seen, including every one, whether of cavalry or infantry, are women. There are not among them any men. The men among us, in this land, till and sow and reap, employing themselves in the cultivation of the land, and the building and the repairing of the towns, and in attending to the affairs of the people, by the pursuit of every kind of art and trade; but as to the women, they are the governors and magistrates and soldiers."

And the young man wondered at this extremely. And while they were thus conversing, the vizier entered; and lo! she was a gray-haired old woman, having a numerous retinue, of venerable and dignified appearance; and the queen said to her, "Bring to us the kadee and the witnesses." So the old woman went for that purpose.

And the queen turned towards the young man, conversing with him and cheering him, and dispelling his fear by kind words; and, addressing him courteously, she said to him, "Art thou content for me to be thy wife?"

LIBRARY OF ST. MARK'S, VENICE.

And thereupon he arose and kissed the ground before her; but she forbade him, and he replied, "O my mistress, I am less than the servants who serve thee."

She then said to him, "Seest thou not these servants and soldiers, and wealth and treasures and hoards?"

He answered her, "Yes."

And she said to him, "All these are at thy disposal; thou shalt make use of them, and give and bestow as seemeth fit to thee." Then she pointed to a closed door, and said to him, "All these things thou shalt dispose of; but this door thou shalt not open; for if thou open it, thou wilt repent, when repentance will not avail thee."

Her words were not ended when the vizier, with the kadee and the witnesses, entered; and all of them were old women, with their hair spreading over their shoulders, and of venerable and dignified appearance. When they came before the queen, she ordered them to perform the ceremony of the marriage-contract. So they married her to the young man. And she prepared the banquets and collected the troops; and when they had eaten and drunk, the young man took her as his wife. And he resided with her seven years, passing the most delightful, comfortable, and agreeable life.

But he meditated one day upon opening the door, and said, "Were it not that there are within it great treasures, better than what I have seen, she had not prohibited me from opening it."

He then arose and opened the door, and lo! within it was the bird that had carried him from the shore of the great river, and deposited him upon the island.

When the bird beheld him, it said to him, "No welcome to a face that will never be happy!"

So when he saw it and heard its words, he fled from it; but it followed him and carried him off, and flew with him between heaven and earth for the space of an hour, and at length deposited him in the place from which it had carried him away, after which it disappeared.

He thereupon sat in the place, and, returning to his reason, he reflected upon what he had seen of affluence and glory and honor, and the riding of the troops before him, and commanding and forbidding; and he wept and wailed.

He remained upon the shore of the great river, where that bird had put him, for the space of two months, wishing that he might return to his wife; but while he was one night awake, mourning and meditating, some one spoke (and he heard his voice, but saw not his person), calling out, "How great were the delights! Far, far from thee is the return of what is passed! And how many therefore will be the sighs!"

So when the young man heard it, he despaired of meeting again that queen, and of the return to him of the affluence in which he had been living. He then entered the mansions where the sheykhs resided, and knew that they had experienced the like of that which had happened unto him, and that this was the cause of their weeping and mourning; wherefore he excused them.

Grief and anxiety came upon the young man, and he entered his chamber, and ceased not to weep and moan, relinquishing food and drink and pleasant scents and laughter, until he died; and he was buried by the side of the sheykhs.

THE DUCK THAT LAID GOLDEN EGGS.

THERE lived once an old man and his wife. The man was called Abrosim, and his wife Fetinia. They were very poor and miserable, and had a son named Little Ivan, who was fifteen years old. One day old Abrosim brought a crust of bread home for his wife and son. He had scarcely begun to eat, however, when Krutschina (Sorrow) sprang up from behind the stove, seized the crust out of his hand, and ran away behind the stove again. The old man made a bow to Krutschina, and begged her to give him the crust back again, as he and his wife had nothing else to eat.

"I will not give you the crust again," said Krutschina, "but instead of it I will give you a duck which lays a gold egg every day."

"Very well," said Abrosim, "I shall be supperless to-night. Do not deceive me, but tell me where I shall find the duck."

"Early to-morrow morning," said Krutschina, "when you are up, go into town; there you will see a duck in a pond, catch it, and carry it home."

When Abrosim heard this, he lay down and went to sleep.

The next morning he rose early, and went to the town, and was very much pleased to see the duck swimming about on a pond. He called it to him, carried it to his home, and gave it to his wife Fetinia. They were both delighted, and put the duck in a big basin, placing a sieve over it. In an hour's time they went to look at it, and discovered that the duck had laid a golden egg. Then they took the duck out, and let it walk a little on the floor, and the old man, taking the egg, set off to town. There he sold the egg for a hundred roubles, took the money, and, going to the market, bought different kinds of vegetables and set off home.

The next day the duck laid another egg like the first, which Abrosim sold

A VENETIAN GARDEN.

in the same manner. So the duck went on laying a golden egg every day, and the old man became in a short time very rich. He bought a large house, a great many shops, all kinds of wares, and set up in business.

His wife Fetinia made a favorite of a young clerk in her husband's employ, and used to supply him with money. One day when Abrosim was away from home buying some goods, the clerk called to have a talk with Fetinia, and it chanced that he then saw the duck that laid the golden eggs. He was pleased with the bird, and, examining it, found written under its wing in gold letters, "Whoever eats this duck will be a czar."

He did not say anything to Fetinia about what he had seen, but asked her to roast the duck for him. Fetinia said she could not kill the duck, for all their fortune depended on it; but the clerk begged her so earnestly that she at last consented, and killed it, and put it in the oven. The clerk then went off, saying he would return soon, and Fetinia also went out in the town. While they were gone, in came little Ivan. He felt very hungry, and looking about him for something to eat, he chanced to see the roast duck in the oven; so he took it out, and ate all of it but the bones. Then he went off again to the shop.

In a little while the clerk came back, and, having called Fetinia, asked her to bring out the duck. The woman went to the oven; but when she saw that the duck was not there, she was terribly put out, and told the clerk that the duck had disappeared. At that the clerk flew into a great rage, and said, —

"You have eaten the duck yourself, of course," and he got up and walked out of the house.

In the evening Abrosim and his son, little Ivan, came home. When Abrosim did not see the duck, he asked his wife where it was; and she told him that she did not know. Then little Ivan said to his father, —

"My dear father, when I came home, in the middle of the day, for dinner, my mother was not in; so I looked in the oven, and there found a roast duck. I took it out, and ate it all but the bones; but I do not know whether it was our duck or a strange one."

Then old Abrosim was in such a rage that he thrashed his wife till she was half dead, and he turned little Ivan out of doors.

Little Ivan began his journey. Where should he go? He determined to follow his nose. For ten days and nights he went on. Then he came to a town, and as he stepped to the gate, he saw a great many people assembled. Now these folk had been taking counsel, their czar being dead, as to who should succeed him. In the end they agreed that the first person who should come in at the city gate, should be made czar. Just then in came little Ivan through the gate; so all the people cried out together, —

"Here is our czar!"

The chief folk took little Ivan by the arms, conducted him to the royal apartments, put on him the czar's robes, seated him on the throne, made obeisance to him as to their czar, and waited for his commands. Then little Ivan thought he must surely be asleep and dreaming all this, but at last he knew that he must be really czar. He was heartily pleased, began to rule over the people, and to appoint his officers. A short time after he called one of them, named Luga, to him, and said, —

"My true friend and good knight Luga, I want you to do me a service. Go to my own country, go to the czar, salute him for me, and ask him to deliver to you the shopkeeper Abrosim and his wife, so that you may bring them to me. If he will not deliver them up to you, tell him that I will lay waste his country with fire, and will make himself my prisoner."

When the servant Luga was come into little Ivan's country, he went to the czar and asked him to let Abrosim and Fetinia go away with him. The czar was unwilling to let Abrosim go, for he wanted to keep the rich merchant in his own country. He knew, however, that Ivan's kingdom was very large and populous, and being therefore afraid, he let Abrosim and Fetinia depart. Luga received them from the czar, and conducted them to his own native country.

When he brought them to little Ivan, the czar said to his father, —

"Yes, Father, you turned me away from your house, and I therefore bring you to mine. Come, live with me, you and my mother, till the end of your days."

Abrosim and Fetinia rejoiced exceedingly to find that their son had become czar, and they lived with him many years, until they died.

Little Ivan ruled for thirty years in good health, and was very happy, and all his people loved him sincerely to the last hour of his life.

THE STOLEN HEART.

ONCE upon a time there stood on an island in the Vistula a great castle, surrounded by a strong rampart. At each corner was a tower, and from these there waved in the wind many a flag, while the soldiers stood on guard upon them. A bridge connected the island with the banks of the river.

In this castle lived a knight, a brave and famous warrior. When the trumpets sounded from the battlements of the castle, their notes announced that he had returned from victory loaded with booty.

SCIOLLO AND COLLEONI, VENICE.

In the deep dungeons of the castle many a prisoner was confined, and they were led out daily to work. They had to keep the ramparts in repair, and see to the garden. Now among these prisoners was an old woman, who was a sorceress. She swore that she would be revenged upon the knight for his ill-treatment of her, and patiently awaited an opportunity to effect her purpose.

One day the knight came back wearied out with his exertions on one of his warlike excursions. He lay down upon the grass, closed his eyes, and was soon fast asleep.

The witch seized the opportunity. Coming gently to him, she scattered poppy seed on his eyes so that he should sleep the sounder. Then, with an aspen branch, she struck him on the breast over his heart.

The knight's breast at once opened, so that one could look in and see the heart as it lay there and beat. The sorceress laughed, stretched out her bony arm, and with her long fingers she stole away the heart so quietly that the knight never woke.

Then the woman took a hare's heart which she had ready, put it in the sleeping man's breast, and closed up the opening. Going away softly, she hid herself in a thicket, to see the effect of her wicked work.

Before the knight was even awake he began to feel the change that the hare's heart was making in him. He, who had till now never known fear, quaked and tossed himself uneasily from side to side. When he awoke he felt as if he should be crushed by his armor. The cry of his hounds, as it fell on his ear, filled him with terror.

Once he had loved to hear their deep baying as he followed them in pursuit of the prey in the wild forest, but now he was filled with fear, and fled like a timid hare. As he ran to his room the clang of his armor, the ringing of his silver spurs, the clatter of his spear, filled him with such terror that he threw all aside, and sank exhausted on his bed.

Even in his sleep fear pursued him. Once he dreamed only of battles and of the prizes of victory, now he trembled as he dreamed. The barking of his dogs, the voices of his soldiers as they paced the ramparts while they watched, made him quake as he lay on his bed; and he buried his head, like a frightened child, in his pillow.

At length there came a body of the knight's enemies to besiege him in his castle. The knight's soldiers looked upon their leader, who had so often delighted in the excitement of the camp and in the victory. In vain they waited for him to lead them forth. The once brave knight, when he heard the clash of arms, the cries of the men, and the clang of the horses' hoofs, fled to the topmost chamber of his castle, and from there looked down upon the force which had come against him.

When he recollected his expeditions in the time past, his combats, his victories, he wept bitterly, and cried out aloud, —

"O Heaven! give me now courage, give me the old strength of heart and vigor. My men have already gone to the field, and I, who used to lead them, now, like a girl, look through the highest loophole upon my enemies. Give me my old boldness, that I may take my arms again; make me what I was once, and bless me with victory."

These thoughts, as it were, awakened him from a dream. He went again to his chamber, put on his armor, leaped upon his horse, and rode outside the castle gate. The soldiers saw him come with joy, and sounded the trumpets. The knight went on, but in his secret soul he was afraid; and when his men gallantly threw themselves upon the enemy, deadly fear came over him, and he turned and fled.

Even when he was once more in his stronghold, when the mighty walls held him safe within them, fear did not leave him. He sprang from his horse, fled to an innermost chamber, and there quite unmanned awaited inglorious death. His men had triumphed over the foe, and the salutations of the guards announced their victorious return. All wondered at the flight of their leader at such a time. They looked for him, and discovered him half dead in a deep cellar.

The unfortunate knight did not live long. During the winter he tried to warm his quaking limbs by the fireside of his castle. When spring came he would open his window that he might breathe the fresh air; and one day it chanced a swallow, that had built its nest in a hole of the roof, struck him on the head with its wing. The blow was fatal. As if he had been struck by lightning, the knight fell down upon the ground, and in a short while died.

All his men mourned for their good master. They knew not what had changed him, but about a year later, when some sorceresses were being put to the ordeal for having kept off the rain, one of them confessed that she had taken the knight's heart, and put in his breast a hare's.

CHAPTER X.

STORIES AND STUDIES WHILE DETAINED IN QUARANTINE.

OUR travellers sailed for Alexandria, Egypt, with the purpose of resting at Cairo, and making an excursion up the Nile. The steamer made a swift and delightful voyage across the Mediterranean, stopped off the quarantine, and was delayed. The health officers came on board.

A day passed. The health officers came on board again. Some mysterious information was passing among the officers of the steamer. The captain looked grave; the stewards troubled and alarmed.

The cause of the detention came out on the third day. There had been a case of supposed cholera on board.

The patient was a passenger in the intermediate part of the steamer. He had recovered, and no other case had followed.

With the shores of Egypt in view, and impatient to land, our travellers were told that they would be detained in quarantine for some time, — certainly a week, possibly a fortnight.

Percy immediately began to study the regulations of quarantine, and the consular duties in regard to them. His father at first explained them, and then he carefully read the book of "Consular Regulations." From this he learned that an Act of Congress of 1878 provided —

That whenever any infectious or contagious disease shall appear in any foreign port or country, and whenever any vessel shall leave any passengers coming from any infected foreign port, or having on board goods or passengers coming from any place or district infected with cholera or yellow fever, shall leave any foreign port, bound for any port in the United States, the consular officer, or other representative of the United States at or nearest such foreign port, shall immediately give information thereof to the supervising surgeon-general of the marine-hospital service, and shall report to him the name, the date of departure, and the port of destination in the United States; and the consular officers of the United States shall make weekly reports to him of the sanitary condition of the ports at which they are respectively stationed.

The book of " Regulations " explained that —

The object of the foregoing section of the law is to secure timely advice of the outbreaks of cholera and yellow fever, and of the probable transportation of the poisons of these preventable diseases in vessels bound for the United States; and consular officers for the United States are directed to put themselves into communication with the health authorities of their respective stations, and from the information obtained from such authorities, or from other reliable sources where no regularly constituted health authorities exist, to prepare and transmit by the mails to the Department of State, for the information of the surgeon-general of the marine-hospital service, on forms prescribed by the department, weekly reports of the appearance, progress, or termination of cholera, yellow fever, small-pox plague, or typhus occurring in their respective localities, and are further instructed to include in said reports information in relation to the prevalence of other preventable diseases, as diphtheria, enteric and scarlet fevers, etc., the prevailing disease or diseases in port, if any, and, when practicable, the annual death rate per one thousand of the population as shown by the official record of deaths for the week reported. Special interest should be taken in the healthfulness of vessels, reporting those arriving from or departing to the United States in a bad sanitary condition; also reporting the facts of any serious sickness or unhealthiness of seamen in port, or of crews arriving from or departing to the United States.

In the event of the outbreak of Asiatic cholera, yellow fever or Asiatic plague, or other contagious disease in epidemic form, the department must immediately be advised by cable or telegraph of such outbreak, using such abbreviation as the department may from time to time direct

The consul will give to every master of a vessel bound to a port in the United States, a bill of health on the form prescribed by the department, giving full information of the number of persons on board such vessel at the time of sailing and the sanitary condition of the vessel so far as known, and also the sanitary condition of the port of departure at the time. At such ports as may

A VISION OF EGYPT.

from time to time be designated by the department, a physician will be employed or detailed to make the necessary inspection of the vessel, her passengers, crew, cargo, and ballast. In case the master of any vessel shall refuse to receive a bill of health, the fact shall be immediately reported to the department by cable, if necessary.

When a vessel having received a bill of health, touches at any other port while *en route* to the United States, the consul at such port shall visa the bill of health and note thereon such changes as may have taken place since its original issue.

Monthly reports of the bills of health issued must be made to the department on the regular forms.

There was, at first, much terror and apprehension among the passengers when the announcement of the infectious disease was made. But, as the case was doubtful, and the patient recovered, the anxiety gave place to hope.

Time grew weary in the long quarantine under the burning sky. Tales of travel and adventures on the sea were told by the English passengers to pass away the slow hours. Some of these "tales in quarantine" were vivid and interesting, and we will give two of them here.[1]

THE GOURD HELMETS.

A YOUNG shipmate of mine, named Montrose Merton, once related to me a queer adventure which he had met with upon his first voyage.

"It happened two years ago, when I was seventeen," said Mont. "Perhaps you may have heard of the brig 'Rainbow,' and how and where she was lost. I was in her at the time.

"We had been freighting about the West Indies for nearly a year, going from port to port with whatever invoice could be picked up, till finally, at Havana, we were ordered over to the little Mexican town of Laguna, where we were to take in a cargo of logwood.

"So we ran over toward the place, and got into the Bay of Campeachy; but the brig never arrived at her port. I suppose it was a piece of carelessness

---

[1] These stories were written by Mr. Coomes for "Golden Days," and are used by permission.

on the captain's part; but, at all events, she struck on a reef, and that was the end of her.

"After a few thumps, away went both masts over the side, and she was very soon full of water. We got off with the yawl and long-boat, saving only our money and clothing, and the next day reached Laguna, where we came under the care of the American consul.

"However, we were in no real distress, as all of us had some specie, and a very little of this would go a long way in such a sleepy port as that old Mexican town.

"We, before the mast, had been permitted to buy and sell some little 'ventures' at the ports the brig had visited, and I, for one, had nearly a hundred dollars.

"The consul was a Mr. Clark, from Connecticut, where he had once been a school teacher. He was a fine man, and he had a son named Richard, who, as it happened, was of my own age to a single day. That, I suppose, was what people would call a 'singular coincidence.'

"Dick Clark seemed as glad to see me as if I had been his own brother, though I was an entire stranger to him. He said I was the first American *boy* he had set eyes on for a whole year, though he had now and then been refreshed with the sight of a few live Yankee *men*, who had come there after logwood in vessels flying the dear old stripes and stars.

"We quickly struck up a warm friendship, and Dick said if I would remain at the place for a time, we would have some fine sport hunting wild animals and exploring the neighboring shores.

"He showed me a dugout that he owned, — a sort of double-ender, about twenty feet long and four feet wide, made from a single tree. Of course it was rather clumsy, as boats go; but then it had been burned down, and hewn down, and chiselled down a great deal thinner and better than you would suppose it could have been. Dick had some tools, and he had given it the finishing touches himself.

"It had a sail and oars and a set of paddles, and there was a canvas cover that could be drawn over about half the length of the hull; so that two or three fellows could sleep under it, if they should happen to be out all night.

"The town was certainly the dullest spot of earth it was ever my fortune to light upon. It smelt of logwood everywhere, just like a dye-house. Nobody thought of dealing in anything else.

"The inhabitants had more time than they knew what to do with, and I don't believe a single one of them was ever in a hurry in his life. No wonder that Dick felt lonesome, I thought.

A CAMPING-PLACE IN SIGHT OF BISKRA.

"As to myself, the case was different. Being at liberty to go or stay, as I pleased, I could feel quite easy and contented; and so I fell in with his proposition at once. In a few days the rest of the 'Rainbow's' crew went over to Havana in a Spanish brig, but I remained behind.

"Dick owned a very good gun; but, as it was the only fire-arm of a modern pattern that he knew of in the place, it seemed at first as if I should have to take up with some old Mexican flintlock. But, finally, I was lucky enough to get a double-barrelled fowling-piece from the skipper of a Dutch bark which was loading with logwood for Rotterdam, and on the next day we started out. Laguna stands on one of a chain of islands at the mouth of Lake Terminos, and we took an oblique course for the main shore, where we hoped to find some large game. Dick thought we should be likely to meet with tapirs, anteaters, sloths, gluttons, and perhaps a bear, besides standing a fair chance of stirring up a jaguar or a herd of peccaries.

"I had seen a good many jaguars behind the bars of cages, but peccaries I knew nothing about, except that they were a sort of small swine. I found, though, that Dick had a real dread of them. They were worse than the jumping toothache, he said, and always looking for a fight. Out of a full hundred, you might kill all but one, yet the hundredth fellow would come right on just as if nothing had happened, clashing his ugly tusks and bristling all over like a little fury.

"After reaching the mainland, we coasted along the shore for two days, sometimes ranging the woods or pampas, at other times off on board our dugout.

"Now and then we would come upon a camp of logwood cutters, and next there would be an unbroken forest or a wide plain, with no human being in sight.

"Our object was to get as many specimens as possible of the skins of curious birds and animals to be carried home as trophies. We wanted, above all things, a jaguar skin, not only for its beauty, but because it could n't be had without the danger of risking our own skins in getting it.

"We killed a sloth, an armadillo, two ant-eaters, and a tapir, all very strange looking creatures, besides bagging two large monkeys and a number of splendid parrots and cockatoos.

"On the third day, while going very quietly through a strip of forest, we got a prodigious start from two ocelots that sprang out of a hollow tree not twenty feet from us. We shot both of them dead on the spot, and they were the most beautiful animals I ever saw. Even the African leopard is n't so handsome.

"They measured about three feet in length, and I have the skin of one of them now.

"However, that day ended our hunt and made us willing to go home, for it was then that the adventure happened that I started to tell you about.

"Within the tropics, you know, everything of the vegetable kind has a rank growth, and Dick and I had several times come upon a species of gourd nearly as large as a peck measure. We had seen, too, a number of dry ones floating upon the water close to the flocks of fowl.

"Dick said he had heard that the natives, by putting the shells on their heads and wading up to the chin, often got right in among the birds, so as to catch them by the legs.

"Here was an idea, and what fine fun it would be to act upon it!

"We discovered a shallow little cove by the lake-side, with hundreds of fowls swimming about in it, and it seemed to us that here was just the place for our experiment. There were a few gourds drifting near the flock, and this encouraged us, for it showed that the birds wouldn't take alarm at our helmets.

"A line of reeds by the water kept us from being seen; and so, leaving our dugout just without the cove, we went looking for gourds to fit our heads.

"Finding two enormous ones, we made eye-holes and mouth-holes in them, and then jammed them over our crowns till they covered our faces completely; then stripped of everything but our duck trowsers, we stood ready for the trial.

"But dear me, what a spectacle we should have made if there had been anybody to see us! As we stood there in the blazing sun, barefooted and bare-shouldered, with our heads feeling as big as bushel baskets, we laughed till I thought we should scare all the ducks out of the cove.

"We were about twenty rods from the water, and just as we began to move toward it, there came some queer little squeaks and grunts from among the trees behind us. We stopped and listened.

"'Oogh, oogh, oogh! quee, quee, quee!' There was a rustling of grass and brushwood, and then, good gracious, if we saw one ugly little snout bearing down upon us, we saw two or three hundred! It was a living wave of tusks and bristles.

"'Peccaries, peccaries!' Dick yelled. 'We must run for it!'

"We still had our guns with us, intending to leave them on the bank while we waded after the ducks; but to have fired just then at that legion of black little demons would simply have been to waste time, and just then we needed all the time there was.

A DAUGHTER OF EGYPT.

"With our helmets on and our chests and shoulders bare, we sprang away like a couple of wild colts. What the peccaries thought we were with the heads we had on, I don't know. It was no doubt the first time they had ever seen the new kind of animal they were in chase of.

"The open ground behind us was fairly alive with the savage little wretches; and how we did run, while they came streaming after us, pulling up with all the power of their stout legs!

"We plunged through the line of reeds and into the water, wading off until it was up to our waists before turning to fire. We had the advantage of them now, for, although they were every one swimming for us, we could touch bottom, while they could not.

"We gave them the contents of our four barrels, and saw that number of them turn keel up; but all the others came straight on, and we were obliged to spring away in lively style, wading along as fast as possible, or they would have had us sure enough.

"They chased us out of the little cove and away around to our boat, though we reloaded and fired a number of times before getting there.

"Once we crossed a deep place where we had to swim, and here they came within an ace of catching us, because it was difficult to carry our guns and make headway at the same time.

"We forgot all about our gourdshell helmets, but floundered and splashed along, looking through the eye-holes like a couple of Cœur de Lion's crusaders right from Palestine. In fact, it was no time to think of our headgear with a whole army of peccaries at our heels.

"A dozen or two of them had got into shoal water, where they could touch bottom, and when we reached the dugout they were almost up with us.

"We grabbed it by the gunwale; but, before the clumsy craft was fairly afloat, we had to spring in and defend ourselves with the oars.

"The little scamps crowded alongside, squealing and snapping their jaws, till it seemed as if they would come right in upon us, in spite of all we could do.

"But we managed to push the boat afloat; and just then something happened that must have surprised them as much as it did us.

"There was a roar and a swaying of the reeds, and, before we could even think, a big jaguar leaped right upon the dugout's bow. He was a powerful fellow, with a great spotted head, and with claws that seemed to sink into the very gunwale.

"But it was n't Dick or me that was wanted. In an instant he whipped up the nearest peccary from the water and was off with a bound. We could see the tall reeds waving, where he sprang through them up the bank.

"The entire herd gave chase to him, and in three minutes there was n't a pig in sight.

"We got off into deep water as soon as possible, and then examined our guns and ammunition. Our powder, being in tight flasks, was not much damaged, but the guns were dripping wet, and we had to let them dry in the hot sun before reloading. But, first, we took off our false heads, and it made us think of Ichabod Crane and the headless horseman.

"After the guns had become dry we loaded them and pulled into the cove, in order to pick up a dead pig or two. We had got out of the boat and were dragging one of the slain peccaries from among the reeds, when we heard close to us a growl that fairly lifted our hair.

"Our guns were up in an instant, and the 'bang!' they made was but a single sound. Through the smoke we saw a large creature tip over backwards and lie with its paws in the air, while two smaller ones scurried away.

"We had killed a female jaguar, and it was her cubs that had run off. They stopped just beyond the line of reeds, and we shot them both very easily.

"It must, we thought, be a rather good day for jaguars, for it was plain that this one could n't be the same that had boarded our dugout, though she answered our purpose just as well.

"The skins of the mother and cubs were perfect beauties, and we lost no time in taking them off.

"The next day we got back to Laguna. An American vessel had arrived there in the mean time, and in her I sailed for home.

"I have never seen Dick Clark since, but you may be sure that neither of us will ever forget the day we wore those gourdshell helmets."

AN UNWELCOME SHIPMATE.

HAD the reader seen the big snake skin which we brought home from South America on board the bark "Cayman," he would probably have wished to know how we became possessed of such a trophy. This I can best relate by describing our voyage.

We had been lying for some weeks at Port of Spain, in the island of Trinidad, which is close to the South American coast, when our vessel was ordered to the river Orinoco, there to load with various products of that region. Our immediate port of destination was the city of Angostura, two hundred and forty miles from the ocean, and in the very heart of Venezuela, so that we looked forward to the trip with no little interest.

A run of a day and night from Port of Spain brought us off the Boca de Navios, the principal mouth of the Orinoco; and then with everything set before the brisk trade wind, we began to stem the mighty current.

Yet, in spite of her broad wings, the bark's progress was tediously slow. There was no steam-tug to give us a lift on our way, and, although the breeze was directly over the quarter, we could not make a mile an hour against the stream at the best; while on many occasions, as the wind slackened, it became necessary to anchor in order to hold our own. In this manner we worked along day after day and night after night.

But the vast river itself was magnificent. Four or five miles wide, and crowned on each bank with a seemingly endless forest, it gave us a profound conception of Nature's grandeur.

And then how deep it was, too! Almost like the sea we had left behind, so that our fellows grumbled at the prodigious amount of chain they had to handle in our many anchorings, though these were always made near one shore or the other.

At such times we could see troops of monkeys and flocks of beautiful birds among the trees; and once we had a plain view of a jaguar as he made his way along the bank, occasionally stopping to look at us.

The captain and mate both fired at him with their revolvers, but were unable to hit him, and he finally disappeared very leisurely in the dark woods.

With our many delays, and our slow creeping against a current that was so often stronger than the wind, it took us eighteen days to accomplish the two hundred and forty miles of river passage; but at last we reached Angostura, and once more stepped on shore.

It required a considerable time to collect all the numerous articles of our cargo, and when they had all been stowed on board, we could have supplied a tannery with hides, a dye-house with indigo, an India-rubber factory with caoutchouc, a grocery with cacao, or a drug shop with sarsaparilla, ipecac, and Peruvian bark; for all these articles were down on our invoice.

After so long a sojourn at the sultry Venezuelan town, there was an exhilaration in once more tumbling the furled topsails from the yards, and feeling that the stanch bark beneath our feet was at last in motion, bound for the open sea and for home.

It would take us four or five days to get out of the Orinoco: for, although the current was now in our favor, the trade wind was against us, so that we should have to make continual tacks from side to side of the river, in order to keep our sails full and avoid coming to a standstill.

But we were off for the dear land of the north, and every one was happy.

Even old Tommy, the captain's big white cat, seemed to purr more affectionately than usual as he rubbed himself against the legs of our wide trowsers and twisted his lithe form into all manner of graceful shapes. Tommy was a great favorite in both cabin and forecastle.

We had another pet, also, — a large, gray parrot, — which hung in a cage by the mainmast, and which had been procured, cage and all, of an English shopkeeper at Port of Spain.

Poll was an everlasting talker. She would cry out, "Eight bells; call the watch; pump ship!" as plainly as any one. And, although at first afraid of the cat, she had got used to him, and would call, "Tommy, Tommy! Come here, old shipmate!" in the most familiar manner imaginable.

Sometimes Tommy would obey the summons, whereupon Poll would drop bits of cracker for him, squalling in a kind of boisterous delight to see him pick them up. The season of flood in Venezuela had commenced, and in passing down the Orinoco we found it much higher than while ascending it. The trees on its banks now rose directly out of the water, which reached we knew not how far back into the forest. We seemed to be sailing on a long lake, shut in by green walls that had no visible foundation. The wind was in our teeth, but, with the friendly current all the while sweeping us along as it crossed our keel, we got on swimmingly.

But on the third day an odd accident happened. We had made a tack somewhat close to the shore, when, just as we were upon the point of going about, our rudder became wedged by a stick of driftwood, of which there were large quantities floating down the river.

Finding the helm unmanageable, we let go an anchor in hopes of bringing the vessel up; but, in spite of this, she went straight in among the trees, snapping off her jibboom, fore-topmast, and main-top gallant-mast.

Here was a tangle, indeed! Vines, branches, and broken spars were all mixed together!

Nevertheless, as we were still afloat, our case was by no means desperate. It is not unusual for the Orinoco to swell twenty feet above its banks, and we judged that this depth of water was still beneath us.

The bark had run over her anchor, and by heaving at the cable, as it passed under her bows and not beyond the stern, we could hope to move her. But an abundance of cutting and clearing must first be done, and, as night was at hand, it would be vain to think of getting out of the scrape before another day.

Our fore-topmast, which had broken just above the cap, had dropped down till its lower end rested upon the deck, while the upper part, with all its hamper, was supported by the trees against which it leaned. The main-top gallant-mast hung to the branches by its rigging, and the jibboom lay under the bows. We succeeded in unbending the fore-topsail, but this was about all we could accomplish before dark. The sail was badly torn, and we piled it in a heap forward.

Meanwhile the mosquitoes put us in a torment. Out on the river we had never been troubled with them, but here in the thicket they swarmed by millions. That night the officers smoked the little pests out of the cabin, and then fortified the entrance with netting, while we before the mast took up our quarters in the top, where — as mosquitoes seldom get much above a ship's deck — we were left in peace.

A lantern was hung on the main-stay, and, from our position aloft, we were to keep a one-man watch for possible contingencies. Some of us were in the fore-top and others in the main. My own lookout, which was in the early part of the night, passed without incident, and it was near daybreak before anything disturbed us, when, all at once, it came to be understood that some unknown creature was stirring on board the vessel.

Instantly we were all wide awake and peering down from the tops with startled faces, while we hurriedly questioned each other as to what it was, where it was, and who had the last watch. The lantern did not light up the deck very well, and the shadows had a weird look to us.

"I see it!" said one of our fellows, at length, in a frightened undertone. "Look! There it is under the port bulwarks. It's a big snake. Keep still, or he'll be up here in a jiffy!"

We could all see it now, though in the dim lantern light its hideous proportions were indistinct. Sometimes, indeed, it seemed as if there were two snakes; but we presently concluded that there was only one, and he a monster.

At intervals he would be wholly lost to sight, and again some portion of his horrid folds would be visible as he crept slowly about the deck, which was well lumbered with wreckage.

At last he went over the bows and disappeared in the darkness, though whether he had gone down into the water or had got hold of a thick-leaved tree that was close to the bowsprit, we were unable to say. At all events, we slept no more that night, and were extremely glad to see the daybreak.

In the morning the officers heard our story with great interest, shuddering to think what would have been their situation had the monster chosen to come through the mosquito netting and explore the cabin.

It made us creep all over to recall the night's experience, and we determined to get the bark out of her berth that day, if work would accomplish it.

We sat, "Turk-fashion," on the forward part of the deck to eat our breakfast, while near us lay the fore-topsail in a pile, as it had been left the evening previous.

The white cat, Tommy, climbed upon the heap of canvas. The next moment he bounded off upon the deck, and with back and tail bristling, whirled around to look behind him.

At the same time there was a movement of the pile, and as we sprang to our feet, the head and neck of a great serpent shot out from the folds of the sail.

An instant of frozen terror, and then how we tumbled over each other! Some ran into the galley, and others into the small house on the booby-hatch. The officers were at breakfast in the cabin. Nobody fled aloft, — we knew better than to do that, at least, nobody did so except Tommy, and he, following the instinct of his race, sprang into the main rigging.

His terrible enemy was rushing after him, and had actually mounted above the bulwarks, when Poll's loud screaming from her cage appeared to attract his attention. The poor bird was in a great fluster.

"Oh, what's the matter now?" she cried.

And this query was followed by a succession of wild outcries that showed her to be dreadfully frightened.

The snake had raised himself for nearly his whole length up the shrouds, but he now stopped, and craning his thin, tapering neck toward the parrot, uttered a frightful hiss.

He had seen that Tommy was too nimble for him, while Polly's flutterings and squallings had put him in mind of other prey.

Down he came from the rigging, making straight for this new object, when "crack, crack!" went the captain's revolver from the cabin door.

He fired two shots and missed with both. Then the mate discharged three bullets, with no better success.

The snake, paying not the least attention to his human enemies struck the cage violently with his frightful jaws, knocking it from its place, but retaining his hold of it as it fell.

Half a minute more, and parrot, cage and all would have been travelling down that living lane had not the two officers improved in their marksmanship. Two of their balls just then struck the reptile, one in the head, the other in the neck, and their effect was instantaneous.

At once disabled, the monster thrashed about in sickening contortions, lashing the deck fearfully, while his two assailants emptied the remaining chambers of their weapons with the steadiest nerve they could muster.

But there was no need of more shots. The furious writhings became less and less, at length ceasing altogether, though the snaky tail showed signs of life for more than two hours.

Then the limp, horrible body was stretched out and measured. We found it to be twenty-eight feet long and about twenty-two inches around in the largest part. The serpent was of the boa family, and checkered with black and yellow.

Probably there had been two of them on board in the night, one crawling away as we had seen at the time, and the other wriggling himself into the loose pile of canvas.

All the shots fired by the captain and mate had been discharged from the companion-way, with the road of retreat well open behind them.

They now stripped off the mottled skin, while we sailors stood looking on, shuddering at the bare thought of touching the hideous thing.

We could reef topsails in the blackest squall that ever blew, but we wanted nothing to do with a snake.

Pretty Poll remained unharmed, in spite of her rough usage, though her cage was sadly battered and bent. It was some hours before she got over her fright, however, and she would keep screaming, —

"Throw him overboard — throw him overboard! I'm most scared to death!"

As for Tommy, he came down from aloft when all was over, but his eyes still looked big and wild, and his tail indicated an unsettled state of mind.

We got the vessel out of her bad predicament before another night, and, anchoring in the river, proceeded to repair damages. After a few days our broken spars had been replaced by others, and the sails again bent, so that everything was shipshape.

Then we beat through the Boca de Navios, and three weeks later arrived safely at New York.

Such is the history of the snake skin which we brought home in the bark "Cayman." It was afterwards stuffed, and, for aught I know, is still on exhibition as a curiosity.

The detention led to the discussion of many topics relating to the consulates, among them "leaves of absence" and "salaries."

The study of the topic "leaves of absence" was interesting, as the schedule furnished by the State Department furnished a kind of geography lesson of *the longest* periods of modern travel, usually *twice* the time needed for ocean voyages being allowed the consul on his journey from the ports of the United States to his place of appointment. The latest "regulation" is as follows:—

LEAVES OF ABSENCE.

Under the authority conferred upon the Secretary of State by law, the following have been established, and determined, and made public, as the maximum amounts of time allowed for transit between salaried consular posts in the several countries named and the city of Washington, and *vice versa*, viz:—

Argentine Republic, forty-five days. Austria-Hungary, thirty days. Barbary States, thirty-five days. Belgium, twenty days. Brazil, forty days. Chili, forty-five days. China (except Tien-Tsin), fifty days; Tien-Tsin, ninety days. Colombia: Barranquilla, sixteen days; Bogota, thirty-five days; Colon, sixteen days; Panama, sixteen days. Congo State, fifty days. Corea, sixty-five days. Costa Rica, twenty-five days. Denmark, twenty-five days; St. Thomas, fifteen days. Ecuador, thirty-five days. Egypt, thirty-five days. France, twenty days. French possessions: Algiers, thirty-five days; Gaboon, fifty days; Guadeloupe, thirty days; Martinique, twenty-five days; Tahiti, seventy days. Friendly and Navigator's Islands, seventy days. Germany, twenty-five days. Great Britain and Ireland, twenty days; British possessions: Aden, forty days; Antigua, thirty days; Australia, fifty days; Barbadoes, twenty days; Bermuda, ten days; Bombay, sixty days; Calcutta, sixty days; Canada (except Gaspé Basin, New Brunswick, Prince Edward Island, Victoria, and Winnipeg), three days; Cape Town, fifty-five days; Ceylon, fifty days; Demerara, forty days; Falkland Islands, seventy days; Fiji Islands, seventy days; Gaspé Basin, six days; Gibraltar, twenty-five days; Hong-Kong, fifty days; Kingston, Jamaica, twenty days; Malta, thirty days; Mauritius, ninety days; Nassau, fifteen days; New Brunswick, six days; New Zealand, fifty days; Nova Scotia, six days; Prince Edward Island, six days; St. Helena, forty-five days; Sierra Leone, fifty days; Singapore, sixty days; Turk's Island, twenty days; Victoria, twenty-five days; Winnipeg, fifteen days. Greece, thirty-five days. Guatemala, thirty days. Hayti, fifteen days. Hawaiian Islands, thirty-five days. Honduras, twenty-five days. Italy, thirty days. Japan, forty days. Liberia, forty days. Madagascar, seventy days. Muscat, sixty days. Mexico: Acapulco, twenty-five days; Guaymas, twenty-five days; Matamoras, twelve days;

Merida, twenty days; Mexico, eighteen days; Nogales, fifteen days; Nuevo Laredo, twelve days; Paso del Norte, twelve days; Piedras Negras, twelve days; Tampico, twenty days; Vera Cruz, fifteen days. Netherlands, twenty days; Batavia, Java, sixty days; Nicaragua, twenty-five days. Paraguay, sixty days. Persia, sixty-five days. Peru, forty days. Portugal, thirty days. Portuguese possessions: Fayal, thirty days; Funchal, thirty days; Mozambique, ninety days; Santiago C. V. I.), forty days; St. Paul de Loanda, ninety days. Russia: Odessa, thirty days; St. Petersburg, forty-five days. Salvador, twenty-five days. San Domingo, fifteen days. Siam, sixty days. Spain, twenty-five days. Spanish possessions: Baracoa, fifteen days; Cardenas, fifteen days; Cienfuegos, twelve days; Havana, ten days; Manila, sixty days; Matanzas, ten days; Puerto Rico, twenty days; Sagua la Grande, twelve days; Santiago de Cuba, twelve days. Sweden and Norway, twenty-five days. Switzerland, twenty-five days. Turkey, forty days. Uruguay, forty-five days. Venezuela, twenty-five days. Zanzibar, seventy days.

The salaries of consuls are as a rule not large. The consuls-general are fairly well paid, but the consuls at the smaller ports rarely receive more than $1500 per annum.

The best paid consulates are as follows, and the study of the schedule will furnish a good lesson of the commercial value of the ports named: —

SALARIES CONSULAR SERVICE.

Consuls-general at Havana, London, Paris, and Rio de Janeiro, at six thousand dollars each, twenty-four thousand dollars.

Consuls-general at Calcutta and Shanghai, at five thousand dollars each, ten thousand dollars.

Consul-general at Melbourne, four thousand five hundred dollars.

Consuls-general at Berlin, Honolulu, Kanagawa, Montreal, and Panama, at four thousand dollars each, twenty thousand dollars.

Consul-general at Halifax, three thousand five hundred dollars.

Consuls-general at Constantinople, Ecuador, Frankfort, Rome, St. Petersburg, and Vienna, at three thousand dollars each, eighteen thousand dollars.

Consul-general at Mexico, two thousand five hundred dollars.

For salaries of consuls, vice-consuls, and commercial agents, three hundred and seventy-seven thousand five hundred dollars, as follows, namely: —

Consul at Liverpool, six thousand dollars; consul at Hong-Kong, five thousand dollars.

CLASS II. — At three thousand five hundred dollars per annum: China, consuls at Amoy, Canton, Chin-Kiang, Foo-Chow, Hankow, and Tein-Tsin; Peru, consul at Callao.

CLASS III. — At three thousand dollars per annum: Belgium, consul at Antwerp; Chili, consul at Valparaiso; China, consul at Ningpo; France, consul at Havre; Great Britain and British dominions, consuls at Belfast, Bradford, Demerara, Glasgow, Manchester, Ottawa, and Singapore; Japan, consuls at Nagasaki, and Osaka and Hiogo; Mexico, consul at Vera Cruz; Spanish dominions, consul at Matanzas (Cuba); United States of Colombia, consul at Colon (Aspinwall).

CLASS IV. — At two thousand five hundred dollars per annum: Argentine Republic, consul at Buenos Ayres; Belgium, consul at Brussels; Danish dominions, consul at St. Thomas; France, consuls at Bordeaux, Lyons, and Marseilles; Germany, consuls at Annaberg, Bremen, Brunswick, Dresden, Hamburg, and Mayence; Greece, consul at Athens; Great Britain and British dominions, consuls at Birmingham, Dundee, Leith, Nottingham, Sheffield, Tunstall, and Victoria (British Columbia); Spanish dominions, consuls at Cienfuegos and Santiago de Cuba; Switzerland, consul at St. Galle; Turkish dominions, consul at Smyrna.

CLASS V. — At two thousand dollars per annum: Austria-Hungary, consuls at Trieste and Prague; Barbary States, consul at Tangier; Brazil, consul at Pernambuco; Colombia, consul at Barranquilla; Costa Rica, consul at San Jose; France, consuls at Rheims and St. Etienne; Friendly and Navigator's Islands, consul at Apia; Germany, consuls at Barmen, Chemnitz, Cologne, Crefeld, Dusseldorf, Elberfeld, Leipsic, Nuremburg, and Sonneberg; Great Britain and British dominions, consuls at Cardiff, Chatham, Cork, Dublin, Dunfermline, Hamilton (Canada), Kingston (Jamaica), Leeds, Nassau (New Providence), Port Louis (Mauritius), Port Stanley and St. Thomas (Canada), St. John (New Brunswick), Sherbrook (Canada), Sydney (New South Wales), and Toronto (Canada); Honduras, consul at Tegucigalpa; Italy, consul at Palermo; Madagascar, consul at Tamatava; Mexico, consuls at Acapulco and Matamoras; Netherlands, consul at Rotterdam; Nicaragua, consuls at Managua and San Juan del Norte; Russia, consul at Odessa; Salvador, consul at San Salvador; Spain and Spanish dominions, consuls at Manila (Philippine Islands), San Juan (Porto Rico), and Sagua la Grande (Cuba); Switzerland, consuls at Basle, Horgen, and Zurich; Turkish dominions, consuls at Beirut and Jerusalem; Uruguay, consul at Montevideo; Venezuela, consul at Maricaibo.

At one thousand five hundred dollars per annum: Brazil, consuls at Bahia,

Para, and Santos; Belgium, consul at Liege and Verviers; Denmark, consul at Copenhagen; France and French dominions, consuls at Cognac, Guadeloupe, Martinique, and Nice; Germany, consuls at Aix-la-Chapelle, Breslau, Kehl, Mannheim, Munich, and Stuttgart; Great Britain and British dominions, consuls at Amherstburg (Canada), Antigua (West Indies), Auckland (New Zealand), Barbadoes, Bermuda, Bristol, Brockville, Cape Town, Ceylon (India), Charlottetown (Prince Edward Island), Clifton (Canada), Fort Erie (Canada), Goderich (Canada), Gibraltar, Guelph (Canada), Kingston (Canada), London (Canada), Malta, Newcastle-on-Tyne, Quebec, Pictou (Canada), Port Hope (Canada), Port Sarnia (Canada), Port Stanley (Falkland Islands), Prescott (Canada), Southampton, St. Helena, St. John's (Canada), St. Stephen (Canada), Stratford (Canada), Three Rivers (Canada), Windsor (Canada), and Winnipeg (Manitoba); Italy, consuls at Florence, Genoa, Leghorn, Messina, Milan, and Naples; Mexico, consuls at Paso del Norte and Tampico; Netherlands, consul at Amsterdam; Paraguay, consul at Asuncion; Portuguese dominions, consuls at Fayal (Azores), and Funchal (Madeira); San Domingo, consul at San Domingo; Spain, consuls at Barcelona, Cadiz, and Malaga; Switzerland, consul at Geneva; Turkey, consul at Sivas; Venezuela, consuls at La Guayra and Puerto Cabello.

CLASS VI. — Belgium, consul at Ghent; Brazil, consul at Rio Grande do Sul; Chili, consul at Telcahuano, France and French dominions, consuls at Algiers and Nantes; Germany, consul at Stettin; Great Britain and British dominions, consuls at Bombay (India), Gaspé Basin (Canada), Sierra Leone (West Africa), Turk's Island, and Windsor (Nova Scotia); Hayti, consul at Cape Haytien; Honduras, consul at Ruatan and Truxillo (to reside at Utilla); Italy, consul at Venice; Mexico, consuls at Guaymas, Nuevo Laredo, and Piedras Negras; Muscat, consul at Zanzibar; Netherlands, consul at Batavia; Portuguese dominions, consul at Santiago (Cape Verde Islands); Society Islands, consul at Tahiti; Sweden and Norway, consul at Christiania.

COMMERCIAL AGENCIES.

SCHEDULE C. — Gaboon, Levuka, and St. Paul de Loando.

And in the estimates for the fiscal year ending June thirtieth, eighteen hundred and eighty-nine, there shall be estimated for specifically, under classified consulates, all consulates and commercial agencies where the fees collected or compensation allowed for the fiscal year ending June thirtieth, eighteen hundred and eighty-seven, exceed one thousand dollars.

CONSULAR CLERKS. — Six consular clerks, at one thousand two hundred dollars per annum each, seven thousand two hundred dollars.

Seven consular clerks, at one thousand dollars per annum each, seven thousand dollars.

CONSULAR OFFICERS NOT CITIZENS. — For salaries of consular officers not citizens of the United States, six thousand dollars.

ALLOWANCE FOR CLERKS AT CONSULATES. — For allowance for clerks at consulates, fifty thousand three hundred and twenty dollars, the sum to be allowed at each consulate not to exceed the rate herein specified, as follows: —

Consul at Liverpool, two thousand dollars.

Consul-general at Havana, one thousand six hundred dollars.

Consul-general at Shanghai, one thousand two hundred dollars.

Consuls-general at London, Paris, and Rio de Janeiro, at one thousand six hundred dollars each, four thousand eight hundred dollars.

Consuls-general at Berlin, Frankfort, Vienna, Montreal, and Kanagawa, and consuls at Hamburg, Bremen, Manchester, Lyons, Hong-Kong, Havre, Crefeld, and Chemnitz, at one thousand two hundred dollars each, fifteen thousand six hundred dollars.

Consuls at Bradford, Birmingham, and Marseilles, at nine hundred and sixty dollars each, two thousand eight hundred and eighty dollars.

Consuls-general at Calcutta, Port au Prince, and Melbourne, and consuls at Leipsic, Sheffield, Sonneberg, Dresden, Antwerp, Nuremburg, Tunstall, Bordeaux, Colon, Singapore, Glasgow, and Panama, at eight hundred dollars each, twelve thousand dollars.

Consuls at Belfast, Barmen, Leith, Dundee, and Victoria, and the consuls-general at Matamoras and Halifax, at six hundred and forty dollars each, four thousand four hundred and eighty dollars.

Consuls-general at Mexico and Berne, and consuls at Malaga, Naples, Genoa, Stuttgart, Florence, Mannheim, Prague, Zurich, Beirut, and Demerara, at four hundred and eighty dollars each, five thousand seven hundred and sixty dollars.

For an additional allowance for clerks at consulates, to be expended under the direction of the Secretary of State at consulates not herein provided for in respect to clerk-hire, no greater portion of this sum than four hundred dollars to be allowed to any one consulate in any one fiscal year, twenty thousand dollars: *Provided*, That the total sum expended in one year shall not exceed the amount appropriated: *And provided further*, That out of the amount hereby appropriated the Secretary of State may make such allowance as may to him seem proper to any interpreter for clerical services, in addition to his pay as interpreter.

The whole consular service of the United States is managed with rigid economy. The times demand a more accomplished representation, with more liberal salaries. Such a reform is sure to come. The American boy, like the English boy now, will one day seek and require a special education for all services in the Department of State.

CHAPTER XI.

THE MEDITERRANEAN AND ITS LEGENDS.

THE Mediterranean!— its history is that of the ancient world. All the mighty events of the past are in some way associated with its shores. It well was called the "midland sea." Europe, Asia, and Africa enclosed it, and around its ports the capitals of the empires that dominated the world for thousands of years, rose, shone, and fell.

The great water-plain has a surface of nearly one million square miles, and is one of the greatest bodies of inland water in the world. The Sea of Marmora, the Sea of Azof, and the Black Sea are properly a part of it. It is twenty-three hundred miles long and more than one thousand wide in its greatest breadth. In some places it is three thousand feet deep, and in some other places five thousand feet. At Nice it is forty-two hundred feet deep close to the shores, and the Straits of Gibraltar, by which it connects with the ocean, are fifty-five hundred feet deep. Some five hundred species of fishes inhabit its waters. Tunny fishing is followed as an industry on its shores. The old tales of the fishermen of the midland sea would fill volumes.

The hot winds from the deserts of Africa affect its atmosphere, and the cool winds of many mountain chains. The giant wind that ships fear is called the levanter. Another wind peculiar to the sea is called the solano. The levanter is a powerful east wind, as its name implies. The solano carries its meaning also in its name.

FLORENCE.

The color of the sea is blue, and a shining blue as it appears in the sun and calm. It changes color; in the Adriatic it is green, and in the Euxine it has a dark hue.

It is beautiful in midsummer, when the winds are laid, and it lies in deep purple under a purple sky, and the clear atmosphere reveals the shores which are the history of the old world. In ancient times, the Pillars of Hercules of the sea, now Gibraltar, were supposed to be the end of the world. The invention of the mariners' compass and the daring of Columbus left the great sea to the realms of history, as opened the ocean world.

The history of the sea, like that of all the empires on its shores, began in fable. Here was the kingdom of Neptune, here were birds with human features, dolphins with wonderful intelligence, monsters, nymphs, and singing shells. The old Greek and Roman poets peopled it with imaginary beings.

Its shores led the first migrations to the West. From the early days of the known world, man has been moving westward. The end of the march of the nations to the West is the Pacific coast of North and South America; then comes the East again. For thousands of years the march of civilization was toward the Pillars of Hercules. When Spain became a great power and expelled the Moors, the sea awaited its Columbus.

Take the map of the Mediterranean, and glance along its shores from Trebizond on the Black Sea to Cadiz. What names that stand for histories! Pass the Bosphorus, and let your eye circle the midland waters. What visions rise!

Constantinople, the city of Constantine, the glittering capital of an empire whose arts and arms followed Rome in the glory of the world! There gleams the crown of St. Sophia, for crescent followed the cross.

Smyrna, Beyrut, Jerusalem, with Joppa, its port, — Jerusalem, near the sea, which has touched all life with the teachings of the fatherhood of God and the brotherhood of man.

Alexandria and the portals of the Nile; — Egypt lifts herself in dusky air. Thence kings went forth to conquer the world. Armies of slaves built the tombs of those kings, whose aims were luxury and a paradise of delights, and who feasted on the spoils of nations from cups of gold, and dreamed of lotus lands in the unseen worlds, and of returning again to the embalmed habitations of their former life.

Tripoli, Tunis, Algiers, — on these shores Carthage once was. Thence Hannibal [how?] drove his elephants over the blue sea. From those fallen cities of splendor and power that lined the southern shore came the war on the Aryan race.

Who are the Aryan race? The Asiatic tribes that moved westward, possessed Europe, produced a Columbus, and found the new world. In a sense, we are a part of the Aryan race. The Aryans followed the evening star. Our country might well have been called the Hesperides.

Sweep along the northern coast of the sea. Granada, Valentia, Barcelona, — they hover on the border of the history of our Western life.

Marseilles, Genoa, and Rome, cities of fate; — for a thousand years Rome was the world.

Naples, Venice, Corfu, Athens; — the blue tides run from the Grecian cities of the arts to the Roman cities of arms.

Imaginary gods arose and vanished with the old empires. Their names haunt the shores. We can almost fancy that we see the horse of Neptune plunging in the sea, and leaving the waves in white foam.

Do we breathe the lotus, we see in it a daughter of Neptune, who was changed into the flower.

Do we pluck the narcissus, we see in it the youth who loved the beautiful maiden whose features were like his own, and whom when she was dead the same youth used to see in his own features reflected in a fountain.

Do we wander in the groves of old trees in the far East, the leaves breathe, "Hylas, where art thou?"

THE DUOMO, FLORENCE.

Do we walk over the ruin of an old Roman villa, the "lar," the fairy of the hearth, starts up before our fancy.

We pass Scylla, to recall the tales of the Sirens, the wandering rocks, and the six men of the crew of Ulysses. You can almost see the monster Scylla, with her twelve necks and six heads, and her long arms reaching out for sea-dogs and porpoises. You have heard in fable that out of each ship she takes a man, and you wonder if that man will be *you*, and down which of her necks you will go.

The fable of Oceanus comes back here, as the first dream of the vast waters of the West. Oceanus was the first-born of the Titans, the offspring of Cœlus and Terra, or the heavens and the earth. The children of Oceanus were the rivers, and the Oceanides, or the three thousand nymphs of the ocean.

Oceanus lived in the West. The poets were right — he did. He came from the West to comfort Prometheus. The allegory came true in history.

Prometheus stole the fire of heaven, and gave it to man to serve the human race. All arts came out of the fire, and so he stands as the benefactor of men. For stealing the sacred fire he was punished by being chained to a rock and by the preying of a vulture upon his liver (heart), which as fast as it was consumed grew again. The appearance of Oceanus to comfort him, as water quenches fire, is one of the most beautiful legends of the Orient.

Another charming tale of the Mediterranean is Arion. We give it in the version of Herodotus.

Arion lived with Periander, king of Corinth. His fame as a poet had filled all lands; and he suddenly felt a desire to travel and to visit those who loved the muse. He went to Sicily and to Italy, and landed on the beautiful coast of the Adriatic. His songs in these countries brought him great wealth. He took sail for Greece, but the sailors on the ship, learning of his treasures, formed a plot to kill him in order to enrich themselves.

"Kill yourself on deck," said the sailors, "or leap into the sea."

"Let me dress myself in my festal robes and sing once more," said the poet.

He presently appeared on the prow with his lyre, and began to play the enchanting Orphean strain. The dolphins heard the music, and one of them swam close to the ship. Arion threw himself overboard, and the dolphin received him on his back and bore him to Greece. When the sailors reached their port they were put to death.

We once arranged this beautiful story for recitation with musical accompaniment. We recommended the use of Rubenstein's "Dying Poet" as the accompaniment. We present this effort at musical story-telling here. Some of our readers may like to use it for a reading as we have arranged it.

ARION.

A Recitation for Piano Accompaniment.

Captain, *loquitur*,—

"Sailors of Corinth, the west winds blow free,
And the wings of the twilight spread over the sea,
And Hesper above us shines mirrored below,
And the moon rises slow, the moon rises slow.
Arion, he stands on the prow, and afar
His poet's eye catches the rose of a star.
Ah, never again shall his young eye behold
Yon crimson star burn in the shadows of gold!

"Sailors of Corinth, night darkens the air:
Go, tell the young bard for his fate to prepare.
The purple-lipped waters more restlessly flow,
And the moon rises slow, the moon rises slow.
Arion, ho, ho! drop thine eye from the star.
The great disk of Dian is rising afar,
Take thy last drink of bliss of the sea and the sky,
Young bard of Corinthia, this night thou shalt die.

"Thy suave lyre has charmed the Etrusian glades,
And sigh for it still the Sicilian maids :
Thou hast led the light dance where the purple wines flow,
When Dian her night-shield held o'er thee aglow.

LOGGIA DI LANZI, FLORENCE.

Thou has haunted the courts of the languorous kings,
In Sicilian airs breathed the raptures divine,
Where gold fell in showers and garlands and rings,
And jewelled cups hailed thee with Samian wine.

" Thou hast harvested crowns, and thy coffers of gold
Weigh down the light ship, and we watch them below ;
But thy gems now are ours, all thy treasures untold.
O'er thy grave in the sea, lo ! the moon rises slow.
Apollo flayed Marsyas for playing too sweet :
To a spider Minerva changed Ariadne, and now,
O subtle enchanter, to spoil thee is meet ;
Get thy harp and attune it once more on the prow.

" Sailors of Corinth, behold him again.
He comes with his crown and his ivy-twined lyre,
He tunes the sweet strings and awakens the strain

[*Piano. Any selection of rhythmic music.*]

To whose rapturous touch his own life shall expire.
What robe has he on. — the Sicilian gown?
No, the robe of Apollo, the mantle of white,
On which the throned Muses look happily down,
And protect from all ill with the ægis of light.

" He stands 'gainst the moon on the light swaying prow ;
Now the glimmering harpstrings his jewelled hands sweep,
And now, lo! he vanishes. Where is he now?
And what melody rises so sweet o'er the deep?
See the dolphins enchanted, — they bear him away.
He rides like a god in a chariot divine,
In the robe of Apollo ; and list, hear him play,
As he played to the kings at the spillings of wine.

" List, — hear it ascend on the heart-beating air,
Enchanting the dolphins, the sky, and the seas :
Now sweet as the love-notes of Orpheus's prayer,
Now light as the dance of the Peloponnese.
Afar now the island of Oxia grows dim,
And the high shield of Dian now melts in the mist ;
Now it soothingly flows like Ionia's hymn :
Now fainter and fainter, — breathe lightly and low,
While the notes ripple low and the still waters flow,
And the domes of the port in the silver stars glow."

[Low pedal, and continuation of music.]

*Morn mingled the blue waves of Corinth with fire,
'Neath the scales of the temple the sailors lay dead;
But Arion awoke to Apollo his lyre.
To the hall of the roses, by princesses led.*

Our travellers went from the port of Alexandria to Port Said, and thence to Suez. They called it a journey to Zag-a-Zig,— a zigzag journey to Zag-a-Zig, as a lively town by the latter name was conspicuous during the construction of the Suez Canal.

Port Said stands at the northern end of the canal, and derives its importance from its connection with the canal. On one side of the port city is Egypt, on the other Ismalia and Arabia Petræa, with Gaza near, and Jerusalem not far from Gaza.

Port Said, which now contains some ten thousand inhabitants, had no existence until 1860. An army of workmen then began to arrive there to build the canal, and it became the depot of the canal company. The construction of the long piers of Port Said was a work of immense difficulty, as the stone had to be brought at first from long distances, and later artificial stone had to be made. One of the great piers has a length of seven thousand feet, and another of six thousand feet. Within the outer harbor is an inner port, and the light-house, with its starlight electric flame, is 180 feet in height.

That was a notable day in the history of the world, when, in 1869, November 16, the Khedive of Egypt, the Empress of the French, the Emperor of Austria, and the Crown Prince of Prussia, formally opened the canal. What a change has passed over the lives and fortunes of these people since then!

The English at first stood aloof from the plan of the canal; even Robert Stephenson looked unfavorably upon it. M. de Lesseps was regarded in England as a visionary. His name afterward became one of the most illustrious in the world, to become almost pitiable with the failure of the Panama Canal.

FOUNTAIN OF NEPTUNE, FLORENCE.

The town of Suez, seventy-six miles from Cairo, with which it is connected by railway, is famous for its bazaars; yet it is situated amid a burning waste of sands.

From Port Said our travellers went to Beyrut, passing Gaza, and touching at Joppa, which connects with Jerusalem by railroad.

Gaza recalled the story of Samson; and as the party passed by it one Sunday afternoon, an old New England clergyman on board related a story which we will give in a story-telling chapter.

CHAPTER XII.

ST. SOPHIA. — THE DERVISH'S FAIRY TALE.

IT was a clear summer morning, and the sky was an uplifting of splendor when our travellers entered the Sea of Marmora, and Constantinople rose before them with the sun. Olympus was burning in the east, in expanding splendors, like a mountain of gold. Terrace above terrace, dark with cypresses, were glimmering in the overflow of light. The city stands upon two seas. It is really three cities, — Stamboul, Galata, and Scutari.

Stamboul, on the tongue of land between the Sea of Marmora and the Golden Horn, is the site of the ancient city of Byzantium.

The city was beginning to be alive. The silence of the night, which had only been broken by the howling of tens of thousands of dogs under the slanting moon, was giving place to the cries of the marketmen. The marble domes of St. Sophia were glittering among groves of eternal verdure, and the muezzins from the rosy minarets were calling the hour of prayer.

Our travellers' first visit was to the mosque of St. Sophia, or the Church of Divine Wisdom, — the architectural glory of the old Byzantine empire, and one of the most beautiful structures that ever arose under the sun. This temple first arose in the reign of Constantine in 325, the year of the Council of Nice. It was destroyed several times, but always arose from its ruins more beautiful than before.

Justinian made the rebuilding of the church the glory of his reign. The beautiful marbles of all lands were gathered for its reconstruction.

The spoils of many of the ancient temples of the world entered into it. It is said that a hundred architects superintended its construction, under each of whom were placed a hundred masons. The emperor

TURKISH WOMAN.

himself was the chief architect, and he claimed to have followed the directions of an angel who appeared to him in dreams. So St. Sophia, the Church of Heavenly Wisdom, was thought to have been planned in heaven.

It was intended to surpass the temple of Solomon. The accounts of the lavish use of gold and gems, of marbles and historic spoils, read like fairy tales. There were forty-two thousand sacred vessels of precious metals and gems, twenty-four sacred books of the evangelists, with gold covers. The doors were of ivory, amber, and cedar, and three of them it was claimed were made of wood from Noah's ark. It was also claimed that the church had the trumpets that overthrew the walls of Jericho.

The dedication of the church was most dramatic. It was Christmas eve of the year 548. The emperor, elated with the completion of this temple, which he believed to have rivalled the past and emptied the future of glory, drove his chariot to the place, and there caused one thousand oxen, one thousand sheep, six hundred deer, and ten thousand birds to be slaughtered, and thirty thousand measures of corn to be distributed among the poor. He entered the church like one bereft of his senses. He ran from the doors to the altar, and with outstretched arms exclaimed, "God be praised! *Solomon, I have surpassed thee!*"

After the Moslem conquest the church became a mosque, and new glories were added to the treasures of the past. Among the holy vessels is a cup said to have been used by the Virgin Mary; also the very cradle of the Saviour. It has a *sweating column*, where miracles are believed to be performed, a *cold window*, where the Koran was first read, and where since the wind has ever blown, and a *shining stone*, which imbibes rays of light so beautifully as to be regarded divine.

Next to the dogs of the city, a boy is interested most in the dervishes and their fairy tales. These story-tellers have an art of their own; they act their wonder-stories and hypnotize the listener, so that he seems to see it all.

Let us give you —

INTERIOR OF A MOSQUE.

A DERVISH'S FAIRY TALE.

ONCE upon a time there were two sisters, — Ellif and Lila. One of them, Ellif, was very beautiful; the other, Leila, or Lila, was a dwarf and hunchback. Now Ellif was very proud of her beauty, and Lila, the hunchback, was abashed at her form, and hid in the kitchen, and did the family work there.

But Lila had a loving heart, and the fairy folk saw her and loved her. The fairy folk were under an enchantment, which only a happy mistake could break.

One night Lila felt a light on her eyelids, and opened her eyes. What a scene! All the fairy folk were there. Her room was as light as day, and the fairy folk were dancing. As they danced they sung, —

> "Wednesday, Wednesday,
> Cheerily, cheerily,
> Wednesday, Wednesday,
> Merrily, merrily."

Lila wished to dance and sing with the fairy folk. She tried to sing, but she made a happy mistake. She sung, —

> "*Thursday*, Thursday,
> Cheerily, cheerily,
> Thursday, Thursday,
> Merrily, merrily."

This little happy mistake broke the spell, and the fairy folk were made free, and were delighted. So they determined to reward her. They rushed toward her, lifted her up. "Sing," said they.

She sung, —

> "*Thursday*, Thursday,
> Cheerily, cheerily,
> Thursday, Thursday,
> Merrily, merrily."

But they sung, —

> "Wednesday! Wednesday!
> Cheerily, cheerily,
> Wednesday! Wednesday!
> Merrily, merrily."

"When you touch the floor again," said the fairy folk, "you will be happy!"

She was. Her hump was gone; her form was light and beautiful; her face was one of the loveliest in all the world; her rags had changed to silk.

She went home, and entered the kitchen. There her proud sister came to see her about her work, and she was filled with envy and amazement as she opened the door.

As they bid her good-by the fairy folk gave her a single hair. "If you should ever be in trouble, burn that and we will come," said they. Lila treasured the hair, and knew that by it she could have anything that she wished.

"Where did you get your beautiful dress, Lila, my sister?" said Ellif.

"The fairy folk brought it to me?"

"Why, my sister?"

"I needed it, and I sung so that it broke their spell."

"What did you sing?"

Lila told her sister the story. The latter was greatly interested and wonderstruck.

"I need a dress," said she, "and now that I know the secret, I will go to the fairy folk to-night and sing too. To-day is Thursday; I will sing *Friday*, and the song of a day to come will break their spell."

Ellif that night waited the coming of the fairy folk. But instead of singing "Friday," she sung, —

> "Tuesday, Tuesday,
> Cheerily, cheerily.
> Tuesday, Tuesday,
> Merrily, merrily."

Now the fairy folk were thrown into horror by the singing of a dead day. They saw that she was selfishly trying to secure gain by having learned her sister's secret. They rushed towards her, and lifted her up, singing, "Thursday, Thursday."

"When you touch the floor again, you will weep," said they.

She did. There was a hump on her back, and her beauty was gone, and she was in rags. She went home, and took her sister's place in the kitchen.

But Lila pitied her sister when she saw her, and wept with her, and sought to comfort her.

"Weep not, my sister, it will yet be well."

"How?"

"Do you see this hair?"

"Yes, my sister."

"The fairy folk promised to help me as often as I should burn the end of this hair. I am going to burn it now."

"Why?"

"So that they will make *you* beautiful."
"And we will both be beautiful in heart."
"Yes, my sister."

She began to burn the hair, and the fairy folk all came. They made the proud sister more beautiful than ever before, and she now had a good heart also. The two sisters were in person and heart the most beautiful women in all the land.

CHAPTER XIII.

BRINDISI. — AN ODD STORY-TELLER.

ROM Constantinople our travellers went to Brindisi, a city of ancient traditions, where Virgil died. There was fever in Rome at this time, and as Brindisi connects by rail with Naples and Rome, they thought it well to rest from their journey here, and to return to Gibraltar by rail.

The harbor of Brindisi is one of the best on the Adriatic, and consists of an outer and an inner port. The country around is most beautiful; and as Brindisi was anciently Brindisium, associated with the Roman wars with Asia, with the glories of the Augustan age, and with the Crusades, it is as interesting historically as it is beautiful. The sea is a charm, and the land a garden, and everywhere the ghosts of historic events arise.

Our travellers stopped at the Grand Hotel de l'Orient, and here their story-telling was renewed amid delightful social surroundings. Visiting Naples and Rome at times, they enjoyed a long rest here.

"We are now in a city mentioned by Herodotus," said an old New England clergyman, who had accompanied them from Alexandria, and who was a classical scholar. "Travellers have rested here for three thousand years or more. Here Mæcenas came on a diplomatic mission, bringing with him Horace. And here was the end of the queen of all Roman roads, the Appian Way."

The Appian Way, — what histories did the name touch with life again, from the beginnings of the celebrations of the Roman seculums

MOSLEM AT PRAYER.

to that barbaric pageant in the days of Philip the Arabian, which commemorated the one thousandth birthday of Rome!

Down this way which armies marched to embark for Greece and for the conquests of Asia, what remnants of armies came back over it, up from the sea! Here the Roman eagles, coming and going, flashed for a thousand years.

Conquerors trod the Appian Way; captives in chains were sorrowfully marched over it towards Rome; poets travelled over it. It was the way of the living; it was the way of the dead, for it was along this way that Rome buried her dead. Here was the place of tombs, funeral torches, and ashes, and human dust. One approached the Rome of the living through the Rome of the dead.

The captive thought, "What does it matter?" as he saw the tombs, and knew that the white palaces of the dead held only common earth.

This end of the Appian Way was really the old port of Rome. The way was paved with stones as solid as the pyramids. It was a long road from Rome down to the glorious Adriatic over this firm-set road. One now passes from Brindisi to Rome in a few hours, but it was not so in the times of Mæcenas, Virgil, and Horace. The length of the Appian Way was a journey then.

But in the days of her glory Rome began at this port by the cool sea. Her longest street reached here, and the Romans loved the way to the Adriatic, where the sea seemed to come up to meet them.

At Brindisi our travellers became intimate with a benevolent old New England clergyman to whom we have alluded. His name was Ware, and he had been a pastor of a church at Scituate, Mass. In his early days he had had poetic ambitions, and had lived for a time in Boston. He was full of benevolence and story-telling, and he became a favorite among the English and American people who were resting at Brindisi.

The people used to gather on the balconies or within the balcony windows in the long evenings and Sunday afternoons to hear "Dr.

Ware," as he was called, or "old Dr. Ware," tell the tales of his simple life. He was one of those people who liked to "make fun of himself," or to freely analyze his own mistakes in life.

One Sunday afternoon he read from the Bible the story of Samson, which had been made newly interesting to him by seeing Gaza as he

APPIAN WAY.

passed along the coast. The old town of Gaza, which is near to Joppa, has still some fifteen thousand inhabitants. It has no walls or gates, as of old. Its white mosque, with its octagonal minaret, rises high over the sandy coast and blue sunny sea. Old Dr. Ware illustrated the incident of the growing again of Samson's hair by a curious and happy story, which we give below.

He one evening, when the stories of Shakspeare that relate to Venice and Verona had been the subject of conversation, told an odd incident of his own early life, in which he pictured Rome as it used to appear to him among the old New England farms. The story prepared the minds of our travellers for the journeys that they were planning to make to Rome, and recalled the associations of their own new land, far, far away.

A MODERN SAMSON, WHOSE HAIR GREW AGAIN.

SUNDAY was a still day in old New England a century ago. People did not ride much nor walk far. It was a still day, even in haying time.

There were few farmers then who regarded labor in the hay-field on the Sabbath as a work of necessity. This idea was of later growth, when farm life on that day began to show greater activity.

How still it was in those old sacred days in the fiery midsummer weather! The church bell rang at ten o'clock, and its notes echoed among the hills and along the valleys. The swarths of cut grass lay as the scythes of the mowers had left them on Saturday. No dinner horn blew; the bells of no bread-cart man came jingling lazily along from house to house; no ox-cart rumbled over the roads.

After church the hired men rested in the half-filled haylofts in the barn or under the shadows of the trees, and, perhaps, discussed the morning sermon, or told the old wonder-tales of the farms and inns. If clouds gathered in the afternoon, the deacon would stand in his door, and shade his eyes, and say, —

"I guess there's goin' to be a shower, and the hay will get a wettin'," and would retire to his lounge with peace of conscience, leaving the ricks and windrows of hay to the mercy of the sky.

It was such a Sabbath afternoon that the Widow Stillwell sat in the door of her cottage, and looked out on the fragrant fields and green woods. Her son, Gideon, or "Gid," as she called him, had just returned from church.

"There's cold victuals on the table, Gid," she said. "The coffee is cold, 'cos I aint goin' to kindle any fire to-day. There's milk and mush and corn' beef, and swamp tarts, and wild strawberries and cream, and that's enough. What did the preacher preach about?"

"Samson!"

"Sho — did he? That was a powerful subject. Where was the text? You tell me, and I 'll find it, and after dinner I 'll talk with you about it, and you must n't go to sleep while your old mother is talkin'. You 'll think of me some day, when I am dead. Where was it, Gid?"

"I don't know where, Mother, but I recollect the words: 'And the Philistines took him and put out his eyes, and brought him down to Gaza, and he did grind in the prison-house.'"

"Good for ye, Gid! What a memory you have got! That does yer old mother's heart good. 'Did grind in the prison-house.' I 'll get the concordance and look it up. You go and get your dinner."

Gideon sat down at a scoured oak-table in the long porch, to a cold Sunday dinner. The door was open, and a hen with a brood of chickens came in, and he fed them.

"What you doin', Gid?"

"Oh, nothin', Mother."

Mrs. Stillwell appeared and saw the hen and chickens, and raised her apron and said, "Shoo;" then added, "'And he did grind in the prison-house;' that 's a mighty improvin' text.

"No matter how good folk a man may have, if he don't do as he ought to do, he will one day find himself at the mill grindin', with his eyes put out. Eh? I 've seen a lot of folks grindin' in my day. Yes, Gid, grindin', grindin', grindin', grindin'.

"Sin puts out the eyes of its servants, and sends them all grindin', grindin', grindin' at the mill, and a sorry spectacle they are at last.

"There 's 'Squire Brown's son; he 's just drinked up his father's farm, and the Philistines have got him; he 's grindin', grindin', grindin'. There 's Ned Gray, he that ran away with the Gratlin gal; he was heady; he 's grindin'. The Philistines have got *him*.

"Gideon, that 's a mighty improvin' text. Be careful that the Philistines don't ever get *you*."

"But, Mother —"

"What, Gid?"

"The parson, he said '*howbeit*.'"

"*Howbeit* what, Gid?"

"'*Howbeit* the hair of his head began to grow after he was shaven.'"

"Yes, but he was n't what he used to be. Don't you ever be a *howbeit* man, Gideon. Have ye eaten all ye want? Well, let us go and set down in the keepin' room, and talk. I 'll wash the dinner dishes to-morrow."

The widow found the text of the sermon in the Book of Judges, and began to give her views upon it. In the midst of a very earnest exhortation she dropped her spectacles and lifted her hands.

"Asleep, Gid? Well, the poor boy has worked hard during the week."

She gazed out of the window under the morning-glories. An old guide-post stood at the corner of the ways.

"Poor boy," she said to herself, "I wonder what course he will take. There are clouds in the sky, and the robins are singin', and I'll go out and see that the cows come up to the apple pasture, so that Gideon will not have to hunt for them if it comes on to rain."

She went out. The clouds passed, and the Sabbath echoed to the golden coronation of a long twilight.

Gideon Stillwell was a bright boy. The widow said that he "favored his father," who came to be at last a justice of the peace. In the Friday evening conference meetings, and at the winter evening debating societies at the school-house, Gideon's voice always awakened expectation, and at the "speaking schools," that held weekly evening sessions at the schoolhouse, he was always received with great cheering when he stepped upon the platform, and honored with greater cheering when he stepped down. At an early age, after attaining his majority, he was elected field-driver and pound-keeper at the town meeting, and at the age of twenty-five he arrived at the high honor of his father, in being made a justice of the peace. These were days that made the widow's heart glad.

But there was a barter store in the neighborhood, where all kinds of commodities were sold, and to this Gideon began to go to spend his evenings, to play checkers and joke and talk. Here he learned to drink liquors and treat and became intimate with some young men who, like the favorite hero of the drinking song of the time, "Rosin the Beau," believed in having a merry time in the world. To use the refrain of one of their songs as a picture: —

> "To-night we'll merry, merry be,
> And to-morrow we'll get sober."

On holidays these jovial fellows became a terror and a nuisance to the community, and they made it a habit to celebrate the evening before the Fourth of July by a frolic, or, as they termed it in country language, by "going off on a spree."

This change of habits led to a great change in Gideon. The community were very charitable towards his weaknesses and lapses, because he was a widow's son, and his father had been a good man, and his own life had opened in such a promising way.

"I'm sorry," said the old parson, "but let us be kindly. He will return to his Father's house again;" and, with this charitable, spiritual figure, he rested the case with hope.

Independence Day, after the victory of Commodore Perry on Lake Erie, was for several years celebrated with great enthusiasm in all American cities and towns. The bands played "The President's March;" floral chariots, with young girls representing goddesses, led triumphal processions; arches spanned the streets, and the country people gathered about the gingerbread-carts in the towns. The nights blazed with bonfires; tar barrels made lurid the sky, and bells and cannon awoke the morn and saluted the sunset. It was a day of fire and noise — the one great day that voiced the exultant political spirit of the time. America stood for liberty in the view of those good times; and liberty was destined to topple all thrones and crumble all crowns, and lead the world to ultimate equality of rights, to a unity of brotherhood and never-ending peace.

The young orator was usually the hero of these unexampled celebrations. He was sometimes a minister, sometimes a lawyer or college student. He usually began his oration with "Ladies and Gentlemen: We have assembled here to commemorate the days on which our fathers fought, bled, and died." Then the eagle began to fly.

Next in honor to the orator was the reader of the Declaration of Independence, who gave that document of Jefferson to the public in an oratorical tone, which was a kind of heroic chant. The grand language, "When, in the course of human events," was thrown on the air like the voice of a trumpet; the arraignment of George III. rose and fell in stately tones, and the effectiveness and eloquence of the reading was a subject of comment for weeks after the event.

It was in one of these grand, patriotic years that Bristol, the town in which the Widow Stillwell and her son lived, had voted at the town meeting to hold a celebration on the coming Fourth of July, and had chosen the then justices of the peace and the old Orthodox clergyman to act as a committee.

The committee appointed the young Episcopal clergyman of the place as orator, and, at the advice of the parson, Gideon Stillwell to read the Declaration of Independence.

A part of the committee made objection to this last nomination.

"Gideon has a grand voice," said the parson.

"But his conduct on past Independence Days has not been an honor to the town," said one. "He carouses."

"This will save him. This will save him," said the old parson. "This

TOMB OF CECILIA METELLA, APPIAN WAY.

honor will go right to his heart, and make a man of him. And," he added kindly, " it will cheer the heart of his mother. The widow is a good woman — a good family; they helped burn the 'Gaspee.'"

This last touch appealed to local patriotism, and the committee unanimously voted that Gideon Stillwell should read the Declaration.

Gideon received this intelligence of this crown of honor with a divided heart. He had spent his evenings much at the store of late, and he and his comrades had agreed to have a frolic on the night of the Fourth, and had formed a strange plan to startle the town.

On the old farms around the town there were, in midsummer, old stacks of hay that had been left over from the foddering seasons. With the exception of the tar-barrel, there is nothing that will fill the sky at night with such a lurid light as the burning of an old haystack. It was the secret plan of the jolly fellows who met at the country store to set fire to all of the old hay-stacks on the farms around the town on the evening of the Fourth, and then to assemble in the old place and enjoy the excitement of the joke, and have a drunken carousal.

If Gideon Stillwell accepted the high honor offered him for the Fourth, he must at once break away from his old comrades and all association with this unlawful escapade.

The sensation of the proposed frolic had been a delightful prospect to Gideon's mind. But the town had appealed to his better nature, pride, and honor. He thought of his mother, his Revolutionary ancestry, and his future; and he accepted the invitation, and began to rehearse the eloquent reading out in the barn and in the woods.

Poor Widow Stillwell used to listen to these rehearsals at the door. She delighted to hear " created free and equal," and " inalienable rights," and " life and liberty and the pursuit of happiness " soaring like eagles over mountain tops into the air. She shut the door softly when " these States are and of a right ought to be free and independent," and sometimes sat down and covered her face with her apron, saying, " Oh, that I should ever be blessed by being the mother of a boy like that ! "

The town of Bristol contained the county jail. In the yard there had been placed a curious machine for the discipline of stubborn prisoners, called a treadmill. Prisoners were not numerous in the county, and there really seemed to be no especial need of this English instrument of torture ; but other officers of prisons were building them to meet the wants of difficult cases, and the officers here were public-spirited men, and did not like to be wanting in any of the improved methods of discipline and compulsory reform.

These treadmills were constructed on the principle of the old-fashioned horsethreshing-machines. The culprit who was placed in one was compelled to tread until he was released.

This clock-work motion soon became very tiresome, painful, and exhausting. The officers of prisons called the discipline "the breaking of the will." Most prisoners so disciplined promised obedience after a very short experience. Of all discouraging inventions to subdue crankiness and perverseness, the treadmill was one of the most effective.

Dr. Oliver Wendell Holmes, in his early years, once wrote a treadmill song, which used to be found in old readers and speakers: —

> "The stars are rolling in the skies,
> The earth rolls on below,
> And we can feel the rattling wheels
> Revolving as we go.
> Then tread away, my gallant boys,
> And make the axle fly;
> Why should not wheels go round about
> Like planets in the sky?"

The treadmill as a prison punishment has long disappeared from penal institutions in England and America.

The evening of the Fourth of July came after a blazing day on the blue bays and green hay-fields. The jolly jokers met early at the store. In an ill-starred moment of weakness Gideon had consented to meet with them, although he had declined to *go* with them. The party were in high spirits, and were enjoying their fun in anticipation.

"Gideon," said one, "go."

"But the reading at the church?"

"No one outside of the party will ever know how you spent the night, and you may be sure that none of us will tell."

"But if we were to be detected? It would ruin my name, and be a disgrace to the town."

"We are not going to be detected."

"I might get over-excited and heated, and drink too much, and that would unfit me for to-morrow."

"We will see to that. We will not let you get drunk."

"I'm heady when I have been drinking; my judgment is warped; I do things that I am sorry for. A little liquor brings out all that is bad in me. When I am half drunk I am fit only for crime. You know how it is. You ought not to tempt me to-night, of all nights. Everything in my life depends upon my keeping straight to-night."

THE BAPTISTERY, DUOMO, AND CAMPANILE OF GIOTTO, FLORENCE.

"But, Gideon, drink a little with jovial comrades."

"Take a little just to wet your whistle," said one.

He did; and then he took a little more to keep it company. Presently he began to grow jovial, and slap his companions on their backs and knees.

He looked out of the door on the green woods that the hills lifted into the air. The moon was rising, shield-like and dusky, like the sun coming up again.

"It's a staver of a night," said he; "just the one for a lark. Boys, I'll go."

The moon rose over the dewy hills and glimmering bays. At about eleven o'clock four great fires, like columns of flame, rose into the air from as many farms. The sky became smoke, then turned into a wannish glare, and the whole heavens seemed to become a sheet of flame.

The church bells in the town began to ring. People rushed out of their houses, both in the town and country. At midnight the whole population was in the streets or roads.

"It is only haystacks," said a fireman on horseback, as he rushed back to the town from the farms.

But a more serious event happened. One of the burning stacks communicated its flames to a large barn, and the burning barn set fire to an old historic farm-house. As soon as the larkers discovered this serious result and began to comprehend that their joke was a crime, they stole back to the store.

The early morning found them here intoxicated, and the selectmen and town constable also found them here. The officers rushed in to arrest them when their eyes fell upon Gideon.

They paused. Their hearts were full of chagrin, mortification, and sorrow.

"We must do our duty," said the constable.

The men were arrested and led amid wondering, humiliated throngs to the county jail.

Once in the jail yard they began to throw off the cloud of drunken stupor, and see their position.

They refused to enter the jail; rough words followed, and then resistance was made to officers, and a fist fight put the custodians of the peace at bay.

The constable sent for help. Strong men came; still the prisoners resisted.

"Force them down, and put them into the treadmill," said the sheriff.

There followed a rough handling of the stack burners, but the officers were soon masters of the place, and the jolly party of the night before found themselves on the revolving cylinder, at the mercy of the common jailer. At the head of this sorry row, who had started a motion that they could not stop, was the appointed reader of the Declaration on this day of national honor, Gideon Stillwell.

The jail yard was surrounded by a fence, and over this the heads of boys began to rise.

"They're in the treadmill. Here's a sight; run, hurry, — oh, oh, they are in the treadmill!"

So shouted a pioneer in the discovery of this strange, odd scene. Boys ran, men ran, and even girls and young women ran, all who could mounted to the top of the fence, some shouting, some jeering, some laughing, and some crying.

The treadmill here was a kind of shed, with stalls for five or six prisoners, and a rail on which the culprits leaned.

If ever a man's face wore an expression of agony, horror, and despair, it was that of Gideon Stillwell on the glowing forenoon of Independence Day. He heard the boys jeering on the fence, and he knew that his disgrace would be the talk of the town for a generation. He could not do anything to mitigate the humiliation of his position.

The high windows and the roofs of the houses around the jail yard filled with people. Gideon heard voices in the air, crackers and horns, and he knew what it meant. But he was in the wheel, and the wheel went round and round, and every revolution made his bones ache and cry out for rest.

One of his fellows began to rail and scold. This caused a great outcry to go up from the fence.

The church bell pealed out on the air. Gideon heard it. It was the bell that he had expected would call him to his place of honor. A boy shouted from the fence, —

"Now, Gideon, give us the Declaration."

At this the boys all along the fence waved their hats and cried, "Three cheers for Independence!"

Another cried, "Three cheers for Washington, Commodore Perry, and Gideon;" which was followed by "Three cheers for Gideon's Band!"

This last volley was repeated amid shouts of laughter. All was excitement, merriment, and sorrow.

Suddenly there fell a silence. The faces were turned backward to the long street, and one boy said, "*She's* coming," and all ceased to jeer. The windows became silent and the housetops. One could hear the robins sing. But the wheel went round.

An old woman on a crutch was coming down the street towards the jail.

All eyes were fixed upon her, and many eyes began to fill with tears. She hobbled slowly along under the elms, her gray hair flying on the light wind out of a funnel-shaped bonnet.

She came up to the fence, and said,—

"Boy, get down, and let *me* see."

The boy addressed dropped upon the ground. The old woman raised herself on her crutch, and slowly lifted her gray head above the fence. There was silence as deep as the air.

Her eyes were dim, but she saw it all. Her gaze was fixed on Gideon, who was near her. And the wheel went round.

"Grindin', Gideon?"

The wheel went round.

"'And the Philistines took him and put out his eyes, and he did grind in the prison-house.' Oh, Gideon, do you remember?"

The wheel went round.

"Gideon, I am in 'the chamber over the gate,' and I wish that I were dead."

The wheel went round.

"Grindin', grindin', grindin'."

The wheel went round.

"Mother?"

"What, Gideon?"

"*Howbeit*, his hair began to grow after he was shaven."

"'*Howbeit?*' Gideon, I will forgive ye. Yer old mother's heart is all that is left you now in the world. When you get through grindin' at the mill in the prison-house, come home, Gideon. I'll mortgage my place, and pay yer fine. And now I'll hobble back and pray. I am all that is left to ye, and God is all that is left to me."

A bell rang. The wheel stopped.

And Gideon — his hair grew again. He lived down his disgrace and became a worthy citizen, and was forgiven by the kind community.

He and his old mother sleep among the slated memorials of the old churchyard near the green, under the elms, where the orioles sing in the summertime.

THE CAMPAGNA.

CHAPTER XIV.

RIENZI, THE LAST OF THE ROMAN TRIBUNES.[1]

> Then turn we to her latest tribune's name,
> From her ten thousand tyrants turn to thee,
> Redeemer of dark centuries of shame,
> The friend of Petrarch, hope of Italy, —
> Rienzi, last of Romans! While the tree
> Of freedom's wither'd trunk puts forth a leaf,
> Even for thy tomb a garland let it be —
> The forum's champion and the people's chief,
> Her newborn Numa thou!
>
> BYRON.

LONG the banks of the Tiber, not far from that part of its course which sweeps by the base of Mount Aventine, a remote and tranquil path wound its leafy way. At a distance could be seen the scattered and squalid houses that bordered the river, from amid which rose the dark high roofs and enormous towers of the fortified mansions of some Roman barons. On the one side the river, behind the cottages of the fishermen, rose Mount Janiculum, dark with massive foliage, from which gleamed the gray walls of many a palace and the spires and columns of a hundred churches; on the other side, the deserted Aventine rose abrupt and steep, covered with thick brushwood; while on the height rolled the sound of the holy convent bell.

[1] I am indebted for this chapter to Miss Florence A. Blanchard.

On a summer evening in the earlier half of the fourteenth century, two youths might have been seen walking through this secluded path. The elder of the young men, who might have passed his twentieth year, was of a tall and even commanding stature. His countenance, handsome though rather thoughtful in expression, was lighted by a wonderful smile. The younger, who was yet a boy, with an expression of great sweetness and gentleness, listened with tender deference to his companion, who talked of the uncertain future and built up his castles of the air, and we hear him say, "But you, sweet brother, though you share not my studies, sympathize with all their results so kindly — you seem so to approve my wild schemes and to encourage my ambitious hopes — that sometimes I forget our birth, our fortunes, and think and dare as if no blood save that of the noblest flowed through our veins."

As they talked a vessel was speeding rapidly down the river, and some three or four armed men on deck were intently surveying the quiet banks on either side, as if anticipating a foe. The bark soon glided out of sight, and the brothers continued their dreams of the future.

As the evening darkened they began hastily to retrace their steps, when the elder remembered that he was to call that evening at the convent for a rare manuscript that had been promised him. Bidding his brother "tarry here a few minutes," he hastened up the Aventine to the convent.

Left to himself, the lad thought over all the stories of ancient Rome which his brother had told him in their walk, as he gathered flowers for his sister and wove them into garlands.

While thus engaged the tramp of horses and the loud shouting of men were heard at a distance. They came nearer and nearer, — a gallant company, their steeds superbly caparisoned. They were all armed, both cavalry and foot-soldiers.

A momentary fear crossed the boy's mind, but it was already too late to flee, — the train was upon him.

Questioning the boy concerning the vessel which had gone down the river in the early evening, they placed him in the thickest of the crowd, and dragged him along with the rest, lest he should prove traitor, and alarm the Colonna.

A winding in the road brought suddenly before them the object of their pursuit; but pushing forward in their eagerness to intercept her, they came upon a small compact body of horsemen, armed cap-à-pie, who dashed from amid the trees and charged into the ranks of the pursuers.

The contest was short and fierce, bringing success to the Colonna. The Orsini turned to fly. Among those who fled onward, in the very path of the horsemen, was the young lad. Fast he fled, and fast behind him came the tramp of the hoofs — the shouts. He was now at the spot where his brother had left him; despairingly he looked up, and, behold! his brother rushing through the tangled brakes.

"Save me, save me, Brother!" he shrieked; a moment more he fell to the ground — a corpse.

The horsemen passed on to new victims. Cola had descended, and was kneeling by his murdered brother.

Presently the advanced guard of the Colonna came by, whose chief in response to Rienzi's impassioned plea for "justice! justice!" promised him that the death of his brother should be avenged. Unfortunately, the cavalier who had murdered the boy proved to be one of the Colonna, and the promise made by Lord Colonna was broken.

The company passed back the way they had come, leaving Rienzi motionless beside his dead brother. His thoughts were dark and stern, — "thoughts in which were the germ of a mighty revolution."

"From that bloody clay Cola di Rienzi rose a new being. With his younger brother died his own youth. But for that event the future liberator of Rome might have been but a dreamer, a scholar, a poet, — the peaceful rival of Petrarch, a man of thoughts, not deeds. But from that time all his faculties, energies, fancies, genius, became con-

THE AVENTINE.

centrated to a single point; and patriotism, before a vision, leaped into the life and vigor of a passion, lastingly kindled, stubbornly hardened, and awfully consecrated — by revenge."

Years passed away. The fame and fortunes of Rienzi were growing amid all the civil strife and contention with which Rome was torn. Her ancient glory had departed. Barbarian tribes had forced their settlements into the city of the Cæsars. The degenerate Roman population possessed all the insolent and unruly turbulence which characterized the plebs of the ancient forum, without any of their virtues. They were ferocious but not brave. The nobles supported themselves as relentless banditti.

For nearly forty years Rome had been deserted by the popes; she had ceased to be the religious capital of the world. The shrines and the reliques of the great apostles and the famous old churches, the Lateran, St. Peter, and St. Paul, were still there; some few pilgrims came from all parts of Europe to the city still hallowed by these sacred monuments. But the tide of homage and tribute which had flowed for centuries toward the shrine of the successors of Saint Peter had now taken another course. Pope Clement VI., more prudent than courageous, had made Avignon, a luxurious town of a foreign prince, the court of the Roman pontiff and the throne of the Christian church.

Rome, thus degraded from her high ecclesiastical position, would welcome with redoubled energy whatever might recall her ancient supremacy. Now republican and now imperial Rome threw off with disdain the thraldom of the papal dominion. The consul Crescentius, the senator Brancaleone, Arnold of Brescia, the Othos, the Fredericks, Henry of Luxemburg, Louis of Bavaria, had all been actors in the drama which proclaimed Rome a new world-ruling republic or a new world-ruling empire.

Despite their retrogression, the Romans still possessed the sense and the desire of liberty. For the last two centuries they had known various revolutions,—brief, often bloody, and always unsuccessful. Yet the empty form of a popular government existed.

Holding their palaces as the castles and fortresses of princes, each asserting his own independence of all authority and law, the barons of Rome made their estate still more secure, and still more odious to the people by the maintenance of troops of foreign (chiefly German) mercenaries, against whom the Italians were no match in discipline and skill.

Of these barons the most powerful were the Orsini and Colonna. Their feuds wer hereditary and incessant; and not a sun set but that the gathering darkness covered the fruits of their lawless warfare, in bloodshed, in rape, and in conflagration.

From these multiplied oppressors the Roman citizens turned with fond and impatient regret to their ignorant and dark notions of departed liberty and greatness. They confounded together the times of the empire and those of the republic; vainly imagining that if both the emperor and the pontiff fixed their residence in Rome, liberty and law would again seek shelter in the city of the seven hills.

Following in the wake of the barons was a crowd of lesser robbers; and more formidable than either were the free-booters, companies of Germans organized for the purpose of shameless pillaging, joined by Romans.

In the year 1343, among the delegates of the people sent on the public mission to Clement VI. at Avignon, was Cola di Rienzi, a son of a Roman innkeeper and a washerwoman, born at Rome, 1313, in a quarter of the city which was inhabited only by mechanics and Jews.

His early youth was passed at Anagni. When about twenty, he returned to Rome and embraced the profession of a notary. But his chief occupation was pouring over those sacred antiquities of Rome, which exercised so powerful an influence on his mind. The first

ST. PAUL BASILICA.

dawn of those classical studies had already been publically welcomed in the coronation of Petrarch. The respect for the ancient monuments of Rome and for her famous writers became a part of Rienzi's soul. His favorite authors were Livy, Cicero, Seneca, Valerius Maximus; but "the magnificent deeds and words of the great Cæsar were his chief delight."

He contrasted the miserable and servile state of his countrymen with that of their free and glorious ancestors. "Where are those old Romans? where their justice? Would that I had lived in their times!" The sense of personal wrong in the murder of his brother was wrought up with his more lofty and patriotic feelings. He had vowed vengeance for the innocent blood. Already had he assumed the office of champion of the poor.

As a result of the embassy to Avignon, the pope granted the jubilee of the fiftieth year, to be held in Rome; and he also promised when the affairs of Rome should permit, to revisit the city.

On Rienzi's return to Rome he heard it openly whispered that the nobles were supported and cherished by the pope himself, that they waged wars with money from the treasuries of the church.

The growing discontent grew more and more outspoken. More and more daring grew the robberies by the nobles. In the streets hand-to-hand fights were frequent. In the times of their greatest disturbances, the one person in Rome who could control the people was Rienzi, who calmed the present by the promise of the future.

Despairing of all alleviation of the calamities of the people from the ecclesiastical power, Rienzi brooded over his hopes of reawakening the old Roman spirit of liberty. He proceeded with wonderful courage and resolution, submitting to every kind of indignity, and assuming every disguise which might advance his end. The worst tyrants with whom he had to deal were no frank and open foes, but men of "shifts and wiles, the subtlest and most deceitful."

Once in his indignation he was betrayed into a premature appeal to the yet unawakened sympathies of the people. The only answer was a blow from a Norman kinsman of the Colonnas; in the simple language of the historian, "a box on the ear that rang again."

Nightly meetings were held on the Aventine (he may have learned from Livy the secession of the people to that hill), where he addressed the people with earnest eloquence, which grew more and more impassioned as their sympathies were awakened.

Allegorical picture was the language of the times. The church had long used it to teach Christian truth. Political purposes had been consummated by it. It was the familiar language of the whole people.

Rienzi seized upon the unrestricted freedom of painting. All historians have dwelt on the masterpiece of his pictorial eloquence, "which, when the people saw, every one marvelled."

"On a sinking ship, without mast or sail, sat a noble lady, in widow's weeds, with dishevelled hair and her hands crossed over her breast. Above was written, 'This is Rome.' She was surrounded by four other ships, in which sat women, who personated Babylon, Carthage, Tyre, and Jerusalem. 'Through unrighteousness,' ran the legend, 'these fell to ruin.' An inscription hung above: 'Thou, O Rome, art exalted above all; we await thy downfall.' Three islands appeared beside the ship; in one was Italy, in another four of the cardinal virtues, in the third Christian faith. Each had its appropriate inscription. Over faith was written 'O highest Father, Ruler and Lord, when Rome sinks, where find I refuge?' Bitter satire was not wanting. Four rows of winged beasts stood above, who blew their horns and directed their pitiless storm against the sinking vessel. The lions, wolves, and bears denoted, as the legend explained, the mighty barons and traitorous senators; the dogs, the swine, and the bulls were the counsellors, the base partisans of the nobles; the sheep, the serpents, and the foxes were the officers, the false judges, and notaries; the hares, cats, goats, and apes, the robbers, murderers, adulterers, thieves, among the people. Above was 'God in His majesty come

SQUARE OF THE CAPITOL, ROME.

down to judgment, with two swords, as in the Apocalypse, out of his mouth.' Saint Peter and Saint Paul were beneath, on either side, in the attitude of supplication."

The morning of the 19th of May, 1347, saw the beginning of the end. The Colonna barons were absent from the city. Rienzi's hour had come.

Over the city brooded a deep silence. The streets were deserted. The shops were but half-open. Toward noon a few small knots of men might be seen scattered about here and there, whispering to each other, but soon dispersing. Suddenly there was heard the sound of *a single trumpet*.

Slowly about the streets paced *a solitary horseman*, winding a long, loud blast of the trumpet suspended round his neck as he passed. Suddenly, as if by magic, the streets became thronged with multitudes — multitudes who broke the silence only by the tramp of their feet and an indistinct low murmur. The Romans were convened for the morrow, at dawn of day, to provide for the good estate of Rome. The call came from Rienzi. This was the commencement of the revolution.

All that night Rienzi was hearing, in the church of St. Angelo, the thirty masses of the Holy Ghost.

On the morrow —

"The Soul of the Past, again
To its ancient home,
In the hearts of Rome,
Hath come to resume its reign."

At ten in the morning he came forth in full armor: by his side the pope's vicar, Raimond, Bishop of Orvieto, and surrounded by a guard of horsemen. Amidst thronging multitudes he ascended the capitol. The laws of the good estate were read. They contained the wild justice of the wild times. The senators were dismissed; the people shouted their approval. Rienzi was invested with dictatorial power — power over life and limb, power to pardon, power to establish the good estate in Rome and her domain. A few days later he took the title of tribune,— an office which had been vacant for more than five hundred years.

The Colonna nobles returned. They all looked on in wondering apathy. All the Colonnas, the Orsini, the Savelli, were compelled to yield up their fortress palaces, to make oath that they would protect no robbers or malefactors, to keep the roads secure, to supply provisions to the city, to appear in arms or without at the summons of the magistracy. All orders took the same oath; they swore to maintain the laws of the good estate.

"Never, perhaps," says Gibbon, "has the energy and effect of a single mind been more remarkably felt than in the sudden, though transient, reformation of Rome by the tribune Rienzi."

A den of robbers was converted to the discipline of a camp or convent. After the death of Orsini, the chief of that tribe of nobles, none who were "conscious of guilt could hope for impunity; and the flight of the wicked, the licentious, and the idle, soon purified the city and the territory of Rome."

In this time (writes the historian) the woods began to rejoice that they were no longer infected with robbers; the oxen began to plow; the pilgrims visited the sanctuaries; the roads and inns were replenished with travellers; trade, plenty, and good faith were restored in the markets; and a purse of gold might be exposed in the highway without danger. Her fame spread. Supreme tribunal and confederate union of the Italian republic might have healed their intestine discord and closed the Alps against the barbarians.

"But the varnish of power brings forth at once the defects and beauties of the human mind." The leap of an hour from a citizen to a prince, from the victim of oppression to the dispenser of justice, is dangerous in proportion to the imagination, the enthusiasm, the genius of the man. The qualities that make him rise hurry him to his fall. The great misfortune of a man nobler than his age is, "the instruments he must use soil himself; half he reforms his times; but half, too, the times will corrupt the reformer."

Rienzi did not so much acquire new qualities as develop in greater contrast those which he already had exhibited. Prosperity made more apparent his justice, his integrity, his patriotism, his virtue, and his genius; but it also brought to light more conspicuously his arrogant superiority, his love of display, and his daring ambition.

He was faithful to his idol of liberty. Even his enemies admitted that. His pomp was the custom of the age. His gorgeous festivals increased the importance of the tribune abroad. Taste grew refined, and foreigners from all states were attracted by the splendor of his court. "And often since then it has been recalled with a sigh by the poor for its justice, the merchant for its security, the gallant for its splendor, the poet for its ideal and intellectual grace."

The secret of much of his greatness, many of his errors, was his great religious enthusiasm. Had there been a brave, intelligent people to back him, Italy's thraldom would have closed; and the bright dream which every great Italian has dreamed from Dante to Mazzini — the unity of Italy and the supremacy of Rome — would have been realized.

But the barons were revolving projects for the restoration of their own power. Incited by the pope, who was jealous of Rienzi, they moved from Palestrina, November 30, and encamped before Rome. A fierce conflict was fought all that day. At eve the battle ceased. Of the barons, who had been the main object of the tribune's assault, the pride and boast was broken; but the slaughter of the citizens had been tremendous.

Needing money constantly to repulse the nobles, Rienzi levied taxes in a tyrannical way. The people rebelled. The pope saw his opportunity, and threatened him with excommunication on the charge of heresy. His followers deserted him in large numbers. He lost heart, and, lacking the daring recklessness which would have held his power, he resigned the office which had been his for seven months, and took refuge in the castle St. Angelo, a Franciscan convent of the Apennines, Dec. 15, 1347, where he remained for two and one half years.

He had reared his edifice on a quicksand, — the Roman people.

HOUSE OF COLA DI RIENZI.

Their passion of virtue had been too violent to last. The virtues of old Rome — frugality, fortitude, love of order, respect for law, — were virtues of slow growth. They had been depressed too long, too low; they were fierce and fickle.

The two years and one-half following his resignation were one long tale of deep and dire disaster to the people. The nobles were again in power. Fires followed earthquakes — the dangers of both were small compared with the power of that terrible scourge, the Black Plague.

In the year of jubilee Rome swarmed with pilgrims. Rienzi stole in in disguise. On his return to the convent, he was induced by the hermit Fra Angelo to undertake a mission to the Emperor Charles IV. for the good of mankind, by the restoration of the power of the emperors. The mission was unsuccessful. He was imprisoned by Charles, at the command of the pope, and sent to Avignon.

After a time interest was again aroused in him. Petrarch even ventured to write to Rome to urge the intercession of the people in his behalf.

In 1354 he was sent to Rome, with the title of senator, by the pope, who proposed to use the talents he possessed for the restoration of order in the capital. Before the end of the year he was killed in an assault upon the capitol, by the people whose defiance was again aroused against him. Disguised as a shepherd, he slipped into the crowd, but, recognized by the golden bracelets which he had forgotten to remove, he was stabbed with a thousand wounds, Sept. 8. 1354. For two days his body was exposed to the assault and indignities of the people, and then burned.

"I loved his virtues, I praised his design; I congratulated Italy; I looked forward to the dominion of the beloved city and the peace of the world."[1]

THE ROMAN HYMN OF LIBERTY.[2]

"Let the mountains exult around!"
On her seven hill'd throne renowned,
Once more old Rome is crown'd.
    Jubilate!

Sing out, O vale and wave;
Look out from each laurell'd grave,
Bright dust of the deathless brave.
    Jubilate!

Pale vision, what art thou? Lo!
From time's dark deeps,
Like a wind it sweeps,
Like a wind when the tempests blow:
A shadowy form, as a giant ghost.
It stands in the midst of the arméd host, —
The dead man's shroud on its awful limbs;
And the gloom of its presence the daylight dims:

---

[1] Petrarch.   [2] Sung at the triumph of Rienzi.

And the trembling world looks on aghast —
All hail to the *Soul of the Mighty Past!*
    Hail! all hail!

As we speak, as we hallow, it moves, it breathes;
From its clouded crest bud the laurel wreaths;
As a sun that leaps up from the arms of night,
The shadow takes shape and the gloom takes light;
    'Hail! all hail!

  The *Soul of the Past*, again
   To its ancient home,
   In the hearts of Rome,
  Hath come to resume its reign.

O Fame, with a prophet's voice,
Bid the ends of the earth rejoice,
Wherever the proud are strong,
And right is oppress'd by wrong,
Wherever the day dim shines
Through the cell where the captive pines:
Go forth, with a trumpet's sound,
And tell to the nations round —
On the hills which the heroes trod,
In the shrines of the saints of God,
In the Cæsars' hall and the martyrs' prison —
That the slumber is broke and the sleeper arisen;
That the reign of the Goth and the Vandal is o'er,
And earth feels the tread of *the Roman* once more!

           LYTTON.

CHAPTER XV.

NAPLES.—ROMAN FAIRY TALES.—THE STORY OF SORDELLO.

HE white city of Naples rises over the blue sea, under a sky all sun and cerulean; and Vesuvius rises over the city, serene and cloudless, except a pearly column of smoke fading in air. The Bay of Naples, with its margin of villas and gardens, is one of the most beautiful in the world. Any one who has seen it will dream of it ever after.

> " My soul to-day
> Is far away,
> Sailing on the Vesuvian bay."

Naples is a picture. It is a city of palaces, churches, and gardens, a little more than one hundred miles from Rome, with which it connects by railway.

Our travellers, with Mr. Ware make one or two visits to Rome from Brindisi. They found the city almost deserted by travellers, and to be hot and presumably unhealthy. There were improvements making in the harbor of Brindisi, and they feared malaria as a consequence. So Mr. Van der Palm, Percy, and Mr. Ware thought it well to go to Naples, and to secure there one of the cool villas overlooking the sea. This they did; and established themselves on one of the hills near the city of palaces, in the clear, cool, and delicious atmosphere. They could now go to Rome and return in a single day.

Story-telling began again in the gardens of the Neapolitan villa. Mr. Van der Palm drew around him his usual consular company, and these were pleased to relate stories of the ports.

Mr. Ware interested Percy in the old fairy tales of Rome. Such tales were usually associated with the Lar, which was the house spirit, or with the Lares and Penates, the household gods.

OLD ENTRANCE TO NATIONAL VILLA, NAPLES.

In old Roman days each hearth had its guardian spirit. The beautiful old stories of Rome were thus full of fairy-land.

Let me give you one of these stories as related to Percy by good Mr. Ware, who lived in ancient Rome in his imagination on the old New England parsonage farm.

THE POT OF GOLD.

In every Roman household, a sort of familiar spirit, or Lar Familiaris, was supposed to reside, having his own little altar near the family hearth, and whose business it was to look after the family fortunes.

The Lar of whom this story tells, presided over an establishment whose owners for a generation had been misers.

Shortly before the grandfather died he had buried under the hearth a

NAPLES AND MOUNT VESUVIUS.

"pot of gold," intrusting the secret only to the house spirit, and praying the Lar to see to its safe keeping.

The son was rather worse than the father, making fewer sacrifices to the Lar than the old man had done. The Lar saw no good reason for discovering the secret to *him*.

The grandson, Euclio, was as bad as either father or grandfather, neglecting the Lar and his own family.

But he had a beautiful daughter who was constantly paying the Lar little attentions, bringing incense, and wine, and garlands, to decorate his altar.

The Lar loved her, and pondered on what he could do to make her happy. She will be expecting a husband soon: the family guardian made his selection for her, — Lyconides, nephew to one of their neighbors, Megadorus.

As the Lar had some good reason to know that the young man would not be acceptable to her father, he contrived that the uncle should ask the girl in marriage for himself, and afterward resign in his nephew's favor.

The miser Euclio knew not how to provide a marriage dowry for his daughter. "Now," the Lar thought, "my opportunity has come;" and he made known to the father the secret of the buried treasure, hoping that out of it he would provide a dowry for the young girl.

But the poor Lar was disappointed, for Euclio had no intention of using the gold in that way or in any other. It became at once his one delight and his perpetual torment. He was in continual terror lest its hiding-place should be discovered. Every noise he heard, he fancied some one was carrying off his treasure. His poor old housekeeper, Staphyla, led a wretched life from his unceasing worry. No offerings were now made to the unhappy Lar.

One day old Megadorus came to ask the hand of his daughter.

"He wants her for the money," he said to himself.

His terrors grew greater and greater. He suspected every one of being a thief. At last, under protest that he was a very poor man, he consented to give Megadorus his daughter. The latter believed him, but was prepared to take her without a dowry; he will even provide out of his own purse all the expenses of the wedding-feast, and will send to the house of Euclio both the provisions and the cooks required for the occasion.

But the cooks are another source of agony to the miser. One of them called for a "larger pot:" he is *sure* they know his secret.

One day he found a cock scratching about the house; he *knew* the newcomers had trained *him* to discover the buried treasure, and in his anger he killed the poor bird.

And last he drove the cooks off the premises under a shower of blows, and digging up his gold, concealed it under his cloak. Then his peril was greater than before; so, carrying the pot of gold to the Temple of Faith, he placed it under that goddess's protection.

Discovering that this proceeding had been watched by a slave of Megadorus, Euclio took the treasure from the temple and buried it in a sacred grove. The slave was more successful this time; he was hidden in

THE AQUARIUM, NAPLES.

the tree beneath which the gold was buried, and when Euclio was gone, he unearthed the pot, and carried it off rejoicing.

The discovery of his loss drove the miser frantic. He is represented in an old play as saying, —

"I'm ruined, dead, murdered! Where shall I run? Where shall I not run to? Stop him there, stop him! Stop whom? Who's to stop him? I can't tell, I can see nothing, I'm going blind. Where I'm going, or where I am, or who I am, I cannot for my life be sure of. Oh, pray, I beseech you, help me! I implore you, do! Show me the man that stole it. Ah! people put on respectable clothes, and sit there as if they were all honest. What did you say, sir? I can believe *you*, I'm sure — I can see from your looks you're an honest man. What is it? Why do you all laugh? Ah, I know you all! There are thieves here, I know, in plenty. Eh! have none of them got it? I'm a dead man! Tell me, then, who's got it. You don't know? Oh, wretch, wretch that I am! — utterly lost and ruined. Never was man in such miserable plight. Oh, what groans, what horrible anguish this day has brought me! — poverty and hunger. I'm the most unhappy man on earth. For what use is life to me when I have lost all my gold? And I kept it so carefully, — pinched myself, starved myself, denied myself in everything. And now others are making merry over it, — mocking at my loss and my misery. I cannot bear it!"

In the midst of the miser's terror there came to him handsome young Lyconides, the nephew whom the house spirit designed that the lovely daughter should marry. He confessed that his uncle had been courting the girl for *him*, and that he himself had stolen his daughter's affections.

The old man cared nothing for his daughter's affections, but only the lost pot of gold.

Lyconides promised to go in search of the gold. The thief proved to be the slave of his uncle.

Euclio gave his daughter to Lyconides; and the pot of gold was her marriage dowry.

Every one was delighted; the beautiful daughter was happy, and the Lar could dance again on the hearth, rejoicing in the gifts with which on family days, holidays, and the Saturnalia he found his altar loaded.

TWELVE FEET OF NOSE.

THE QUEEREST OF THE ROMAN FAIRY TALES.

THERE was once an old father. His last sickness came. He had three sons, and he called them about his bed to make his will.

"I am about to leave this world of trouble," he said. "I have no gold to leave you, but I have three gifts for you that have magic power. I give to you," he continued, addressing the eldest, "this old hat."

"But what good will it do me, Father?"

"As often as you put it on it will make you invisible."

To his second son he said, "I give you this purse."

"But, Father, it is old and empty."

"Yes, but as often as you put your thumb and finger into it, you will find a scudo there."

To his third son he said, "I leave to you this horn."

"But what good will it do me, Father? It is only empty air to toot a horn."

"As often as you sound that horn, my son, it will bring you whatever you wish."

"And now," continued the old man, "you are all well provided for. Let no man rob you of these things, and you will all be prosperous and happy.

The magic One will ever be at your call." And he turned his face to the wall and died.

The eldest brother went one day to the palace, and found that the queen was fond of cards.

"Go play with the queen," he said to his second brother. "You have the purse that never fails."

The young man went. The queen beat him at the game, but said, —

"You are poor; I will not demand payment of you."

MONUMENT OF VICO, NAPLES.

"But I have money at my command. I have only to do this, and the One will come." And he opened the purse, and took out fifty scudi.

"That is a strange purse," said the queen. "Let me look at it."

He gave it to her to examine, and as often as she put her thumb and finger into it she found a scudo there.

"Give it to me," said the queen.

"I cannot; 't was my father's last gift."

"Then I will keep it;" and she called the guard to lead the young man out of the palace.

He went home and told his brother how he had been treated.

"I will go to the palace and recover the purse," said the eldest.

So he put on his magic hat and went to the palace. He demanded of the queen the return of the purse.

"Who are you to command me?" said the queen.

"I can make myself invisible," said the young man.

"How?"

"By this magic hat."

"Let me look at it."

He showed her how as often as he put it on he became invisible, and when he took it off, he appeared again.

"That is very strange," said the queen. "I wonder if it would make me invisible; let me see."

The youth handed her the hat. She put it on and disappeared. He could not find her anywhere; but the same guard came to him as had seized his brother, and led him out of the palace.

He went home sorrowful, and told his two brothers what had befallen him.

"I will go to the palace with my horn," said the third brother, "and will recover both the hat and the purse."

So he went to the palace and blew his horn, and summoned the One. "An army," he said; and an army came.

The queen was terribly frightened. She called the youngest brother to her and said, "How did you get your army?"

"With this horn."

"It would be a good thing for me to have. Let me blow it, only just once."

He handed her the horn. She blew it, and the One came with magic power.

"Let the guard appear," she said.

The guard appeared as before, and led the young man out of the palace, and the queen now possessed the purse, the hat, and the horn.

The three brothers were now woful and poor, but the One did not fail them in their need.

The youngest brother one day being very hungry came to a wonderful fig-tree, and began to eat the figs; but every fig that he ate caused his nose to grow a foot in length. His nose became so long that it reached to the ground, and he did not know what to do. He went to a cherry-tree and began to eat cherries. Every cherry that he swallowed caused his nose to shorten, and at last it was as before.

"I will go and sell some of these figs to the queen," he said. "I will see how she will look then."

So he went under the palace windows and cried, "Figs." The queen purchased a basketful and ate twelve, and her nose became twelve feet long, so that it dragged on the ground.

"And now I appear as a doctor," said the youth.

"I would give half of my kingdom to be cured," said the queen.

"Give me only the hat, purse, and horn, and I can cure you if I will," said the youth.

The queen restored to him the cap, purse, and horn.

"But I will *not*," said the youth. "You shall reap as you have sown. Wear your nose as a warning." And he put on the hat and was invisible; he blew the horn, and was borne away from the palace; and he went home, and they had a feast out of the magic purse.

They never parted with their treasures after that; and the One always came when wanted.

As for the poor queen, she dragged about the twelve feet of nose until her dying day; and no one would marry her, as we may imagine; and we hope that no one in her kingdom ever dared to be greedy or insincere again, with such an awful warning before him. Think of a queen with twelve feet of nose; but however badly she may have looked, she appeared no worse than do others who have been deformed in character by selfishness and insincerity.

The company made a study of Browning in their villa. The poems of Browning are like a guide-book in Italy.

Among these poems was "Sordello." The poem was written by Browning in his early life, and was greatly ridiculed at the time of its appearance for its supposed obscurity. It is stated that Tennyson said of it, "There were only two lines in it that I could understand, and they were both lies. The first was—

"'Who will may hear Sordello's story told.' And the other—

"'Who would *has* heard Sordello's story told.'"

What was Sordello's story?

Percy undertook the study of the poem. His first efforts to interpret it were not satisfactory. He read it a second time with a daughter of one of the consuls, named Blanche.

"How do you understand it?" he asked of her one evening at Naples.

"It represents a life of good inspirations ruined for a time by vanity, but made noble in the end by the return of the first inspiration," said the girl. "Sordello in his years of opportunity thought more of receiving praise for his work than of the work itself."

"It then represents a lost opportunity?" said Percy.

"But Sordello saved himself at the end. These poems of Browning," added Blanche, "make me feel as though I were near the judgment day. When I read 'Sordello,' I find myself continually asking myself if I am living a true and sincere life."

"You are not the first person who has been troubled over 'Sordello,'" said Blanche. "Let me tell you an incident related in Powell's "Living Authors of England."

Blanche gave the incident from the book, which is as follows:

"Douglas Jerrold was recruiting himself at Brighton after a long illness. In the progress of his convalescence a parcel arrived from London, which contained, among other things, this new volume of 'Sordello.' The medical attendant had forbidden Mr. Jerrold the luxury of reading; but owing to the absence of his conjugal 'life-guards,' he indulged in the illicit enjoyment. A few lines put Jerrold in a state of alarm. Sentence after sentence brought no consecutive thought to his brain. At last the idea crossed his mind that in his illness his mental faculties had been wrecked. The perspiration rolled from his forehead; and smiting his head, he sat down in his sofa, crying, 'O God, I *am* an idiot!' When his wife and sister came, they were amused by his pushing the volume into their hands, and demanding what they thought of it. He watched them intently while they read. At last his wife said, 'I don't understand what the man means; it is gibberish.' The delighted humorist sank in his seat again: 'Thank God, I am *not* an idiot.' Mr. Browning, to whom we told this, has often laughed over it; and then endeavored to show that 'Sordello' was the clearest and most simple poem in the English language. This experience it was, perhaps, which made Jerrold say of Browning's style, that he 'wrote Greek in shorthand.'"

"Carlyle," said Blanche, "once wrote, 'My wife has read through "Sordello" without being able to make out whether Sordello was a man, a city, or a book.' Poor Jane Carlyle."

"Suppose you make an analysis of the poem," said Percy, "and give it to me; then I will try to read it again."

Blanche wrote out an analysis, having studied Mrs. Dall and other works, and combining all of the authorities she could find on the subject, and quoting much from the poem itself. The result was as follows: —

THE LEGEND OF SORDELLO.[1]

"Who wills may hear Sordello's story told:
. . . .
Sordello, compassed murkily about
With ravage of six long, sad hundred years."

The thirteenth century was remarkable for its brilliant virtues and atrocious crimes. Men lived on no medium ground; they were either heroes or monsters. The Crusades, which for two centuries had kept all Europe in a tumult, were drawing to a close. Attended by all the disorder, license, and crime with which war is always accompanied, they were nevertheless productive of much lasting good in the progress of civilization. Three direct results were noticeable. Feudalism received its death-blow. By its fall the kings and the people came into prominence. The wealth of the church had been increased, and the power of the papacy had been strengthened. A fierce struggle between the church and the empire — the struggle between religious and secular authority — had long been raging. The Guelfs fought for the church and the people; the Ghibellines fought for the emperor, opposing the rule of the church in secular matters.

"The strife in the reign of Frederick II. was not," says Dean Milman, "for any specific point in dispute, like the right of investiture, but avowedly for supremacy on one side, which hardly deigned to call itself independence; for independence on the other, which, remotely at least, aspired after supremacy. Cæsar would bear no superior, the successor of Saint Peter no equal."

In the midst of the din of political turmoil, the smoke of war and intrigue,

[1] I am indebted to Miss Florence A. Blanchard, a young teacher and author, for this elegant analysis.

THE LEGEND OF SORDELLO

at the very close of the twelfth century, the hero of our story, Sordello, named now with only one name — that of Dante — was born.

The biographical difficulties which surround him are too numerous to mention, and too conflicting to be unravelled. Little is now known about him and that little is much obscured by tradition and legend. Two persons may have been mixed together in the accounts given of him. One of these persons was a poet, and the other was a man of action and political intrigue.

"He was plainly a distinguished person in his time, a cunning craftsman in the choice and use of language ; but if this was all, his name would only rank with a number of others, famous in their time, but under the cloud of greater successors. He may have been something more than a poet: he may have been a ruler, though that is doubtful. But we know him, because in the antechamber of purgatory he was so much to Dante." [1]

> "Nothing whatever did it say to us,
>   But let us go our way, eying us only
>   After the manner of a couchant lion :
> Still near to it Virgilius drew, entreating
>   That it would point us out the best ascent ;
>   And it replied not unto his demand,
> But of our native land and of our life
>   It questioned us : and the sweet guide began :
>   'Mantua,' — and the shade, all in itself recluse,
> Rose towards him from the place where first it was,
>   Saying : 'O Mantuan, I am Sordello.
>   Of thine own land !' and one embraced the other."

"He leads his companions to the secret and guarded valley where kings and princes of the earth, who have meant to do their duty, but in the end have not fulfilled their trust, must wait outside of purgatory the hour of mercy: when Dante sees their still sadness, and learns their names, and hears their evening hymns. And here we learn Dante's judgment on Sordello himself; he is placed among those who had great opportunities and great thoughts, — the men of great chances and great failures." [2]

Six hundred years ago the river Mincio formed around Mantua a great marsh, which separated the city from the low mountains, covered with firs, larches, and rings of vineyard. Among these mountains stood Goito. —

> "Just a castle built amid
> A few low mountains."

[1] Church. [2] Church.

Pass within. You wander through "a maze of corridors contrived for sin," and on through "dusk winding stairs," through "dim galleries," till at last "you gain the inmost chambers, gain at last a maple-panelled room." A sunbeam floats about the panel, and in its golden light the graven characters unfold "the Arab's wisdom everywhere." But the main wonder is a vault, and in its midst —

"A dullish gray-streaked cumbrous font."

Four shrinking Caryatides encircle it.

For many a year, every evening just at sunset, a slender boy, in a loose page's dress, emerged from the castle to sit in turn beside each one of the patient, marble girls who crouched beneath the font, and prayed that they might win pardon for the sins for which he fancied them to be doing penance in stone.

"'T is autumn." With an earnest smile he watched the noisy flock of thievish birds at work among the yellowing vineyards.

"'T is winter, with its sullenest of storms." Lifting a light with both hands to the embroidered forms of the arras, he studied the proud barons and fair dames of the house of Romano, the ancestors of Ecelin da Romano, surnamed il Monaco, a Ghibelline prince, whose wife Adelaide was mistress of Goito. He turns away. Yourself shall trace the delicate nostril, the sharp and restless lip, the calm brow; and you can believe —

> "Sordello foremost in the regal class,
> Nature has broadly severed from her mass
> Of men, and framed for pleasure."

> "Who will may hear Sordello's story told,
> And how he never could remember when
> He dwelt not at Goito."

To the world he was known only as the orphan child of El Corte, an archer who, soon after the lad's birth, in 1194, when the imperialists were driven out of Vicenza amid great slaughter and conflagration, had laid down his own life in saving his mistress, Adelaide, and her new-born son, afterward famous as Ecelin the Cruel.

Calmly his youth glided away. Beyond the glades on the fir-forest border, and the rim of the low range of mountains, which looked toward Mantua, was for him no other world. Over these he wandered at pleasure and alone.

The castle, too, seemed empty. Far and wide might he roam save through the northern wing. His only clew to the world came from some foreign women-servants, very old, who tended and crept about him.

And first a simple sense of life engrossed him, — "content as the worm that strips the trees, the day's adventures for the day sufficed." His whole life was in his fancies. To all he saw that was lovely, he gave fresh life from his own soul. His ruling desire was to find something to worship, and bury himself in each external charm. No new form of loveliness within to match each one without was developed.

> "As the adventurous spider, making light
> Of distance, shoots her threads from depth to height,
> From barbican to battlement: so flung
> Fantasies forth and in their centre swung
> Our architect,— the breezy morning fresh
> Above, and merry, — all his waving mesh
> Laughing with lucid dew-drops rainbow-edged."

His life was blended with that of land, sea, flower, bird, and insect. Springs, summers, and winters quietly came and went. Time at length put an end to this period of content. The poppy and linnet had their day. Something informed the boy that others desired a portion in his joy. Where shall he find his public? Forth glided not only each painted warrior, every girl of stone, and Adelaide and Palma, upon whom he stumbled in the arrased glooms, but the entire outer-world: whatever scraps and snatches, song and story, dreams, perhaps, which he had given to flower and tree, were now given to the streams of life-like figures which passed through his brain. Ere he could choose they surrounded him, — lord, liegeman, vavasor, and suzerain. He lived the life of each. As he let his rough-hewn bow of ash sink from his aching wrist, he imagined that he had sent a golden shaft hissing through the Syrian air to strike down some defender of Jerusalem against the crusaders. As he picked grapes and filberts, he dreamed of himself as the young emperor Frederick II., quaffing wine with the soldan, or looking at the bunch of dates which the titular king of the Holy City sent his imperial son-in-law, to remind him of his promise to reconquer Palestine.

He compared his life with that of the warriors on the arras. "Will no career open for him also?" Those men are older: his call is yet to come. The pageant thinned. From futile boy attempts to emulate his heroes in reality, he passed to imaginary feats, in which he excelled them all, and finds in the passing —

> "The Apollo in his own soul."

Time stole on. By degrees the Pythons perish off; his votaries sink to respectful distance — their dismissals seem emphatic; only girls are very slow to disappear, — his Delians.

> "Glance the bevy through, divine Apollo's choice, his Daphne!"

He heard the servants talk of how Palma, the daughter of Ecelin and niece of Este, had been promised by her father to the Guelf chief, Count Richard Saint Boniface, one of the Capulets of Verona; "but the maid rejects his suit," those sleepy women said.

She, scorning all beside, deserves the most Sordello. So, conspicuous in his world of dreams sat Palma, whose tresses of gold were like "spilt sunbeams."

But fate is tardy with the stage and crowd she promised. His fancies cease to soothe him. The earnest smile is gone.

Long years of life like this were broken up by an accident, "which opened the veritable business of mankind."

As the first pink leaflets bud on the beech, and the larches brighten in the spring sunshine, Sordello goes forth buoyantly, hoping that to-day's venture will secure his visioned lady, —

> "Whose shape divine,
> Quivered i' the farthest rainbow-vapor, glanced
> Athwart the flying herons?"

On he goes through the brakes of withered fern and over the great morass shot through and through with flashing waters, each footfall sending up a diamond jet. Still Palma seems floating on before him: he thinks that when he has passed the next wood he will hear her own she loves him, — Boniface to hear, to groan, to leave his suit! He clears the last screen of pine-trees before Mantua; and there, under the walls, amid a gay crowd of men and women, sits his lady, enthroned as the Queen of the Court of Love, at which the troubadour Eglamor contends for her prize against all comers.

Naddo strings a lute for Eglamor, who sings of Elys. Sordello's brain swam; for he knew a sometime deed again: many a foolish gap and chasm does it supply. He longs to speak. Before the people's frank applause was half done, Sordello was beside him, spite of indignant twitchings from his friend the trouvère, singing "the true lay with the true end," taking the other's names and time and place for his. On flies the song in a giddy race after the flying story, word making word leap forth, and rhyme, rhyme. As he closes, the people crowd around and shout, "The prize! the prize!"

He had gained something then; and into a soft slumber would gladly have

MORNING IN VENICE.

sunk, " but one sight withheld him." The crowd opens. He sees Adelaide sitting silent, and at her knees the very maid of the north chamber.

With just six words and no more Palma laid the scarf upon him, warm with her own life. Her golden hair touched his cheek.

He knew no more till he awoke some furlongs off, at home, crowned, — with that scarf about his neck, and curious women kindly peering round. They tell him that the jongleurs, Naddo, Squarcialupe, and Tagliafer, had brought him home, and that Palma had chosen him for her minstrel.

Sordello, who had hitherto *perceived*, now began to think, and naturally enough, of his own poem. How had the people come to feel its beauty?

As he pondered this question, sounds low and drear stole on him, and a noise of footsteps broke his revery. Some friends led by Naddo were carrying the body of Eglamor to the grave, a few loose flowers in his hand. Poor Eglamor had died of sorrow. He loved his art, and stood faltering before it. His new song had been dear to him, but he shouted for Sordello with the rest; and bending to lay his withered crown beside the fresh one, left tears and a kiss upon the singer's hand. Nay, he even sang, at the careless bidding of bystanders, the very song with which Sordello had outshone him; then went home. Friends used to wait his coming. Now they were already with the rising star, the new Sordello.

Weary and puzzled by his uncertain future, at length he said, —

    "'Best sleep now with my scorn,
    And by to-morrow I devise some plain
    Expedient.' So he slept, nor woke again."

They found as much, those friends, who went to gossip heartlessly before him of Sordello's life and song.

Sordello laid his fresh crown upon the dead man's breast, and in sweet song besought Nature still to hold him dear.

And the prayer was answered. A plant, which bears a three-leaved bell, that ripens to its heart ere noon, " its soft, pure petals falling noiselessly as the last breath of the trouvère," still bears the name of Eglamor.

Beneath a flowering laurel thicket, in the sunrise of blossoming and May, Sordello lay, wondering why the old castle hid so the secret of his birth. This was the story he knew.

Years before, when at Vicenza, both her counts banished the Vivaresi kith and kin, those Maltraversi hung on the skirts of Ecelin's army, reviling him, he in anger set all their homes on fire, forgetting that his wife was there. There in the flames did Adelaide give birth to Ecelin the younger; and the mother and her babe were rescued from the mob by a poor archer, named El Corte. There was no one left to thank, when they thought of it years later, but his young son Sordello. This child Adelaide carried off to Goito, — a retreat where she went when times were rude, when Este schemed for Palma, or Taurello, who had lost all his family in those dreadful flames, came to the Mantuan court.

Apollo vanishes; and there remains a low-born youth, who has just been made his lady's minstrel.

In the midst of his musings a letter came from Naddo, praying him to visit Mantua, and supply a famished world. "The evening star was high when he reached Mantua, but his fame arrived before him."

But his song soon turned to a source of annoyance — 't was the song's effect he cared for, scarce the song itself. He tried to rise above the singers who simply tell of the forms they see around them, and to become a poet who, through such pictures, reveals the loveliness of his own nature, so that his hearers shall love in him the love that leads their souls to perfection. He failed. His *heroes* were on the people's lips, but no one cared for *him*. They would not see in Sordello any trait of his meanest hero. If he tried to give original ideas, he was blamed for being too abstruse, and not building on the common heart as a bard should, — who was no philosopher. His native Italian was too crude for the expression of his thoughts. He coined new words, but they proved too artificial and cumbrous. He took less pains with his verses, and they gained less and less applause.

> "Weeks, months, years went by;
> And lo, Sordello vanished utterly,
> Sundered in twain; each spectral part at strife
> With each: one jarred against another life;
> The Poet thwarting hopelessly the Man."

Meanwhile the world rejoiced ('t is time to explain), because a sudden sickness set it free from Adelaide. A rustle forth of daughters and of sons blackened the valley. Romano entered the cloister, and as he did so proclaimed a truce between the imperialists, who had been his partisans, and the adherents of the pope. A letter from him informed his friend Taurello that three weddings were to put an end to Guelf and Ghibelline strife. His two sons, Alberic and Ecelin, are to marry Beatrice d'Este and Giglia St. Boniface, while Palma is to be given to Count Richard, as the old rumor said.

His letter found Taurello at Naples, sworn to sail next month with the emperor for Syria. "Never thunder-clap so startled mortal!" "I absent, and she to die!" exclaimed Taurello; and half a score of horses were ridden dead, ere he stood, with reeking spurs, before Romano at Vicenza.

"Too late," the chieftain stammered. "Boniface urged me; Este would not wait. Forgive! As you found me first, so leave me now. You have my Palma. Retain that lure — only be pacified!"

To Mantua, Taurello hastened for Palma; and ere he reached the city, Sordello was chosen to greet the triumphal entrance into Mantua of the famous Ghibelline soldier with his song.

> "'Take a friend's advice,'
> Quoth Naddo to Sordello, 'nor be rash
> Because your rivals (nothing can abash
> Some folks) demur that we pronounced you best
> To sound the great man's welcome: 't is a test.
> Remember! Strojavacca looks asquint. —
> The rough fat sloven; and there 's plenty hint
> Your pinions have received of late a shock —
> Outsoar them, cobswan of the silver flock;
> Sing well!'"

Fast the minutes flit; vainly Sordello seeks for inspiration. Another day will bring the soldier, and he cannot choose but sing. So, a last shift, he quits Mantua, — slow, alone. Out of that aching brain, — a very stone, — song must be struck.

> "And thus he wandered, dumb
> Till evening, when he paused, thoroughly spent,
> On a blind hill-top: down the gorge he went,
> Yielding himself up as to an embrace.
> The moon came out; like features of a face,
> A querulous fraternity of pines,
> Sad blackthorn clumps, leafless and grovelling vines
> Also came out, made gradually up
> The picture: 't was Goito's mountain-cup
> And castle."

Back rushed the dreams of old, enwrapping him wholly. 'T was Apollo now they lapped, those mountains, not a pettish minstrel meant to wear his soul away in discontent, brooding on fortune's malice. Heart and brain swelled; he expanded to himself again. The slim castle had dwindled of late years, — gone to ruin, — trails of vine through every loop-hole. Nought avails the night as, torch in hand, he must explore the maple chamber. "Palma was gone that day," said the remaining women. Last, he lay beside the Carian group reserved and still.

> "The Body, the Machine for Acting Will,
> Had been at the commencement proved unfit;
> That for Demonstrating, Reflecting it,
> Mankind — no fitter: was the Will itself
> In fault?"

His forehead pressed the moonlit shelf beside the youngest marble maid awhile; then, raising it, he thought, with a long smile, "I shall be king again!" as he withdrew the envied scarf; into the font he threw his crown.

> "'Next day, no poet! Wherefore?' asked
> Taurello, when the dance of Jongleurs, masked
> As devils, ended; 'don't a song come next?'
> The master of the pageant looked perplexed
> Till Naddo's whisper came to his relief.
> 'His Highness knew what poets were: in brief,
> Had not the tetchy race prescriptive right
> To peevishness, caprice? or, call it spite,
> One must receive their nature in its length
> And breadth, expect the weakness with the strength.'
> So phrasing, till, his stock of phrases spent,
> The easy-natured soldier smiled assent,
> Settled his portly person, smoothed his chin,
> And nodded that the bull-bait might begin.'

And the font took Sordello's laurels; let them lie. A dream is o'er, and the suspended life begins anew. Over a sweet and solitary year is wasted in the lonely castle. One declining autumn day he sauntered home complacently, their moods according, — his and Nature's. Every spark of Mantuan life was trodden out. Harsh the earth's remonstrance followed. 'T was the marsh gone of a sudden. Mincio in its place laughed, a broad water, in next morning's face. And here was Nature, bound by the same bars of fate with him!

> "No! youth once gone is gone;
> Deeds let escape are never to be done.
> Leaf-fall and grass-spring for the year; for us —
> Oh, forfeit I unalterably thus
> My chance? nor two lives wait me, this to spend
> Learning save that? Nature has time, may mend
> Mistake, she knows occasion will recur:
> Landslip or sea-breach, how affects it her
> With her magificent resources? — I
> Must perish once and perish utterly.
> . . . .
> Ay, happiness
> Awaited me; the way life should be used

> Was to acquire, and deeds like you conduced
> To teach it by a self-revealment, deemed
> The very use, so long! Whatever seemed
> Progress to that, was pleasure; aught that stayed
> My reaching it — no pleasure. I have laid
> The ladder down; I climb not; still, aloft
> The platform stretches! Blisses strong and soft,
> I dared not entertain, elude me; yet
> Never of what they promised could I get
> A glimpse till now!
> . . . .
> "I die then! Will the rest agree to die?
> Next Age or no? Shall its Sordello try
> Clue after clue, and catch at last the clue
> I miss?
> . . . .
> "Why fled I Mantua, then? — complained
> So much my will was fettered, yet remained
> Content within a tether half the range
> I could assign it?"

"Palma sent your trouvère" (Naddo, interposing, leaned over the lost bard's shoulder), — "and, I believe, you cannot more reluctantly receive than I pronounce her message: we depart together. What avail a poet's heart Verona's pomps and gauds? five blades of grass suffice him. News? Why know you not the world's tidings?"

Then was told the tale from the beginning: how Taurello found in Palma a kindred spirit, and they secretly agreed to postpone the marriage as long as possible, and the first pretext for a rupture promptly seized; how Palma still delayed her journey to Verona, where she had promised to marry the count in his palace; how, made bold by Salinguerra's absence, the Guelfs had burned and pillaged till he unawares returned to take revenge, setting street after street on fire, and riding in blood to his horse's fetlocks; and how Count Richard hastened with his friend Azo, Marquis of Este, and other leading Guelfs to drive Salinguerra out of Ferrara, but permitted himself to be decoyed to a parley, at which he was treacherously taken prisoner; how the whole Lombard League of nearly twenty cities, that took the side of the popes against the emperors, rose in arms to deliver him from Salinguerra, who strengthened himself at Ferrara with great bands of mercenaries.

"And they want you doubtless to contrive the marriage-chant ere Richard storms Ferrara," Naddo added.

Sordello rose, a new man, to seek the world once more.

It was the autumn of 1224 when Sordello, now thirty years old, hastened to join Palma at Verona. She had timed her journey so cunningly as to arrive just after Richard's departure, and thus gain a plausible pretext for charging him with breach of faith.

Sordello reached the city while "a last remains of sunset dimly burned o'er the far forests." 'T is many years and more since that autumn eve in Verona. The second Friedrich wore the purple, and the third Honorius filled the holy chair. "A single eye from all Verona cared for the soft sky." Trumpets were pealing and alarm-bells booming. The Carroccio — a car which carried the city's standard, the crucifix, and a great bell into battle — was being dragged into the market-place, where the people were crowded, listening to the fiery speeches of their magistrates, and eager to march against Salinguerra and show that Verona was no unworthy member of the great league.

In the count's palace was a dim closet, which overlooked this tumult; and there Sordello and Palma sat with fingers interlocked, while she told him, with a coy, fastidious grace,

"Like the bird's flutter ere it fix and feed,"

How she had longed for some out-soul, which should direct all the force that was expanding within her; and how she had accepted him as her lord ever since that spring morning when his face, not unknown to her, burst out from all the other faces at the Love Court.

"I was vainly planning how to make you mine," she says, "when Salinguerra showed me how to break loose from Count Richard and the Guelfs. My father and brother have given up the leadership of the Lombard Ghibellines, the best part of our inheritance. You and I will take the vacant place. To-morrow morning, disguised in some gay weed, like yours, we will flee to Ferrara. Let Taurello's noble accent teach the rest. Then say if I have misconceived your destiny, too readily believed the Kaiser's cause your own."

And Palma fled before Sordello, dumb with joy at the prospect of becoming a king, and thus embodying his own will in this "aggregate of souls and bodies" as he had dreamed of doing, could express his rapture at the knowledge of her love.

Meantime Ferrara lay in rueful state; the lady-city, for whose sole embrace her pair of suitors struggled, felt their arms a brawny mischief to the fragile charms they tugged for.

A young Guelf was mourning at the sight of a shrivelled hand nailed to the charred lintel of the doorway, within which he had seen his father stand, bidding him farewell.

An old Ghibelline howled over a little skull with dazzling teeth, which he had dug up in the heap of rubbish where his house was burned.

THE TOWER OF ST. MARKS.

A deserter from Salinguerra came back to find his palace razed so adroitly, that he did not know the spot, but sat on the edge of a choked-up tank ploughing the mud inside with his feet and singing the song with which the Ecelins rode into battle, until one fierce kick brought up his mother's face, caught by the thick gray hair about his spur.

Another Ghibelline had murdered his brother. A woman of Ferrara offered to sell her own daughters to Sordello; and he heard Salinguerra boasting of burning hostages alive.

The sight of all this suffering led our hero up from dreaming of ruling men to aspiring to serve them. He confessed to Palma, as they talked that night alone beside a smouldering watch-fire, his unwillingness to join the Ghibellines. She urged that the Guelfs were just as cruel; but he longed to find some better way than that pursued by either faction.

One of the sentinels came up, and bade him sing of Rome. To Sordello Rome was the point of light from which rays traversed all the world. In her he saw embodied a plan to put mankind in full possession of all their rights. Visions of her laws and her new structures crowded upon him.

He knew how zealously the popes and bishops had taken the part of the Lombard cities, and defended them from the emperors and nobles. This cause seemed that of the people against the princes, and of the future against the past. He faltered as he remembered how slowly Rome was built; his courage returned as he remembered how rapidly Hildebrand built up the papal power, and how mightily his successors labored in the crusades, — "almost dispensing with the truce of God." At last he resolved to imitate these great workers, and to begin by making a convert of Salinguerra.

> "Is it the same Sordello in the dusk
> As at the dawn?"

Just before sunset he found the old warrior sitting with Palma in his own dreary palace. He had been giving audience to the emperor's envoy, the pope's legate, and the league's ambassadors, and was now complacently planning his next move, and considering what use he should make of the new badge of authority just sent him by the emperor. After sixty years of fighting he was still young, —

> "So agile, quick, and graceful turned
> The head on the broad chest."

But thirty years of idle dreaming had left Sordello stunted and worn out, — the shadow of a man. He stammered, and was so awkward and bashful that his speech at first only deserved scoff. Salinguerra, a master of the right words in the right places, listened with good-natured contempt to one whom he knew only as an archer's orphan son and Palma's too much favored minstrel. Indeed, the Ghibelline veteran showed such scorn of the advice to release his prisoner, open his gates to the league, and turn Guelf himself, that Sordello was moved to eloquence. He pleaded the cause of the people, whose faces he saw filling the dim chamber, so powerfully, that Salinguerra began to admire him, and at last determined to make him his ally. Suddenly he flung the emperor's badge around the orator's neck, and welcomed him as Palma's husband, head of the Romano family, and leader of the Lombard Ghibellines.

And now springs to light a secret which Palma had heard from her dying step-mother, namely, that Salinguerra's wife and child, who were supposed to have perished in that Vicenza massacre, had both been rescued, and the son was living under the name of Sordello.

Sordello sat pale and silent; but his father laughed with joy as he told how the emperor was going to destroy the papal power and place all Lombardy under a prefect, whom he himself had leave to name. His son must take this office, in virtual independence of Frederick himself. So he ran on, until Palma drew his iron arms away from the shrinking shoulders of his son, who rose, tried to speak, and then sank back. In order to give him time to recover, she led the father, who staggered, in his joyful excitement, down the narrow stairs into a dim corridor, lighted only by a grating, which showed in the west one ragged jet of fierce gold fire. There he sat down on a stone bench, while Palma sang her lover's poems, and told him how the world loved him, and thought his wan face eclipsed even that of Count Richard's. Salinguerra drank in every word; and as she finished, —

> "He drew her on his mailed knees, made
> Her face a framework with his hands, a shade,
> A crown, an aureole: there must she remain
> (Her little mouth compressed with smiling pain
> As in his gloves she felt her tresses twitch)
> To get the best look at, in fittest niche
> Dispose his saint. That done, he kissed her brow."

Then began schemes with a vengeance, schemes on schemes, — "not one fit to be told that foolish boy," he said. "But only let Sordello Palma wed. Then — "

Above the passage suddenly a sound stops speech, stops walk.

"'T is his own foot-stamp; — your hand; his summons!'" Out they two reeled dizzily.

Sordello sat gazing at the river, while eve slow sank down the near terrace to the farther bank, and only one spot left out of the night glimmered upon the river opposite, — a breath of watery heaven like a bay, a sky-like space of water, ray for ray, and star for star, one richness where they mixed as this and that wing of an angel, fixed, tumultuary splendors folded in to die. Yonder the slow moon to complete heaven rose again; and naked at his feet, lighted his old life's every shift and change, effort with counter effort. He had needed some steady purpose to uplift his soul, as the moon sways the ocean. Others made pretence to strength not half his own; yet had some core within, submitted to some moon, and were able therefore to fulfil a course, while he had missed life's crown.

He would fain serve the people; but really doing it seemed so doubtful that he was sorely tempted to accept the crown his father offered him, and live only for present pleasures, leaving the future out of sight. He thought of the sages, champions, martyrs, who dashed aside the cup of pleasure, and so gained the better life which this conceals. His mental struggle was fierce. He would dash this badge, and all it brought, to earth. He will think *once* more, however. With his last remaining strength he stamped on the emperor's badge, — his great temptation.

Dash the veil aside, and you divine who sat there dead, —

> "Under his foot the badge: still, Palma said.
> A triumph lingering in the wide eyes,
> Wider than some spent swimmer's if he spies,
> Help from above in his extreme despair,
> And, head far back on shoulder thrust, turns there
> With short, quick passionate cry: as Palma pressed
> In one great kiss, her lips upon his breast,
> It beat."

They laid him beside his mother in the stone font he loved. Nothing now remains of him but a name in the Mantuan chronicles and a few verses still sung at Asolo.

"A nature of magnificent possibilities, whose work for the world was lost, though he himself was saved, just for the want of a love divine enough to inspire, human enough to direct and control its service for the world," — a life ending at the point and with the same hopes with which it started.

Is there no more to say?

"In the bright summer morning, while the lark sings, mounting heavenward above the castle-walls, a merry boy brushes the dew from the grass as he passes, and glad at heart he sings, — his song one fragment of the old Goito lay, that spoke the praise of Elys."

"Who would has heard Sordello's story told," in the hope that it may help —

> "Some souls see All
> — The Great Before and After, and the Small,
> Now, yet be saved by this the simplest lore."

"My life will not be ruined by vanity," said Percy. "I never could have analyzed the poem like that; it takes a girl to find out the mysteries of the poets."

The charm of the afternoons and evenings at Naples, especially in a villa overlooking the bay, cannot be well described. It exists in the purple air, the gardens, and the sea. The gardens are sweet with orange and lemon trees, cool with the green olives, and everywhere bright with flowers.

Afar lies Capri, some twenty miles distant, — a garden of the sea, with mountains and rocks. It commands, with the city of Naples and Vesuvius, one of the most enchanting scenes on earth. Only eleven miles in circumference, it has a population of some six thousand souls.

It is, as it were, a mountain peak in the sea, and it has an elevation of nearly two thousand feet.

The old Roman emperors loved it for its beauty, and the ruins of their aqueducts, gardens, and villas are still seen. Tiberius lived here in his wickedness. The remains of the twelve palaces that he built to the twelve deities are shown, as though the building of temples were a compensation for a cruel, dissolute, and ruinous life.

Vesuvius slumbers over all the calm sea and serene hills. It is a long time since he awoke in his power. Solitary and majestic, he arises from the plain of Campania, having a circumference of thirty miles, and some four thousand feet high.

It lost some of its height and beauty in the great eruption of 1822, when some eight hundred feet disappeared.

Vesuvius was not suspected of being a volcano until near the time of the destruction of Pompeii. Its sides up to that time were covered with vines, and on its top was a lake. Here was the stronghold of Spartacus, the gladiator.

It buried Pompeii under twenty feet of ashes.

The eruption of Vesuvius in 1779 was most remarkable. The clouds of smoke arose to a height four times that of the mountain, and the streams of fire were two miles high. A single mass of rock that was ejected was more than one hundred feet in circumference and seventeen feet high. The last great eruption was in April, 1872.

CHAPTER XVI.

THE WHITE-BORDERED FLAG

MR. VAN DER PALM and Percy bade adieu to Mr. Ware at Naples early in autumn, and took up their residence in Rome, intending to pass the winter there. Here they beheld in the holiday week one of the most brilliant festivals in the world.

In Rome Mr. Van der Palm was introduced to some of the most progressive minds of Italy, and became a member of one of the many Peace Societies in Italy, which were composed partly of Italians and partly of Englishmen living in Rome and other art cities. In no country has the Peace movement and the new education of Peace made a deeper impression than in Italy.

While in Rome he was made a delegate in America to one of the great Peace Congresses that was to be held in the city. It was to number leading men from England, France, Germany, and the United States.

The Pan-American Congress, of which Mr. Blaine had been the inspiring spirit, had discussed the union of all republics in one grand treaty to settle all their international difficulties by arbitration. Some of the delegates had suggested that those nations who would enter into such an agreement should border their flags with white. The Human Liberty League, which became a voice of the Pan-American Congress after the latter had dissolved, has favored this idea, and their societies have done a good educational work.

It was at this Italian Peace Congress that the first white-bordered flag was shown. The display of the new flag, which was the Stars

CAPRI.

and Stripes, was followed by a very dramatic incident. The speaker threw the flag back over a statue near him, not knowing probably what the statue was intended to represent. It was the statue of the Gladiator. The audience hailed the picture of the statue of the

NATIONAL VILLA, NAPLES.

Gladiator covered with the American flag wearing the white border of peace as a happy omen.

At one of the receptions given to this Peace Congress by the women of Rome, Mr. Van der Palm gave an address. It was well received, and we give a part of it here. His subject was, "The New Education of Peace."

THE NEW EDUCATION OF PEACE.

WE are standing on the threshold of a new age, which is preparing to receive new influences. The supreme century of the world is now rising before us. In that century education will be peace, and the kingdom of the new education is passing over to the control of women. The world has waited this humanizing and pacific influence through all the generations. It was of such an era that Virgil in his "Pollio" sung. To women is coming the trust of the education of the new arts of peace.

The beginnings of this new education for peace are seen everywhere, but they await a noble leadership. The educational systems of Frœbel and Pestalozzi are superseding old forms; and the ideas of these educators were that education stood not for the arts of money-making, but for character and for the whole of life, and that in true character was the harmony of the world. The crowning of the names of the martyrs of liberty and human progress is a part of this new peace education. Every monument that rises for virtue enriches life. The setting of the flag in the skies over every home and school-room and church, as the French place "liberty, equality, and fraternity" everywhere, is a part of this pacific work of education. The village improvement societies, the thousand societies for human improvement, are all companies waiting to join the grand army whose final march is unity and peace. Poetry is singing the Song of Peace; art awaits the new impulse; and science in her mighty progress is a friend of man and a missionary of humanity. The world awaits the deeper meanings of the teachings of the Sermon on the Mount. The best of all ages is now; and better is to come; and the strength of this new peace education by women will be the strength of our republic.

A generation ago there arose on the peaceful shores of the Connecticut, above the green valley and elm-shaded streets, a mighty arsenal. Charles Sumner, in his oration on the "True Grandeur of Nations," which Cobden pronounced the greatest contribution that human scholarship had ever made to the cause of peace, said that the arsenal at Springfield was chiefly useful in that it had inspired an immortal song whose voice was for peace. That song was written by Longfellow, the poet of hope, home, and history, who, because he felt most deeply for humanity, will outlive his brother singers in the sympathies of time. Entering the arsenal one day in his early life, these thoughts came crowding upon him: —

This is the Arsenal. From floor to ceiling,
  Like a huge organ, rise the burnished arms;
But from their silent pipes no anthem pealing
  Startles the villages with strange alarms.

Ah! what a sound will rise, how wild and dreary,
  When the death-angel touches those swift keys!
What loud lament and dismal Miserere
  Will mingle with their awful symphonies!

I hear even now the infinite fierce chorus,
  The cries of agony, the endless groan,
Which, through the ages that have gone before us,
  In long reverberations reach our own.

Is it, O man, with such discordant noises,
  With such accursed instruments as these,
Thou drownest Nature's sweet and kindly voices,
  And jarrest the celestial harmonies?

Were half the power that fills the world with terror,
  Were half the wealth bestowed on camps and courts,
Given to redeem the human mind from error,
  There were no need of arsenals or forts:

The warrior's name would be a name abhorred!
  And every nation, that should lift again
Its hand against a brother, on its forehead
  Would wear forevermore the curse of Cain!

Down the dark future, through long generations,
  The echoing sounds grow fainter and then cease;
And like a bell, with solemn, sweet vibrations,
  I hear once more the voice of Christ say, "Peace!"

Peace! and no longer from its brazen portals
  The blast of War's great organ shakes the skies!
But beautiful as songs of the immortals,
  The holy melodies of love arise.

War came; and humanity and justice demanded that the arsenal at Springfield should pour forth its arms on another contest that was to lead the work on to peace. But the peace principles of Sumner, Longfellow, Cobden, Bright, Lucretia Mott, and Harriet Martineau, whose statue once stood in this church, remained the same. At the World's Fair at Chicago there is to assemble in August the most glorious Peace meeting this world has seen since the disciples sat down to listen to the Sermon on the Mount. To this cause humanity calls women; and of all women, the daughters of Rome should lead in this movement, and hasten the day when the work of their great ancestors shall yield its ultimate and eternal harvest.

Rome celebrated her Seculums, and Horace sang his "Carmen Seculare." Arches arose, but they were arches of war. Captive kings and queens grovelled in their chains at chariot wheels. Cæsar celebrated the conquest of Europe, Asia, and Africa in a single triumph. At the Seculums the heralds marched down the Appian Way, and the trumpets rang with the exultant but solemn words: "Come, see ye a day that no man ever before saw, and that no man living will ever see again." There was a different triumph on the banks of the Mississippi a few days ago. The East had wedded in bonds of iron the Pacific Ocean. Arches arose, but they were crowned with grain; chariots moved through the streets, but they were the cars of human progress. It was Peace education.

Men die, but institutions continue, and the spirit of one generation grows into another. The pilot of the "Argo" may come not again, but the Argo will ever return with the golden fleece. The new age tends to unity of humanity; and woman's patriotic mission is the education of all the arts of peace, — character education for the whole of life. The time has come to repeat Garrison's words with new meaning: "My country is the world, and my countrymen are all mankind." Over the steel-blue waters of Plymouth, Mass., in my own land, rises the faith monument, — an eternal teacher. At the other end of the continent, in Buenos Ayres, rises the white peace monument of San Martin, the real liberator of South America. Having won the freedom of Argentine and Chili and Peru, he said to the three nations that offered him their highest places and honors: "The presence of a fortunate general, no matter how disinterested he may be, in the country where he has won victories, is detrimental to the state. I have achieved the independence of Peru. I have ceased to be a public man." He marched down the Andes, where his armies had put to flight the condors for the last time. He did not return like Cincinnatus to his plough, or like Washington to his home, for the good of the republic. He went into voluntary exile; and after thirty years of silence for the sake of the peace of his country, he died in Boulogne.

His country wished to bring home his body, and crown him dead. Grand was that day when Buenos Ayres received the dead body of her hero. They had built for him a tomb; it represented not the battle of Maypu, nor what he did in war, but what he did for peace. The angels of human progress were those that the sculptor made to guard his tomb.

From the Faith Monument near Plymouth Rock to the marble angels of peace in Buenos Ayres is a mighty arch of the republics of liberty. Progress is marching beneath it under the northern constellations and the southern Cross. The republics await the new education of peace, that will crown the work of all their heroes, — Washington, Bolivar, Juarez, and San Martin. To this work the daughters of the patriots of all lands may well give their hearts and hands, as the women of Venezuela drew into Caracas the chariot of Bolivar. Heaven awaits the consummation. "Lift up your heads, O ye gates, and be ye lifted up, ye everlasting doors, and the King of Glory shall come in!" The greatest work of the world awaits the patriotism of women, the work that shall place the brightest crown of all on the achievements of all heroes, — the new Education of Peace.

The armies of war began their march to the west from Rome. So may it be with armies of peace. Out of Rome women led the way of the heroes of old. So may it be now. So as we saw in yonder hall, may the white-bordered flag cover the gladiators of every land, till a new race shall possess the earth, whose only struggle will be to make power of themselves by the noblest and holiest development.

Percy, with the new education of the arts of peace in view, saw Rome as probably no boy ever looked upon it before. Rome, in its ruin, is one vast monument of wars. The Roman wars were waged, not for defence as a rule, but for conquest. Rome mowed the world.

Everywhere that Percy went in the Roman winter and spring he beheld the reminders of the human slaughters of thousands of years. The Tiber ran red with the legends of battles. The *Forum Romanus* was an echo of the voice of war. The bridge of Horatius Coacles, the triumphal arches of Septimus Severus, of Titus, of Constantine, the castle of St. Angelo and the field of Mars, the Coliseum, the Palatine, the Forum, and the column of Trajan, and the statues of all the emperors except Antoninus, were to our young traveller's eyes, in his new education, like so many evidences of a barbarous selfishness, when the city of the Tiber sought not the good of mankind, but the gold of mankind, and crowned ages of robbery with the arts that only are merited by the conquests of peace.

To him Christianity there took a new coloring. The voice of the Great Teacher in Galilee was the only one that rose for peace amid all these worthless struggles for power and sheddings of human blood. "Blessed are the peacemakers!" Percy heard that voice crying in the wilderness of the world in the silence of time, and felt its meaning there.

There arose to him one solitary place of interest amid all these monuments of cruelty, injustice, and human woe, which he wished to see. It was the Temple of Concord. It represented an idea,— the new idea. Where was it? Only pictures of it, with a few relics, remained.

The Temple of Concord was first built at the time of Furius Camillus, in commemoration of the reconciliation between the patricians and plebeians. In this temple the senate used to meet. It fell into decay; but was restored by Livia, the wife of Augustus. This latter temple was burned.

Two other temples of concord were built, but they disappeared.

But the pictured goddess still is to be seen. She is represented as a matron holding in her right hand an olive branch, and in her left a horn of plenty.

There was one house in Rome that Percy sought with interest. It recalls the democratic and republican revival in the Middle Ages. It was the traditional house of Rienzi, or Rienzo,— a house that brings thoughts of the Gracchi, the Fabricii, the Scipios, Cato, Antoninus, and all the glorious deeds, or deeds that were glorious in the olden time. It stands near the Temple of Fortune, and is built out of the ruins of a long past. It is called to-day the house of Pilate, and has associated with it a legend of the old governor of Judea. Here, according to another tradition, lived not only Rienzi, the leader of the tribune,— the tribune of "the orphan, the widow, and the poor,"— but Crecentius.

Who was Crecentius?

He was a Roman leader who became consul in Rome in 980, and

who aspired to restore the empire to its former state of liberty and glory. He dreamed the dream afterwards dreamed by Rienzi. The emperor Otho III. entered Rome with an army in 998, and defeated him, and put him to death. His end was heroic. Miss Mary Russell Mitford has grandly described it in one of her noblest poems.

THE ROMAN CONSUL.

"We are now in the city of the early consuls," said Mr. Van der Palm. "The consuls of to-day hold their name from the officers who governed the old Roman republic; and there is in the consulates of all lands a resemblance to the ancient form of power. The consuls of Rome were first elected after the expulsion of the kings, about 510 B.C. The office existed more than one thousand years."

"How were consuls appointed?" asked Percy.

"They were not appointed at all; they were elected, as I said. They were really elected kings. They were at first elected only from the rank of the patricians. After a time the plebeians, asking for representation, began to elect tribunes with consular power."

"What did the consuls do?" asked Percy.

"They commanded the army, framed the laws, and presided over the senate. And they controlled much of the world through pro-consuls; and it is from the pro-consuls that the consular service of all governments to-day descends. The American consul to-day is like the pro-consul of the Roman empire."

Mr. Van der Palm further explained —

"The Roman consuls were first termed *prætores*, or leaders of armies. The title of consul was introduced some three hundred years before the Christian era.

"The symbol of the authority of the old consuls was the ivory sceptre, surmounted by the eagle. When they went to their high seats as judges, a bundle of rods with an axe in the centre was borne before them by twelve lictors.

"They were inaugurated by grand processions and a religious festival. In the empire the office became merely a title of honor conferred by the emperor.

"The pro-consuls, who administered affairs in the provinces, were commonly chosen from those who had been consuls, as in the great growth of the empire especial prudence and experience were needed for this office.

ROMAN GATE, GENOA.

"The office of mercantile consul, or commercial consul, originated in Italy about the twelfth century. Its purpose was to protect trade, vindicate the rights of commerce, and to make reports in the interests of the government. The office thus created in Italy, on the model of the pro-consul of the days of the times of the republic, was adopted to carry on the commercial relations of most European countries.

"The duties of the foreign consuls are assigned to them in printed instructions. The consul exhibits his commission to the state to which he is assigned, and receives a document from that state called an *exequatur*, which endorses the commission.

"The European consul is expected to know the laws and language of the country to which he is assigned, and to protect the rights of his countrymen there.

"A great service of the British consular office has been to protect the rights of seamen.

"There is a curious fiction about these consulates, which follows the old proconsular idea. It is, the consulate *is a part of the country from which the consul is sent.* America followed the idea. I could never be out of America when in my own consulate. Hence I can execute deeds, and even perform the marriage ceremony among my own people. An Englishman is not *supposed* to be out of England or her provinces whenever he is in any consulate under his own flag."

PILO GATE, GENOA.

SOUTH BASTION, GENOA.

"And so," said Blanche, the consul's daughter, who undertook to explain to Percy the meaning of "Sordello," "and so the consulate is a kind of myth or fairy tale. It has a touch of the poetic about it. I always love to see the flag of a consulate in any port. It recalls to me the old homes of the country for which it floats; and so it seems that there is always, and for every man, be he a merchant or a wayfarer, a hospitable welcome at the consulate."

Percy visited Genoa, the birthplace of Columbus, of which city we have spoken in other volumes. He was somewhat surprised to find there *several* birthplaces of the ocean hero.

> "Thirteen towns contend for Homer dead,
> In which the *living* Homer begged his bread."

Our travellers returned to New York, and arrived off the Nevasink Highlands on the first day of the great naval parade, on the 25th of April, 1893. There was spread over the front of the great gray fortress, as they were passing, a flag with *a white border*. Above it, the representatives of a patriotic organization, called the Lyceum League of America, were raising a banner to welcome the world.

The ceremonies were most impressive, following as they did the incident of the throwing of the white-bordered flag over the statue of the Gladiator in the Roman hall. They gave to our consular traveller and his son inspiring views of the mission of America.

www.ingramcontent.com/pod-product-compliance
Lightning Source LLC
Chambersburg PA
CBHW030809230426
43667CB00008B/1132